THE SLIPPERY SLOPE

CONTEMPORARY SOCIETY THROUGH THE LENS OF APPLIED ETHICS

VOLUME I

BUDDY THORNTON

Contemporary Society Through the Lens of Applied Ethics

Observations from the
Slippery Slope-Volume I

Revised and Expanded
Second Edition-October 2022

"Have the courage to say no. Have the courage to face
the truth. Do the right thing because it is the 'right thing to do.'
These are the magic keys to living your life with integrity."

— W. Clement Stone

"The law of evolution is that the strongest survives!'
'Yes, and the strongest, in the existence of any social species,
are those who are most social. In human terms, most ethical.
There is no strength to be gained from hurting one another.
Only weakness."

— Ursula K. Le Guin

The Slippery Slope
Contemporary Society Through the Lens of Applied Ethics-Revised Edition I

Published and distributed in Winterville, North Carolina, USA: Elite Publications and Gifts Of Legacy LLC: Scottsdale, Arizona, USA
All attempts have been made to ensure the accuracy of the information presented in this book, but this is not a guarantee.

ISBN: 979-8-88831-483-8 - Print Hardback
ISBN: 979-8-88831-485-2 - Print Paperback
ISBN: 979-8-88831-486-9 - Print- eBook
ISBN: 979-8-88831-487-6 - Audiobook

If you would like to do any of the above, please seek permission by contacting Elite Publications at +1 (919) 618-8075 or via email to info@elitepublications.org

Publisher: Elite Publications
Language: English
Library of Congress Control Number: 2022911308

Editor - Buddy Thornton
Interior design by: Amit Dey – amitdey2528@gmail.com

FOREWORD

by Isaiah Drone III

Founder of Brokenness to Healing Foundation

I have been working with Buddy Thornton for the last four years, and he has been a key figure in transforming communities within the southwestern United States. Buddy's passion for prosocial change through coaching and mentoring, and with his wife Sharon's support, our organization, **The Brokenness to Healing Foundation**, has directly influenced middle and high school boys' lives in the Dallas-Fort Worth, Texas area. Buddy has assisted in custom-made and collective professional approaches to oversee that all mentees consistently achieve transformative mentorship skills, experience, and leadership competency. Buddy has invested countless hours as a Positive Social Change Agent.

It is no wonder why I wasn't at all surprised when he handed me *CONTEMPORARY SOCIETY THROUGH THE LENS OF APPLIED ETHICS* "Observations from the Slippery Slope-Volume I" to read. As I read through this book's chapters, I intuitively knew that this literary work would be controversial to some but essential as an eye-opening tool, especially during the outbreak of COVID-19. So many unethical treatments like social inequities and minority disenfranchisement have manifested across the American social landscape during this pandemic. This book addresses the trauma that triggers microaggressions during social interactions. Buddy coaches the readers on how to mediate ongoing conflict and navigate from the subconscious and intrinsic biases to extrinsic bias and beyond through a healthier and more redefined positive social lens.

TABLE OF CONTENTS

ACKNOWLEDGMENTS

The author would like to thank the many people who debated the issues or supported his efforts through his creative journey. Without their influence and persistence, the work would lack many details. In addition, the author would be inconsiderate if he failed to emphasize how the author's spouse (who chooses not to be named herein) kept the home fires burning, allowing the writing project to sustain a semblance of momentum.

Dr. Sunny Liston, the author's committee chair from Grand Canyon University (and a reluctant participant who prefers a push toward completion of the author's dissertation and taking a walk across the stage with the elusive DBA), has been gracious enough to read and comment on the author's work. Thank you for your perseverance.

Isaiah Drone III, a peer and fellow doctoral candidate at Grand Canyon University, has spent considerable time commenting on the portions of the book relating to how disadvantaged populations suffer through various injustices due to mandates at the hands of the majority in power. Across the American social landscape, due to the limited adherence to virtuous, ethical pursuits and the habituated norms inherent to minority disenfranchisement, social inequities exist, which Isaiah attempts to mitigate through the non-profit, Brokenness to Healing Foundation and his support for social influencers like the author. I am highly pleased and eternally grateful he agreed to write the foreword: many blessings and much love, my brother in Christ.

My collaborative partners, Natalie McQueen and Lindsey Scholta, deserve well-earned credit for their efforts to assist in the revision of this second edition. Through their efforts, the author gained valuable time and perspective while researching and writing the new material. It is remarkable how others influence someone by practicing an ethical approach, essentially taking a "practicing what you preach" mantra and role modeling it daily. Thank you for sharing the load.

Finally, I want to thank the readers who chose my book as their conduit to ethical perspectives. Without the potential for an engaged audience, the book would not exist.

FROM THE AUTHOR

Starting the Slippery Slope series has been a singular passion driven by my motivation to be a positive social change agent since I returned to my academic pursuits in my late 50s. As a navy veteran from the Vietnam War era, a husband, father, grandfather, and now great-grandfather, I have experienced many social interactions that expose two oft-repeated commonalities.

The first is how making choices, from optimal to average to indifferent daily, creates barriers or pathways dictating our future options. Optimal choices are the catalyst for enhancing our lives. Anything less than optimal becomes problematic, although degrees of importance accompany all choices. When considering what choices to make, everyone must navigate the incidental alternatives. These choices usually have no long-term consequences, like which road to take to work, what movie to select for recreation, or what to consume for a meal. These are the "small c" choices.

The more significant "capital C" choices are those decision-tree types leading up to critical life-altering events. Examples are the what or why of career choices, who becomes the quality world participants in your life, and what risk-reward paradigm is correct for your personality type. More in-depth options have significant artifacts, factors often leading to how future choices expand or contract based on actual outcomes.

The second commonality is how society has minimized the value constructs embedded in relationships across all groups and cultures. The degradation of humanity can be tracked to egoism, narcissism, and self-aggrandizement. I have asked myself often, "Why are relationships failing, sometimes miserably, across many critical paradigms?"

My reading and studies have led to many potential answers about failure. William of Ockham projected what should be considered a universal starting point for most discussions on relationship failure when he said, "The simplest answer is often the correct answer." Based on Ockham's Razor (William's theory), humanity is falling prey to poor choices aligning with the debasement of ethics and morals. No other context crosses the entirety of the human species, specifically, our failure to maintain optimal social behavior. Thus, the compelling drive to create the Slippery Slope series.

I have discussed and debated where to start this journey with many peers, and the consensus is to start with a discourse on applied ethics and morals. Many books exist with many historical perspectives on both behavioral philosophies. Hence, the chosen course of action was to throw out some topics with ethical and moral dilemmas, leading to a contemporary debate on the issues and how they fit into people's everyday lives. Therefore, books one and two are ethics (this book) and morals (the next volume). Foundationally, the chosen literary path appears reasonable, but where does a treatise on choice-making enter the picture?

Book three will be on Family Choice Dynamics, and book four will explore social choices in "hot topic" areas. I intend to encourage debate and get people engaged in the discussions, people who can make a broad social impact on humanity, and gaining a dedicated community, a following of like-minded people who embrace these topics as relevant and timely would be fantastic and subsequently fulfill my mission as a positive social change agent. You can visit my website, www.bctmediationsplus.com, or send me an email to any of the following with a subject line of "slippery slope reader": bthornton2@my.gcu.edu; bct@bctmediationsplus.com; or buddypscapro@gmail.com.

DEFINITIONS AND CONCEPTS WHEN APPLIED TO ETHICS:

The following definitions and concepts are a compendium of ancient roots and evolved perceptions of ethics the author includes to increase reader understanding. Many books list definitions in an appendix; however, leading with this knowledge expands the utility and establishes a knowledge base specific to this book (the historical root of each definition or concept shall appear in Appendix A):

Absolutism/Despotism: theory of only one correct course of action without regard to whom, what, where, or culture

Action Potential: emerging avenues giving rise to multiple choices across all contexts

Altruism: self-less concern for the well-being of others without expectations of value

Autonomy: self-governance

Axiology: *a* philosophical study of value, synthesis of ethics and aesthetics, one's notion of self-worth

Beneficence: actions aligned with mercy, kindness, or charity holding significant intrinsic value

Business ethics: a code of behavior encompassing all aspects of interactions between stakeholders in any defined commercial enterprise, which allows the exploration, synthesis, and implementation of sustainable processes while preventing exploitation leading to harm

Confidentiality: the act of keeping information private, a duty of

Consequentialist: one who judges the acceptability of actions based solely on results

Deontological: duty-bound to act with virtuous intent regardless of outcome or consequence for oneself

> **Act Deontological:** each circumstance is measured based on its merits due to variance in individuals

> **Rule Deontological:** non-consequentialist principles applied as rules which determine whether an action is right or wrong

Duty: a required task or action

Ethos: ethics or ethical approaches

Eudaimonia: a state of well-being or happiness one pursues universally based on the virtuous living ideals present in one's society

Facts and Values: "knowledge of" is objective and worthless without subjective utility

Fairness: impartial treatment without bias

Fidelity: trustworthiness

Focus on Collectivist Values: Eastern honor-centric system

Focus on Individualist Values: Western truth-centric system

Honorable: *projecting as a* principled worldview of note

Integrity: the quality of being honest and exhibiting honesty

Interests: one's focal point of primary concern

Intrinsic goodness: the human trait with action potential for the emergence of virtuous behavior

Justice: the presumed legal or philosophical path to social fairness

Law of Unintended Consequences: results inconsistent with expectations

Logos: logic or logical approaches

Maleficence: Exhibiting evil or harmful behavior

Morality: one's worldview of rightness or wrongness along a continuum of individual considerations

Motivation: a power leading to the action potential for doing something

> ***Affective Motivation:*** an influence to act based on experience

> ***Extrinsic Motivation:*** an influence to act based on external factors

> ***Intrinsic Motivation:*** an inner drive to act based on the self-choice

> ***Rational Motivation:*** an influence to act based on knowledge absent experience

Non-maleficence: avoiding evil and preventing actions harmful to others

Paternalism: intervention by those in power aligned with preventing personal choice, most often with promoting an alleged version of "best interests of the governed."

Pathos: empathy or suffering (two ends of the feeling continuum)

Pejorative: disparaging or exhibiting contempt for others or a policy through deception

Personal ethics: one's code aligned with matters of choice-making dynamics, optimally aligned with one's moral conscience and existing legal frameworks

Phronesis: practical wisdom

Ren: the Confucian concept of benevolence toward other beings

Rights: principles of freedoms or entitlements owed through legal mandate or social convention

Teleological: the morality of an action is dependent on results and leads to a justification-focused society

Telos: an ultimate objective or goal

Utilitarianism: aligns with optimal results for the broader society

> **_Act Utilitarianism:_** an act is ethical only if it produces maximal happiness or pleasure

> **_Rule Utilitarianism:_** an action is ethical only if it benefits a more significant percentage of society

Veracity: accuracy with habitual correctness or the pursuit thereof

Virtue/Virtuous: a pure unbiased approach to one's worldview

Virtue ethics: a dynamic social code of behavior governing all aspects of intentions, perceptions, or actions based on honoring one's life through servant leadership and sacrifice for others, without or before seeking personal needs fulfillment

EXAMPLES OF ETHICS:

Some Examples of Acceptable Ethical Behavior would be:

"When someone tells a significant other the hard truth about anything, regardless of personal cost."

"Helping a person you don't know to get to the hospital in an emergency (has a moral component)."

"Turning a conflict situation between others into a meaningful intervention despite personal risk."

"Exhibiting selflessness toward less fortunate people when the opportunity arises."

"Profits are derived by enhancing someone else's needs without exploitation or causing harm."

"Giving professional consideration to clients and staff at all times."

Some Examples of Unacceptable Ethical Behavior would be:

"Cheating to win at anything for any reason."

"Focus more on your own needs over those less fortunate selfishly."

"Stealing someone else's lunch in an empty break room."

"Lying to get around one's competition for a coveted goal."

"Taking liberties with trusted peers behind their backs."

"Projecting contempt or disdain for clients and staff while in a professional role."

HISTORICAL QUOTES ON ETHICS:

"A man is ethical only when life, as such, is sacred to him." - Albert Schweitzer (1875-1965), French-German Philosopher and 1952 Nobel Peace Prize Winner (Albert Schweitzer Quote: A Man Is Ethical Only When Life (n.d.). Retrieved from https://www.azquotes.com/quote/596478)

"Live so that when your children think of fairness and integrity, they think of you." -- H. Jackson Brown, Jr., American Author (H. Jackson Brown, Jr. Quotes -- Brainy quote. (n.d.). Retrieved from https://www.brainyquote.com/quotes/h_jackson_brown_jr_135055)

"Integrity is telling myself the truth. And honesty is telling the truth to other people." -- Spencer Johnson, American Author, Professional Speaker, Management Expert

"Have the courage to say no. Have the courage to face the truth. Do the right thing because it is right. These are the magic keys to living your life with integrity." -- W. Clement Stone (1902-2002), American Businessman, Philanthropist, and Self-Help Book Author (Honesty and Integrity -- Random Acts of Kindness. (n.d.). Retrieved from http://materials.randomactsofkindness.org/cde/en/5-Honesty-and-Integrity.pdf)

"Even the most rational approach to ethics is defenseless if there isn't the will to do what is right." Solzhenitsyn

"There is no sickness worse for me than words that to be kind must lie."-Aeschylus

ETHICAL CONTEXTS

The definitions and concepts of ethics are being utilized in this literary creation to project a broad picture of the overarching socio-cultural impact of applying or ignoring ethical paradigms. Importance should be attached to efforts to expand widespread knowledge and utility aligned with ethical considerations globally and understand the inherent difference between ethics and morals (the subject of the next volume). Most authors seemingly interchange them indiscriminately. Based on most available teaching, two seminal forms of western ethical discourse exist one should explore, with many divergent theories following in their wake.

The following section will include a table of many philosophers throughout history, although focused on western philosophers, and not intended to be an exhaustive list of all philosophers, only the most relevant ones based on historical context. Following the chart is a summary of several philosophers who impact the worldview of ethics applicable to modernity. Many philosophers in the table have historically influenced contemporary western social behavior and the rule of law through the application of their collective teachings.

Table of Western Philosophers

Philosophers in bold print are considered noteworthy, and the list is not exhaustive, serving only as a representation of the field:

Western Philosopher Timeline and Theory			
Philosopher Name	B-D	Origin	Theory
Heraclitus	535-475 bce	Greece	Change Dynamics
Archelaus	500-??? bce	Greece	Conventional Ethics
Empedocles	490-430 bce	Greece	Elementals and Eternal Forces
Socrates	**470-399 bce**	**Greece**	**Socratic Reasoning**
Thrasymachus	459-400 bce	Greece	Sophistry
Antisthenes	446-365 bce	Greece	Cynicism
Aristippus	435-356 bce	Greece	Physical Hedonism
Plato	**428-348 bce**	**Greece**	**The Forms**
Aristotle	**384-322 bce**	**Greece**	**Eudaimonia/Teleology**
Epicurus	341-270 bce	Greece	Indulgent Hedonism
Chrysippus	279-206 bce	Greece	Stoicism
William of Ockham	**1285-1347**	**England**	**Ockham's Razor**
T Hobbes	1588-1679	England	Lack of Moral Sense
R Descartes	1596-1650	France	Dualism
Spinoza	1632-1677	Spain	Four Knowledge Theory
J Locke	1632-1704	England	Empiricism
Leibniz	**1646-1716**	**Germany**	**Theory of Uniqueness of Being**
B Mandeville	1670-1733	England	Selfish Salvationist
A Ashley-Cooper	1671-1713	England	Unfailing Moral Sense
G Berkeley	1685-1753	Ireland	Perception and Reality
F Hutcheson	1694-1746	England	Unfailing Moral Sense
D Hume	1711-1776	Scotland	Emotivism/Idealism Vs Realism
JJ Rousseau	1712-1778	France	The Moral Sentiments
I Kant	**1724-1804**	**Prussia**	**Rules-based Deontology/Categorical Imperatives**
J Bentham	**1748-1832**	**England**	**Utilitarianism**
JS Mill	**1806-1873**	**England**	**Utilitarianism**
Nietzsche	1844-1900	Germany	Sophistry
Frege	1848-1925	Germany	Analytical Philosophy
F. de Saussure	**1857-1913**	**Swiss**	**Diachronic versus Synchronic Linguistics**
B. Russell	1872-1970	England	Skepticism
G.E. Moore	**1873-1958**	**England**	**Moral Sense**
L Wittgenstein	**1889-1951**	**Austria**	**Certitude Treatise/Ethical Fuzziness**
C.L. Stevenson	1908-1979	USA	Emotivism
EN Lorenz	**1917-2008**	**USA**	**Chance and Chaos Theory**
A. Bandura	**1925-**	**Canada**	**Determinism versus Choice**

SUMMARY OF THE PHILOSOPHER TABLE

Beginning with Heraclitus, whom scholars credit with some of the earliest recorded western philosophical thinking, and moving through Chrysippus, one of the last identified philosophers from ancient Greece, the extant western philosophers established a credible foundation for seeking what humanity is "all about." Taking a journey through the early philosophical underpinnings is essential to understanding the thinking of the more recent "intellectual thinkers."

Going through the chart, one should discern a significant gap between Chrysippus and William of Ockham; almost fifteen centuries passed while philosophy took a long holiday. Philosophy and religion converged synchronously due to the influence of Roman domination and their overwhelming presence in western and central Europe, creating an extended period of socially stagnating "enforced entropy." Any philosophical thinking not aligned with the Church was treated as a threat to the word of God. After the Roman influence's demise, the historical period referred to as "The Dark Ages" further suppressed philosophical thought.

The Renaissance and the Enlightenment period created environments more favorable to philosophy and alternate thinking outside the Church. As the chart illustrates, many noteworthy thinkers emerged and put forth ethical theories that exist in some form, being evolved or relatively intact to this day. Of note are Immanuel Kant and his categorical imperatives. The first, "Act always in such a way that your action could become a universal rule," and the second, "Always treat other people, not as a means to an end, but as an end in themselves."

For either of Kant's categorical rules to be effective, people must act ethically. One aspect of note about following Kant's treatise is contrary to modern thinking. Kant insisted on an ethical act extended from duty. Deriving pleasure from the action would invalidate the duty aspect, thereby damaging the sense of worth one might gain by engaging in an otherwise ethical act. Regardless of Kant's position, the modern concept of Choice Theory uses Kant's two rules as a foundation. For example, Choice Theory utilizes a behavioral foundation extending from Maslow's Hierarchy of Needs platform for building one's self-worth and self-image to support proper behavior, which depends on Kant and his rules espoused almost three centuries ago.

The scope and breadth of philosophy are hard to grasp. The chart of noted philosophers only scratches the surface and omits eastern philosophers. Imagine, for a moment, a world where the historically relevant thought leaders from all historical periods synthesized an ethical and moral path for humanity. Unfortunately, the most one can hope for is a platform where one might get a piece of one or two of the most relevant philosophies with the action potential to impact one's quality world and existence.

PROLOGUE

"Ethical Pursuits: The Challenge of Being an Optimal Version of Oneself"

So, why a book on contemporary ethics? Society generally lacks a perspective on applied ethics from the author's viewpoint. What are we doing here? The author is seeking to increase ethical dialogue across social groups. What is the author trying to say? Social interaction would improve locally and globally if humans understood, embraced, and applied more effective ethical choices within their daily lives. What problem is being solved or exposed? Let's explore these questions:

First, the author is not solving or revealing one specific problem within the book. Instead, he asks the readers to utilize the knowledge imparted and the questions raised within the manuscript to open and engage in essential dialogues within their respective spheres of influence aligned with the general lack of ethical consideration within contemporary society. Many contexts offer at least one perspective on a topic within the existing ethical discourse and leave a door open for opposing viewpoints to emerge, hopefully, to continue expanding the applicable dialogue.

The author does not take a position on any topic, stating at least one, if not two, opinions to consider as a proverbial "conversational ice-breaker." No one book can cover such an expansive topic, putting the author in a hopeful position to influence readers to explore and engage in civil discourse with others about ethics and stimulate the masses to act. The author selected topics emerging from many contexts. He understands topical relevance within the reader's domain and hopes to encourage readers' feedback on matters to include in later texts.

The book starts by exploring a historical and practical foundation of ethics. The author offers historical facts and definitions and includes some positive and negative examples in the ethics domain. Incorporating the chart of philosophers through the ages, arguably quite convoluted, builds a picture of how the ideology surrounding ethics traversed the human social sphere of influence across several millennia, eventually arriving intact within the contemporary world. The foundation emerging from the chart seeks to project the breadth and scope of the philosophy behind ethics and attempts to represent how humanity has approached the importance of ethical pursuits throughout the ages.

Chapter One explores basic ethical reasoning, followed by some aspects of commonplace ethical objectivity in Chapter Two. Chapter Three dives into the self and how perspective works, and Chapter Four applies concepts from the first three chapters to contemporary social reality. Chapter Five offers several ethical scenarios to stimulate the reader's critical thinking skills. The rest of the book gives the reader support material and ideas for further research.

The advisable approach to reading this book is with an open mind and a focus on understanding how ethics applies to every aspect of contemporary life. The author understands that each reader is unique and has the right to hold individual opinions about ethics. The author's only request is for each reader to understand the existence of distinct differences between ethics and morals, and one should not confuse or conflate the two. Enjoy the book!

FRAMING THE BASIC OVERARCHING CONCEPTS OF ETHICS

*E*thics stems from human interaction, and the contemporary discourse centers on two basic styles or contexts, Deontological and teleological, with modern variants emerging from various scholars down through the ages. To act with consideration for only one or the other would be an anomaly or an outlier. Deontological and teleological are the opposing ends of a broad ethics continuum, and every form of ethics exists within the continuum.

Deontological worldviews (often referred to as virtue ethics) require one to act with noble intent regardless of personal cost, and two distinct types of Deontological treatises are equally prominent. "Act deontology" is where humans, defined as unique, perceive each circumstance or context on its own merits. "Rule deontology" seeks to apply universal rules (Kantian, for example) and compartmentalize the rightness or wrongness of any act.

Whether one applies broad deontological ethics principles as rules to determine right or wrong regardless of cultural artifacts or narrowly defined personal behaviors, the binding agent for all deontology is a traditional virtue context. Aristotle projected deontological actions as an inevitable duty in the strictest sense, aligning with choosing to be universally virtuous in life's pursuits while persistently exhibiting intrinsic goodness without considering adverse outcomes.

Teleological (Telos -- end or goal; logos-reasoning) worldviews, an "end justifies the means" perspective, is often referred to as normative consequentialist ethics. The means-driven form of ethics measures an action's value based on whether a choice produces maximal social benefit, happiness, or pleasure for the largest number of social members. Social actors prefer justifiable outcomes focused on a broad approach to social beneficence, meaning one projects a significant existence of ethics only when one creates the highest social benefit, or *Telos*, the Greek conceptualization of a goal.

Aristotle, who is often the most recognized of the ancient philosophers, with ample apologies to Plato and Socrates, measured *ethos*, the Greek word for ethical approaches, based on the magnitude of virtue within an act. Aristotle believed fairness was a righteous human concept secondary to duty or fidelity. Pursuing *Eudaimonia*, a state of well-being central to Aristotle's discourse, depends on a blending of *phronesis* and *logos*, the Greek ideology of practical wisdom based on logical thought. Before moving into the contemporary social environment, one should explore the origins of the ethics continuum as a basis for enhancing one's comprehension of the concepts included in this book.

CONTEMPORARY ETHICS–"WHERE DO WE START?"

$\mathcal{H}$uman existence depends upon the DNA building blocks of cytosine, adenine, guanine, and thymine when considered through the lens of biology. Add enough sustenance, water, and oxygen, and humans as a species are functionally in an ideal biological growth space. Perhaps, if biology was the whole equation, many other psychosocial factors influence functionality, relegating biology to an essential but isolated origin process.

Slightly less than 8 billion humans (plus or minus a few million) live on "Planet Earth" circa 2020. The planet, comprised of 70% water, with 13% habitable land versus 17% inhabitable land, is incapable of sustaining humanity, especially when one must also consider the vast number of other species competing for space and resources. The resulting permanent scarcity of resources has created existential-level competition between all living creatures. Fortunately for humanity (but not so much for other species), humans sit at the top of the global "food chain."

So, you ask, "What does this have to do with basic contemporary ethics?" In a word, "Everything." Competition leads to conflict on many levels. Managing any dispute requires a set of artificially constructed rules formulated to maintain order while mitigating conflict and chaos. Before the emergence of critical thinking and modern philosophy, humanity followed a "might makes right" simplistic mentality. During the shift to a form of "consideration for others," occurring over the past three-plus millennia (give or take a few hundred years), modern humans have evolved from small, independent pockets of competing groups to become an overcrowded, highly interdependent global society, and yet, through asymmetric power dynamics, a "might makes right" context persists. Many factors influence globalization, and globalization creates many artifacts. Some significant elements are forced migration of refugees due to ever-present wars, cultural exchanges leading to acculturation, assimilation, or the amalgamation of one group with others, and the discovery, exploration, and exploitation of emerging sources of natural resources still occur today. The artifacts include increased interdependence, which also increases the complexity of every working model of human socialization, necessitating a burdensome, complicated system for establishing acceptable behavioral norms.

Occasionally, humans contemplate their existence and assess the level of "rightness" within their social condition, such as when a pandemic like COVID-19 creates a shared social crisis. The resulting knowledge is what researchers and scholars label "philosophy." Regardless of the path taken to arrive at the current social context and based on resource scarcity's proven reality, humans must often coexist in a less-than-optimal environment. Doing so means co-creating a harmonious existence, living with a constant level of competition-driven conflict, making sacrifices for the benefit of others, or suffering dire consequences. One does not have to be an academic historian to know which side of the conceptual continuum the norm has occupied. Conflict is universal and challenging to navigate. The struggle is not with eliminating all possibility of disagreement since paths leading to universal accord, however well-intended, do not exist, but by understanding the causes of conflict and choosing to adhere to some code of behavior with significant potential to mitigate conflict substantially. The search for answers is a primary concern for every "global citizen." The solution to the quest is exploring how to achieve global harmony, starting with an investigation of oneself and extending into society.

Chapter One

ESSENTIAL TREATISES ON ETHICS

"There was a group of blind beggars lining one side of the road enjoying the warmth of the midday sun when a man came upon them with an elephant. As the man passed alms into their bowls, he offered to let each beggar touch his elephant for good luck. As the first man reached out, he felt the elephant's trunk. Then, in succession, each touched an ear, the great heaving side of the beast, a leg, and the tail. Once the elephant handler continued his way, the beggars spoke of what they had touched. Since each had touched a distinctly different part of the animal, they argued over exactly what the elephant was. Perception, it turns out, is everything."

Ancient Indian Tale

"My biggest problem with modernity may lie in the growing separation of the ethical and the legal."

Nassim Nicholas Taleb

"From the ethical point of view, no one can escape responsibility with the excuse that he is only an individual on whom the world's fate does not depend. Not only can this not be known objectively for certain, because it is always possible that it will depend precisely on the individual, but this kind of thinking is also made impossible by the very essence of ethics, conscience, and the sense of responsibility."

Georg Lukacs

"The answer is that there is no good answer. So as parents, doctors, judges, and society, we fumble through and make decisions that allow us to sleep at night because morals are more important than ethics; love is more important than law."

Jodi Picoult

"Your life is a trajectory. Every choice you make alters that trajectory positively or negatively. Will you categorize that dinner with friends as a business expense? Will you be honest with your daughter? Will you take more credit than you're due? These are just the small questions that we face every day, and little by little, the answers influence the trajectory of our lives and beings."

Donald Van de Mark

Readers would engage in an exercise in futility when opening any discourse on ethics or morals without first asserting how philosophers of all historical periods, from the ancient past to the contemporary academics, struggle to settle on one comprehensive theory about the "rightness or wrongness" of human behavior based on available facts from their era. Just as the beggars in the introductory story struggled with defining their elephant, humans struggle with defining ethics, religion, and many other abstract concepts. However, the challenge in understanding ethics and morals is not unique to the modern era; the struggle to define and apply behavioral contexts has been part of the human social dynamic throughout recorded history, with equal considerations and discourse from all ancient cultures.

Self-defined Western cultures focus on the ideologies emerging from historical philosophers such as Socrates, Plato, and Aristotle with a behavioral slant toward collectivist value constructs. Other global cultures have similar discourses and focus on noteworthy historical figures. For example, Buddhism and Confucianism, included from Eastern belief systems, and the Code of Hammurabi from the

Babylonian Empire has added abstract ideology and are prominently embedded in any human discourse on the evolution of ethics.

Each Eastern philosophy projects a behavioral slant toward collectivist, collaborative value constructs anchored on honor. For example, the Confucian concept of *Ren*, defined as beneficence toward other beings, is similar in context to many global behavioral code conceptualizations, such as the *Oneness of Ātman*, the immortal "true self" from the Hindu faith. The Islamic principle of love for God and God's creatures is also an exemplary example. However, radical extremists globally bastardize many Muslim belief contexts, functionally invalidating society's benefits through moderate Islamic behavior when creating conflict and turmoil for many humans.

The Hindu faith gave the world the *Trimurti*, a conceptual belief trinity. The triad includes *Shiva*, the destroyer of evil, the transformer of the universe, *Brahman*, the original creator, and *Vishnu*, the restorer of moral order in humankind. Compare the Trimurti and Shiva as the Supreme Being with the Hindu belief system of *Shakti*, the embodiment of fertility and feminine creation. Shakti represents a Supreme Being responsible for being the agent of all change. Confucian followers offer the concept of *Ren*, which requires benevolence toward all other beings.

Another potential exploration is a concept originating in Africa, *Orisha*, believed to have existed in the spirit world or evolved from humans revered due to extraordinary feats. Orisha is a Yoruba religious precursor to many Latin American religions such as *Santería, Candomblé*, and *Trinidad Orisha*. Orisha's primary goal is the attainment of *Ashe*, a conceptual life force derived from gentle and virtuous behavior. Orisha migrated to the New World from Nigeria as an artifact of the slave trade, alongside *Serer* of Senegalese origin, the *Akan* from Ghana, and *Vodun* of the Gbe tribes, which became the precursor of many modern voodoo sects in North and South

America. These African-based religious and spiritual belief systems expand the base of what the Western world has discerned about the rich cultures emerging from humanity's birthplace and make one wonder how infinitely broad the ethical continuum must be across society based on the discernible diversity present within disparate belief systems.

The Abrahamic religions, Islam, Judaism, and Christianity, are more familiar to Westerners. During the last three centuries, colonial influences and global migration patterns have diffused these three belief systems, allowing them to exist in every corner of the globe, along an ever-evolving landscape with many iterations. First, Christianity alone has the Catholic faith plus multiple versions of Protestantism, called denominations, worldwide. Second, Judaism centers on the ancient Hebrew faith and adheres to a form of implied ownership and jurisdictional supremacy over their people's ancestral home. Conversely, juxtaposed against the traditional forms of Judaism, a Messianic version has emerged, which attempts to bridge the gap between Christianity and the traditional Jewish people. Finally, Islam has multiple versions aligning with various sects throughout the globe, such as Shia, Sunni, Wahhabi, and Sufi. Experts support the existence of more than 150 variants of Islam, with a hybridized version, Bahaiism, and the Nation of Islam made up mostly of members identifying as African-American.

With the multiple variants of the three Abrahamic belief systems, plus hundreds of other religious groups worldwide, it is no wonder humanity has a challenging time becoming "one people." The reality of a religious belief, the "ought" instead of the "is" should be a "live and let live" form anchored in the Golden Rule; however, the reality is one of fracture and conflict. For example, the conceptual differences and seemingly limitless types of expressed beliefs separating the three defined Abrahamic faiths dominate media outlets.

The media focuses on Islamic extremists and their attempt to force their radicalized beliefs on others. The level of conflict emerging from the strict interpretation of Islam and how the radical followers treat non-believers or infidels is significant and newsworthy due to the shocking nature of the violence extending from their actions. The negative impact should not be surprising to believers of other religions worldwide, given how commonplace the brutality has become. Comparatively, one should note the continued existence of many radicalized groups within all global faith systems, not only the groups extending from Islam. Indeed, much of the armed conflict in the 21st Century has been due to the friction between believers of the Abrahamic faiths and other groups and centers on the broad continuum of approaches to how spiritual beliefs manifest in one's life.

The primary point of exploring ancient and contemporary ethical beliefs is to demonstrate how society reinvents itself across time. An artifact of reinvention is how all groups evolve while maintaining secure connections with a universal, identifiable human past. All humans, when isolated or separated from other parts of the world, social groups concurrently develop or have adopted similar conduct codes, although some become perverted or extreme over time. Many hold up as examples of humankind's efforts to civilize, allowing modern scholars to compare origins and outcomes objectively.

Historically, smaller, more isolated populations from global prehistory exhibit commonality. Humans traditionally develop and follow distinctly similar belief systems, including honor, sacrifice, and a sense of duty, continually striving to be considered productive, participating group members during their era. An author could create an entire book with examples of how believers, non-believers, and non-conformists interact consistently throughout history.

For this book, the focus shall be on how contemporary humankind has adapted the ancient concepts of ethics to fit within modernity and explore the artifacts from various social adaptations. The utility realized through the emergent changes is, at times, reasonably sufficient. Yet, many contemporary people take a minimalist approach to ethics, creating a pervasive, self-serving behavior pattern the ancients would barely recognize. Moreover, the correctness of the emerging perversions in behavior is subjective, encouraging debate and potential conflict about how modern humans view applied ethics. Let's explore the social implications.

The ongoing discussion has become mostly academic since many contemporary social constructs do not consider ethics a primary component, relegating ethical considerations to an "include only when necessary" position. Therefore, the book's secondary focus is a deep dive into how shifting or limited ideas of ethics have influenced the contemporary world for better or worse, suggesting pathways to returning society's thoughts to a more relevant ethical discourse.

This book on ethics is not intentionally prescriptive. The follow-up book, Volume II in the "Slippery Slope" series, which focuses on contemporary society's morals, shall follow the same pattern. The author is not seeking to judge others by exploring right or wrong behavior. Instead, the author suggests pathways or action potentials for how humans might debate ethical issues and what topics should be pertinent to subjective choices based on applied ethics. The author advocates choice theory dynamics, which restricts oneself to a litany of self-appraisal and self-correction while wishing to avoid the contemptible contemporary social habituation aimed at socially policing others.

Another point of emphasis to consider is the exclusion of academic citations by the author. The author's position seeks to provide readers with a compelling point of inspiration to join this debate and create enough energy to make positive social change aligned with Volume

I's ethical considerations and Volume II's moral concerns. Asking readers to dive into the debate without encouraging them to feel compelled to conduct research aligned with their interests would be contrary to the author's purpose. References provided after the appendices should be sufficient to jump-start the motivation to research and engage from an informed position socially. Change has a chance when people seek and gain insightful knowledge and choose to be influential for society's sake based on their passionate causes. When a solid foundation for positive change as self-defined by the participants is created because participants acquired the knowledge through a written text and subsequent research, the author has met the challenge of his self-imposed task.

"HISTORICAL AND CURRENT PERSPECTIVES ON ETHICS"

"Alexander the Great, arguably one of the greatest military minds in human history, drove his army east from the Hellenic regions conquering nations and people. During his journey, he encountered many puzzling artifacts. One was the Gordian Knot in Phrygia. Legend implied the person who untied the knot would conquer the world, so Alexander tried his hand at the task. After struggling with the problem for a few moments, Alexander cut the knot apart with his sword. Although modern scholars know Alexander failed in his military attempt, he did conquer a significant portion of his known world and secured his place in history. His teacher before assuming the Macedonian Throne? Aristotle, who is often considered the most substantial philosopher and teacher of ethics known in the Western world."

Buddy Thornton

"Perhaps, indeed, there are no truly universal ethics: or to put it more precisely, how ethical principles are interpreted will inevitably differ across cultures and eras. Yet, these differences arise chiefly at the margins. All known societies embrace the virtues of truthfulness, integrity, loyalty, fairness; none explicitly endorse falsehood, dishonesty, disloyalty, gross inequity."

Howard Gardner

*"The whole interest of my reason, whether speculative or practical,
is concentrated in the three following questions: What can I know?
What should I do? What may I hope?"*

Immanuel Kant

The evolution of ethics (and morals) in ancient Greece emerged and gained prominence as an antecedent of the growth of democracy and the city-states around 600 BC. It is one of the foundational human constructs from which all Western individualistic cultures derive social structure. One must become aware of the older civilizations which preceded ancient Greece, one being Mycenae in the same general geophysical locale. However, knowledge of the Mycenaean culture is limited, so contemporary historians anchor their earliest western-oriented philosophical findings in Greece and the emergence of the modern concept of democracy. The spark leading to the dialogue on ethics came from opposition to prior teachings, notably the protestations of Thrasymachus, an early Sophist who spoke of justice as merely obeying the laws of society established by whatever group holds power, strongly aligned with the idea that "might is right." Socrates, followed by Plato, and finally, Aristotle, debated the wisdom inherent to Grecian social orders based on the Sophist vision of power and control. Aristotle arrived at how ethics should be an internal construct based on proper individual behavior aligned with defined virtues along a *Pathos* continuum stretching from empathetic responses to pathetic suffering across humanity.

Aristotle occupied a unique place in human history. Royalty stood on the one hand; war, socially rigid stratification, and slavery were commonplace, and yet, here stood Aristotle, teaching royalty about many subjects while writing about the need for ethical behavior and equitable outcomes.

Similarly, Eastern collectivist ethics (and morals) emerged from the earliest Indian writings, the Vedas, around 1500 BC. Like Mycenae before Macedonia and Greece, the Akkadian Empire predates much of what one recognizes as the eastern Indo-centric civilization. Again, like Mycenae, most of the culture of Akkadia has disappeared into antiquity, leaving modern experts to start with the Vedas. The Vedas were foundational to Hinduism, Buddhism, Taoism, and Confucianism; these eastern belief systems focus on postulating social "ideals" for living optimally amongst other humans. Through various discourses, the Eastern religions concentrate on man's purity and ultimate perfection through virtues like Aristotle's envisionment in Greece and Macedonia.

Concurrent with Eastern philosophy and religious tenets, Western and Middle Eastern philosophies rose to social prominence. The rise of ancient philosophy had a substantial hand from traders who practiced their craft while traversing their world seeking profits through commerce along the Silk Road, the trade routes between the West, the Middle East, and the East. Examples of shared innovative, emergent influences in the evolution of modern ethics and morals over the millennia exist globally. The Abrahamic faith-based triumvirate of Christianity, Islam, and Judaism in Western history aligns with Buddhism, Taoism, Confucianism, Hinduism, and other faiths as "parallel codes of expected behavior," regardless of which belief system one adheres to, has issues with, or one's level of tolerance.

Although quite fascinating, these religious influences over time will not be part of this treatment on the subject, with one exception. Ancient man held all people to be equal within context, unlike modern man; specifically, one academic ideal was the concept of *paideia*, the Greek belief in providing access to primary education for the masses. Paideia ensured utility would be derivable from knowledge universally. The Greek ethos aligned with the viewpoint that each citizen must be willing and competent to lead regardless of their socioeconomic beginnings; therefore, each "citizen" (defining who a citizen was is arguably another excellent point of discussion) strove to gain the necessary utility. During the era of Greek and Indo-European cultural diffusion, the concept of race or color meant nothing; one's education (cognition combined with demonstrated competency) presents as the foundational differentiation marker between people linked to the Silk Road cultures. Instead of exploring paideia-bound educational theories, this book shall primarily focus on evolving contemporary ethical and moralistic contexts that align with socio-cultural shifts in norms and behaviors that are emerging across all known cultures organically. So, let us begin by touching on basic modern ethics.

In most definitions, ethics are aligned with right or wrong concepts, subject to cultural or social interpretation, and hold action potential as the framework for one's moral perspective. Most defined professional groups, such as doctors, attorneys, mediators, and financial planners, have well-established ethical codes of conduct. Within the established norms for behavior in most professions, ethics become member-defined frameworks to project honest, fair, and predictable professional performance. Removing the ethical constraints from contemporary professional structures makes behavioral margins harder to discern. Questionable ethics would exponentially increase, such as the plethora of unproven claims surrounding the 2020 election cycle and how social media and the courts are misused daily.

A specific non-political example exists in the current treatment of pass-fail in many modern school systems (although ample districts are willing to hold a student back for cause), creating a dual standard when comparing the various levels of support for standards across distinct locales). Established norms aligning with pass-fail are easy to identify, yet virtually all students move seamlessly through the system, regardless of whether they meet the criteria. The threat of lawsuits aligned with claims of psychological harm to the child, the deflection of bullying by parents, or the hope of student self-correction through maturity over time are examples of many "justifications" for not holding a failing student back. The author withholds judgment about whether the process is effective or not; instead, he will only suggest two groups of questions based on ethics.

The first group of questions: Is it ethical to lower the bar and ignore standards established to ensure when students "graduate" and enter mainstream society? Would bypassing the established standards allow teachers and parents to ensure students gain enough competency to function as self-sufficient adults? A subset of the questions, whether it is ethical to hold some students to a rigidly held standard while other students get a "pass," is essential to social equity's core issue, especially for disadvantaged populations. Suppose a contemporary norm of "pass all students regardless of potential costs" is the new standard. The broader community would be burdened with caring for many insufficiently prepared adults based on risk-avoidant choices by educational decision-makers. From an ethical perspective, the contemporary norm aligns with decision-makers taking a "path of least resistance" by not adhering to or anchoring policy on generally aligned optimal standards.

The second group of questions: Is it ethical to reward an academic failure at the same rate or magnitude as an academic success? Does a high school diploma hold social weight as a measure of eventual success as an adult? Arguably, it should project value. Unfortunately, the modern-day normative view of the present educational system has reduced a high school diploma's perceived value to minimal consideration. People ask a qualifying question after, "Did you earn a high school diploma?" The follow-up invariably becomes, "What was your GPA?" The GPA system becomes problematic when considering how the system should project as the success scale for graduation standards (and beyond); however, multiple factors cloud the issue, such as bonus points awarded for honors classes.

Many in society also ignore the derived utility GPA differentiation offers due to the subjective nature of how teachers have tremendous latitude in grading contexts. Again, with emphasis, no effort shall be made to denote any perception of value. Infinite reasons exist to support the present-day system's existence, and the justifications for the support given are explorable in many other forums. In modern contexts, a debate on social choices within the educational sphere of influence rarely hinges on ethics alone.

Before moving forward, be mindful that the educational example is only one of an infinite number of contexts one may utilize to project how minimal adherence to standards has eroded how ethics are socially applied. Minimizing consideration for the "concepts" of right or wrong has become skewed within the context of modern ethics, not the ethics themselves. Some "skewness" misaligning ethics with modernity comes from utilitarianism. Like the two contexts noted within deontology artifacts, utilitarianism also exists as either act-based aligning with acquiring maximum happiness or rule-based focused on widespread socially beneficial outcomes. If the contexts are correct, exploring contemporary applied ethics should suggest a corrective pathway, eventually supporting the adoption of a worldview aligned with compelling behavior models based on redefining and applying an evolved theory of ethics one finds between the virtue of deontology and the utility of teleology.

With the suggested exploration in mind, the author has compiled this book as a vehicle to stimulate debate while avoiding any suggestion of implied certitude. The author supports his position with a section on the fallibility of certainty. Volume I on ethics and Volume II on morals expand both contexts beyond the common mistake of juxtaposing the two as being permanently linked or aligned. Readers should begin their journey through the book by imagining a construct like a mind map where ethics and morals may or may not be present, together, separated, synthesized, or overlapped (think like a Venn diagram), but never as synonyms of each other. One must consider the broad continuum of potential within any social discourse. Those entering the debate should recognize whether an action or thought is moral, amoral, or immoral based on accepted cultural norms. Likewise, whether either purposeful, intentional, or unintentional acts or innovative ideas are ethical, unethical, or lack any principled component or basis, acknowledge the conceptual reasoning behind separating the two contexts.

"FOR WHOM DO YOU SERVE?"

"Jesus called them together and said, "You know that those who are regarded as rulers of the Gentiles lord it over them, and their high officials exercise authority over them. Not so with you. Instead, whoever wants to become great among you must be your servant, and whoever wants to be first must be slave of all. For even the Son of Man did not come to be served, but to serve, and to give his life as a ransom for many."

Luke 22:25

"Servant leadership means being the optimal choice when your people need you, but that also includes yourself. Be present, seek growth, listen to everyone before choosing, gather a community around you, and be willing to let others teach you."

Buddy Thornton

"I devote my life in service of humanity."

Lailah Gifty Akita

The search for practical answers to this question has led to many debates about motivation and whether one owes any level of responsibility or accountability beyond one's needs and wants. Scholars and researchers cite *Abraham Maslow's Hierarchy of Needs* (1943) as a dynamic contemporary theory linked to human motivation. Although 75 years have elapsed since Maslow first published his treatise on human behavior, "A Theory of Human Motivation," the method applies to all motivational discourses which followed. As a seminal article, Maslow's Hierarchy bears exploration due to its foundational alignment with contemporary ethics. Suppose one is to explore Maslow's theory; modern academics view the hierarchy as a working

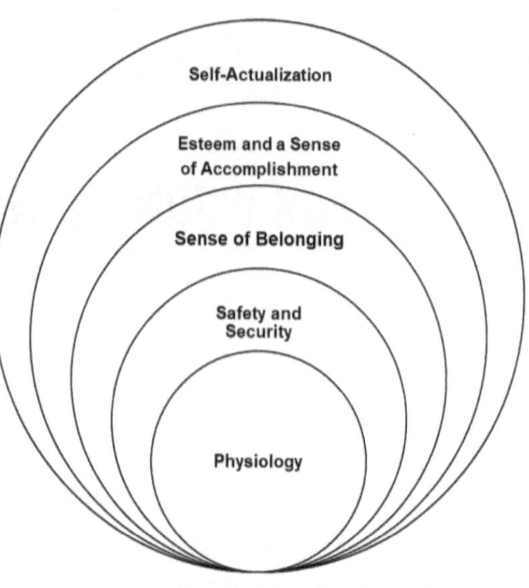

explanation, a behavioral model, or a framework instead of a theory. One would discern a similar orientation with several propositions of Aristotle's Ethics and the concept of *eudaimonia*, the belief aligning with pursuing a well-lived existence allowing a man to earn the highest virtue. Both Maslow's theory and Aristotle's treatise should be equally applicable within the boundaries of a timeless continuum reaching from one man to the whole of society.

Many scholars consider the original conceptualization of Maslow's Hierarchy as a pyramid with five attainment levels; however, Maslow perceived a fluid continuum where participants could occupy each needs area simultaneously. The illustration presented represents Maslow's original Hierarchy of Needs: Maslow's model holds relevance for an infinite number of undergraduate psychology classes, remarkable considering eight-plus decades have passed since its inception. The work has enjoyed multiple iterations since Maslow's inception and publication, with an expanded example appearing later in this chapter.

"BASIC NEEDS-PHYSIOLOGICAL AND SAFETY"

"One thousand days define a human's existential opportunity experience over each lifetime. From conception to the second birthday, research shows the physical and psychological development which occurs 'presets' each child's life journey. Scarcity in any area diminishes a child's entire existence more than one may imagine. UNICEF"

"By looking at the world through the eyes of a child, you may begin to experience, then understand, the unique viewpoints they have of their world, which are vastly different from how adults see their world. What might their eyes be missing if they focus solely on the hunger in their belly? How might constant fear disrupt their worldview? Listen, and you will hear. Remember, their perception IS their reality!"

Buddy Thornton

"The ache for home lives in all of us. The safe place where we can go as we are and not be questioned."

Maya Angelou

"The desire for safety stands against every great and noble enterprise."

Tacitus

"I won't get into details, but the greeks are a loud people because they have been occupied for centuries by different peoples on different occasions, and so the best way to keep the 'bear' away is to make it think twice before approaching."

Monaristw

"I had always thought of home not as a house, or even a place, but a feeling of safety and acceptance, a warm light when the rest of the world was a dark, forbidding place. Whenever my family was around, wherever we were, I felt like I was home."

Elizabeth Haydon

The first level, physiological needs, is the universal pursuit of each human's existential biological artifacts. The minimal needs "primacy" effect aligns with every construct of man's competition to share the planet's consumable resources. All species, including humankind, compete for these resources. When put into Aristotelian terms, seeking eudaimonia would shift a single man's pursuit of physiological resources to an ethical requirement to secure minimal needs for his family, village, city, or state as a foundation for a well-lived existence.

A similar pattern appears at the second level, the procurement of safety and security. Again, humans have the propensity to take risks associated with achieving the needs aligning with necessary sustenance. However, once those needs are satisfied, humans default to a strong focus on "preservation of self." Without question, the survival instinct extends from one of singular focus to a desire to propagate the species, which aligns the second as a foundation for the third level, seeking to belong to an in-group and be loved.

Aristotle's treatment of ethics requires the sacrifice of oneself for the in-group's safety and security, again as an antecedent of a well-lived existence. In the context of Ancient Greece and Macedonia, the concept of an in-group was fluid, meaning the in-group might include family, the city, or the entirety of Greek civilization, depending on the immediacy of threats. Based on this concept, social norms would expect one to voluntarily act on the action potential aligned with servitude or sacrifice for the sake of others and possibly pay the ultimate price for the safety of one's compatriots, which is a blended universal construct of both deontological ethics (doing the "virtuous" right thing) and teleological ethics (achievement of results or ends justify the means, in this case, one's sacrifice). In contemporary terms, one would be ethically bound to act with benevolence toward others.

Also included within the second level is an intense debate over "whom does one serve?" For example, if one would achieve safety during a threatening event without regard for others, can this be ethically correct? There are many sides to this question; however, the ultimate problem is one's focus based on context. On one side, for example, if a man preserves himself to ensure his family's existence, believing they would otherwise become victims, the choice should be considered ethical. However, on the opposing side, if the same man provides for his survival at the cost of another in his in-group, the act may be perceived as unethical.

One construct addressing the servitude domain is a continuum of action versus inaction. Imagine an environment where one chooses to act for others with little risk, where maleficence is manifest and may allow the omission of overt acts entirely yet remain effective. Extend the environment to an overt act of goodwill, which may also manifest with minimal involvement, but often requires one to endure sacrifice for others, such as in the context of servant leadership. Either choice may allow one to achieve an optimal social effect. The entire continuum aligns with Eudaimonia if one consciously addresses servant leadership based on the commission or omission of acts as an honorable, ethical trait.

Distinct conflict contexts, such as war, tend to make the question moot, with both sides balancing social duty and individual needs. War scenarios subsequently shrink the value of safety and sacrifice down into a discussion of level one minimal needs constructs. Throughout history, the existence of war has forced entire groups of people into level one existence. The issue shifts from one's understanding of ethical behavior to one's perception of morality aligned with complicated "right or wrong" choices one faces at the end of a gun barrel. In volume II, the book on morals, readers shall explore and expand the morality context of armed conflict. Arguably, armed conflict scenarios create environments with limited existential choices, and ethical considerations are of little importance.

The first two levels of Maslow's Hierarchy project prioritized basic needs essential to all humans, especially in the early years of life, as projected in this section's introduction. In the contemporary mindset, achieving both needs levels allows the emergence of skewed ethical considerations. Does one focus on one's unique needs, or should the needs of loved ones take precedent? Are both achievable to a degree? Does someone choosing to achieve needs at a minimal level diminish their self-image or self-esteem? The possible responses to these questions are infinitely debatable. Based on religious worldview, cultural norms, legal considerations, and personal choice, the answers lie on a continuum described on one end as objectivism, with the other being subjectivism. Objectivism aligns with making decisions based solely on measurable variables and logic-based thinking about possible outcomes. Subjectivism aligns with making decisions based on an individualized mental construct with minimal consideration for extrinsic facts. Objectivity stifles creativity, while subjectivity will always suffer from limitations inherent to an incomplete information reality. Humans optimize the objectivity/subjectivity context by avoiding the extremes and finding a balance within the middle ground, the perceptual "gray" area of moderation.

Similarly, humans pursue existential needs by creating a broad range of "achievement pathways" with action potential leading to success. At one end lies the teleological perspective of "acceptable outcomes at any cost excuses any behavior taken to acquire those outcomes." At the other end lies the deontological perspective of "required unequivocal but acceptable sacrifice" to ensure others' needs. When considering the skewed ethical considerations in the previous paragraph, where would each answer lie on the achievement continuum?

Please note that the questions are rhetorical with no correct answers. Regardless of how one answers these four questions, the benefit derived is aligned with whether the questions stimulated critical thinking. Go for a walk. Think about how an opposing perspective may be more accurate than your thoughts on the topic. Take the time to write a short paragraph on both (or more) potentialities for clarity. This exercise in critical thinking is foundational to the next section on psychological needs.

"PSYCHOLOGICAL NEEDS FRAMEWORK: BELONGING, LOVE, AND ESTEEM"

"You cannot change any society unless you take responsibility for it; unless you see yourself as belonging to it and responsible for changing it."

By Grace Lee Boggs

"The Greeks found love to be so important; they developed eight different versions of the emotion, namely Eros (passionate), Philia (affection), Agape (universal and selfless), Storge (familial), Mania (obsessive), Ludus (playful crush), Pragma (enduring), and Philautia (self-love). The Christian Bible elevates Agape as the highest form of love, the love that Jesus Christ professed to his Father and all of humanity."

Buddy Thornton

"Associate with men of good quality if you esteem your reputation, for it is better to be alone than in bad company."

George Washington

"Freedom on the inside comes when validation from the outside doesn't matter."

Richie Norton

*"Owning our story can be hard but not nearly as difficult
as spending our lives running from it. Embracing our vulnerabilities
is risky but not nearly as dangerous as giving up on love, belonging,
and joy, experiences that make us the most vulnerable. Only when
we are brave enough to explore the darkness will we discover
the infinite power of our light."*

Brene Brown

*"I didn't understand then what a profound act of generosity this was; to see
another person as a part of your tribe when they don't see themselves that
way is an act of kindness. It requires that you extend yourself to another."*

Elamin Abdelmahmoud

Some people say, "Love makes the world go-'round." Psychologically, the belief has merit, but biologically speaking, the statement is incorrect. Procreation would be the correct answer. In most Western cultures, attracting a mate is a considerable "rite of passage" for both sexes. In many Eastern cultures, love is secondary to attaining an exploitable and socially significant familial position with status through arranged pairings. From an ethical perspective, there is no strong push or pull in either direction.

Maslow's original hierarchy asserts that gaining a sense of belonging is the first step beyond essential needs. One may effortlessly isolate a "sense of belonging" from other "needs" constructs such as love or passion. First, a sense of belonging aligns with primal biology. "Belonging" is the foundation of any esteem construct and is the quintessential mental boundary between needs and wants. Second, understanding the right way to belong, in a relationship, in a family, or in a group emerges from the application of *phronesis*, one of three components of an earlier version of the current action cycle, portrayed as the Greek ideology of practical wisdom, and aligning with Aristotle's adherence to the pursuit of *eudaimonia*.

Intimate dyadic relationships, unique within human social constructs, lie along a distinct continuum, from the "Eros" to "Pragma" of Greek descriptions of love, but sometimes reaching to "Mania" and beyond. The beneficial end of the continuum thrives on an environment of universal positive regard, regardless of social or cultural pretexts.

Beyond "mania," an obsessive form of harmful love, is eternally bound to the destructive end of the continuum where ethics lacks substance and morals are absent from thought. A sense of ownership of one person by another, jealousy, controlling behavior, and many abuse contexts make the harmful end of the dyadic relationship continuum ethically untenable. In contrast, the pairing co-ownership makes the intimate dyad incredibly durable, creating the context where pragma emerges. Within the arranged marriage context of many collectivist societies, harmful behaviors are generally unacceptable; despite the early absence of eros, love finds a way to thrive, with cultural norms leading to positive outcomes.

When speaking of thriving, beginning with intimate relationships, most dyadic contexts successfully exist as a form of collaborative symbiosis, referred to as "dyadic entanglement." Humans continually move into and out of dyadic relationships based on a constant shift in perceptible needs. Maslow's concept of "esteem" requires bidirectional balance and each party's ability to focus on maintaining some form of universal positive regard. Any construct offsetting or upending the balance within the dyad reduces both parties' motivation to remain in the relationship. In most cases, the constant shift occurring within non-intimate dyadic relationships allows humans to continually evolve toward optimal existence, supporting Aristotle's virtue construct.

Humans tend to project within "schemas" of expected behavior aligned with the environment they occupy with minimal consideration for other human interactions outside basic dyadic constructs. Intrinsic self-esteem increases or decreases in proportion to how well individuals perceive their environmental "fitness" and contribution to a group. "Fitness," in this case, is how well one blends into an environment's social structure. The drive to achieve fitness within a specific social context forces an evolution of one's perspective on Maslow's original model regarding how self-esteem and self-actualization work in contemporary society, leading one to view Maslow as a dynamic interactive model.

First, humans conceptualize a subjective definition of success individually while being influenced by social norms within a narrowly defined sphere of influence. The pursuit of success context is where cognitive (knowledge-based) processes lead to schemas designed to increase social fitness. Social fitness and mental needs are particular to an individual, followed by a similar focal target: aesthetic needs. Whether aesthetic needs are a projection of social "fitness" or simply following one's preference for how to project one's competence range or physical image is immaterial to the foundational aspect of how aesthetics affect self-esteem. A blended model chosen to boost one's intrinsic self-image includes synthesizing all artifacts involved with one's vision of "fitness."

"SELF-ACTUALIZATION, TRANSCENDENCE, AND ETHICS OF CHOICE"

"Transcendence refers to the very highest and most inclusive or holistic levels of human consciousness, behaving and relating, as ends rather than means, to oneself, to significant others, to human beings in general, to other species, to nature, and the cosmos."

By Abraham Maslow

"Across all human religions, one's version of God is, by faith and belief, transcendent and unknowable. Whether faithful or unbelievers, humans universally pursue self-actualization, a 'somewhat' acceptable substitute for the unattainable transcendence of God."

Buddy Thornton

"What you have to decide is how you want your life to be. If your forever was ending tomorrow, would this be how you'd want to have spent it? Listen, the truth is, nothing is guaranteed. You know that more than anybody. So don't be afraid. Be alive."

Sarah Dessen

Thus far, Maslow has suggested concrete, identifiable stages within his hierarchy of needs paradigm. Although the steps are recognizable, they are malleable, overlapping, and highly interdependent, with every human experiencing the potential for concurrently occupying all levels within the model depending on one's needs and environmental context. The original model was simplistic, while an evolved model illustrates more depth and breadth, allowing one to increase utility by exploring the expanded concept.

The original model suggests that self-actualization, a subjective, individualized mindset of what constitutes a healthy self-image based on achieving positive self-esteem, is the pinnacle of human achievement. The original model lacks a "why," which the newer model addresses by inducing action potential for including psychological needs as an essential context. Maslow objectively defined a subjective framework. The model requires a level of flexibility aimed at supporting unique choices. The framework allows an individual to find the best way to reach and then breach each level within the model, with the breach creating enough momentum to conquer each level effectively. Since self-actualization is a subjective construct, the newer model had to include an answer to the "why," which is how to establish "motivation to achieve" within the self as a variable. Achieving transcendence became the answer to why, which suggests the newer model has found an optimal human target, the contemporary "best version" equivalent of Aristotle's *eudaimonia*, a life well-lived.

The ethics inherent to the concept of choice dynamics become applicable to Maslow's hierarchy at this point as a referent to the motivation variable. Is it ethical to dictate another person's choices? Is an attempt to dictate actions beyond oneself tenable to most modern social constructs? The ethics of choice supports how the only person one can control is oneself. By visualizing choice dynamics as the primary moderator, one may seek to internalize a transcendence pathway and align the selected path with ethical choices. When considering the topic of ethics and the upper levels of human growth potential, Maslow's hierarchy depends on humanity's adherence to "Choice Dynamics." Once existential needs are met, individual choice drives every level of the motivational construct.

Expanding or maintaining flexible options for seeking and achieving "fitness" becomes critical to creating unique pathways leading to an individual's optimal success. Any perception of failure during one's projection of aesthetic choices or during the affirmation of those choices becomes a psychological barrier. Flexibility is foundational to one's self-actualization; inflexibility blocks any potential outcome aligning with optimization. Since individual choice is the primary foundational component of motivation-specific behavior, one should explore an expanded version of Maslow's hierarchy model aligned with contemporary social contexts.

The updated version shared in this chapter is only one of many possible adaptations. The original model, consisting of five levels, has evolved into eight. The potential exists within Maslow's model for infinite stages when considering that each base level may include numerous sub-levels. For example, how does one internalize aesthetic needs? To some, physical beauty is optimal. Within another group, mental efficacy reigns supreme. Most people would link aesthetic to a visual manifestation of beauty; however, any artifact may hold the perception of "beauty" for any beholder, such as music to the ears, the elegance of a cheetah traversing the African plains at high speed, or the beauty ascribed to overcoming a barrier once perceived as unconquerable.

Self-actualization and transcendence also depend on one's perception of what one should optimize within one's focus. What should become apparent here is how flexible the model becomes as it adapts to individual needs and allows an in-depth choice analysis. A demarcation line between deficit needs and growth needs lies within the model, aligning with one's perspective and dividing the eight levels into four needs and four wants areas of motivation. Take the time to deeply explore what each stage means to yourself, discussing your thoughts with others to get a broad outlook of how vastly different humans choose to perceive what began as a simple model of human motivation. Remember to consider each level's options based on different needs environments, such as the unique needs of a single person versus the expansive needs of a family, especially given the additional duty each family member owes to the others within the in-group. Also, be open-minded to others' perspectives and be willing to allow your ideas to evolve and grow, enhancing your ability to acquire each rung within the model.

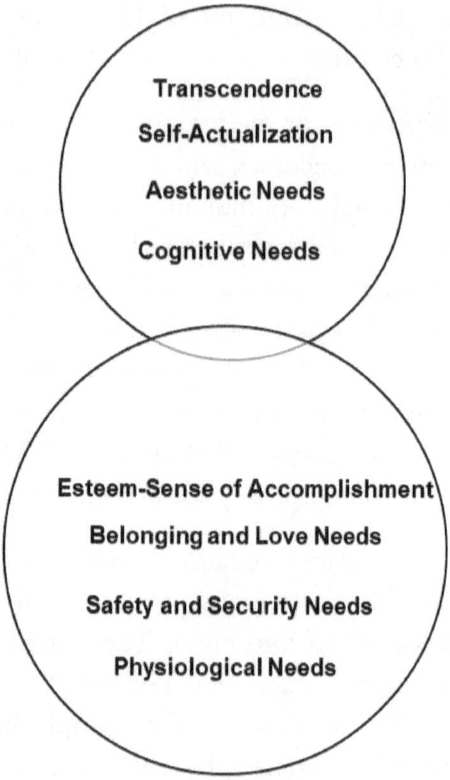

Transcendence

Self-Actualization

Aesthetic Needs

Cognitive Needs

Esteem-Sense of Accomplishment

Belonging and Love Needs

Safety and Security Needs

Physiological Needs

Note how the newer model sets four levels of needs as deficiency needs, leading to a different reference line for where personal choice becomes part of the cycle. The original model supported an archaic thinking mode, which ignored emergent levels of psychological needs as essential to "being." The newer model supports fundamental belonging as a critical part of human existence, with positive self-esteem being an "all-important" steppingstone to consistent, sustainable growth.

The deficiency needs context also supports how achieving the first four levels should be perceived as an "amoral" journey requiring only a cursory ethical construct. Breaking down the journey one chooses to traverse in seeking the pathway for attaining one's growth needs depends on an individual's intrinsic motivation level. However, all humans are motivated to reach and sustain viability within the first four levels, as portrayed by Maslow, given those needs' existential nature. Upcoming sections of this book will explore how contemporary society has shifted ethics to fit the motivation model, as portrayed here. The exploration requires a foundational understanding of Maslow's expanded motivation model. One must also explore the motivational context from a cross-cultural position to gain a validated perspective leading to an equitable exploration of individualistic and collectivist societies, the two most researched forms of socially identifiable groups globally.

"EXPANDING MASLOW TO A CONTEMPORARY MOTIVATION MODEL"

*"Do what is right, not what is easy nor what is popular.
Attitude is a choice; happiness is a choice; optimism is a choice;
kindness is a choice; giving is a choice; respect is a choice.
Whatever choice you make makes you; choose wisely."*

RT Bennett

*"Live your truth. Express your love. Share your enthusiasm. Take action
towards your dreams. Walk your talk. Dance and sing to your music.
Embrace your blessings. Make today worth remembering."*

Steve Maraboli

"Life always begins with one step outside of your comfort zone."

Shannon L. Alder

When humans consider the concept of "motivation," they begin the process by understanding that motivation is subjective and highly individualized in every culture. There are many motivation research models to explore, as the Venn diagram illustrates. The best research on how "motivation" fits Maslow's Hierarchy comes from the Expanded Cultural Intelligence Scale (E-CQS) due to the increasing rate of globalization within society and the inclusion of a continuum linking intracultural to cross-cultural contexts. The study validating the E-CQS focuses on how cultural intelligence artifacts influence organizational structure and strategy. The results of the initial and subsequent studies project a distinct pattern suggesting the prominence of motivation within predictable human behavior. The model identifies artifacts aligned with exploring how humans pursue goals, a journey based on four primary components to every goal-oriented approach. These components separate into cognition and metacognition, the mental portion of the four-factor model, with motivation and actionable behavior being the model's functional portion. Research demonstrates that the E-CQS model is cyclical, omnidirectional, and creates a constant feedback loop.

First, one must have or acquire knowledge to pursue any goal. The E-CQS labels this as a cognitive need. Once knowledge is acquired, one must add or assign structure to how the acquired knowledge enhances one's ability to engage in the pursuit. The E-CQS labels the resulting strategy-based configuration as a metacognitive need. "Meta-"denotes the ability to combine or synthesize knowledge into a construct with utility. These first two essential aspects are foundational to building mental competency, which creates an environment where an ever-present action potential leads to the two defined functional components.

The first functional component is motivation, which is the "why" for pursuing any goal. Without "affective" (self-enhancing experiential) motivation, the final element, behavior, would not be triggered. Knowledge acquisition often prompts rational (knowledge-based without any experiential basis) motivation, which may counteract affective motivation's positive effects. Moving from rational to affective motivation requires the insertion of personal acceptance, often called "buy-in," and the ability to cope with bias. Affective motivation is the action potentiator, compellingly driven by a fundamental belief that an objective aligns with an optimal personal choice capable of providing access to an adequate fulfillment of needs. Once motivation is intrinsically stable, prompting one's will to act, behavior takes on a life of its own and virtually flows unchecked until one achieves the target goal. The resulting action cycle complements Maslow's Hierarchy. (See Appendix C for a complete article on the design and potential utility of the Action Cycle.)

In this context, Cultural Intelligence (CQ) explores how motivation works. The choice of CQ is arbitrary since the four-factor model works equally with any of the contemporary "intelligence" paradigms, such as Emotional Intelligence (EQ), Social Intelligence (SQ), or any of the other defined types of recognized intelligence (explore three representative models displayed in appendix C to explore how the concept is quite broad, but note how CQ, EQ, and SQ are absent). One aspect inherent to any version of measurable "intelligence" is the difference between exhibiting the attainment of knowledge and any level of action potential for derived utility from the acquired knowledge, which is where motivation sits as an essential component to triggered behavior associated with each type of intelligence.

When synthesizing motivation into the model, one must turn to the demarcation line between existential needs (deficiency causes barriers) and growth environments to explore the concept of ethics. All humans must achieve basic existential needs to survive, making individual motivation during the need's attainment portion of the model an essential existential focus for anyone mired in a self-perceived deficiency area. Once one crosses the Maslow model demarcation line, the point where growth becomes the primary focus and the "wants paradigm" begins to manifest, one's motivation becomes subjective and individualized. Moving beyond the "must do" to the "choice dynamics" paradigm empowers humans to embrace a subtle "doubling down on protecting what we have" effect. One effortlessly demonstrates how navigating Maslow's Hierarchy explains why humans either ignore or adhere to the concepts of ethics dependent upon where in the model they find themselves. The human needs-wants context always impacts every notion of ethics.

The scarcity of global resources is a reality, although resource distribution is inconsistent across populations. Therefore, overcoming deficiency needs and exploring growth needs is not a personal guarantee based on the asymmetric context of global scarcity. In many parts of the globe, human populations must spend excessive time and resources to overcome the deficiencies they endure; in other areas, the abundance of riches suggests humanity needs to spend more time and energy on essential resource allocation. Keeping this in mind, one may conclude that having or earning an opportunity to climb above the demarcation line depends on one's access to resources and the motivation to trigger one's action potential.

When the opportunity to climb does not exist, to what extreme may someone who desires more than a minimal existence go to reach the growth paradigm, even on the bottom rung? How one perceives the question and answer is where ethics, or a palpable lack of ethical consideration when one fears failing where needs fulfillment are in question, plays an essential role. How ethics is perceived depends highly on where one exists on the action potential continuum. Is it ethical for the "haves" to maintain their existence at the cost of the "have-nots?"

Exploring the dynamics of ethics when taking the journey through Maslow's Hierarchy becomes an existential question for many global citizens, requiring exploration of socioeconomic stratification and how dehumanization mitigates or negates ethical thinking.

There are many motivation models to explore; Maslow is not the first, nor possibly the best, but it stands the test of time because of academic diffusion and adoption. For the enterprising readers who want another model to peruse, try Promotion Versus Prevention Orientation (Higgins), Self-efficacy (Bandura), or Self-regulation (Zimmerman).

"THIS IS NOT ONE WORLD"

"You may travel the whole world yet not feel one with it. It is not about moving your feet; it is about moving your mind."
Abhijit Naskar, *Aşkanjali: The Sufi Sermon*

"One World is not abolishing frontiers, which would lead to a surge in migration, create tension, and destabilize life on our planet. One World is abolishing the concept of borders in people's minds and replacing devotion to individual nations with belief in one united world, home to one race: the human race."
Mouloud Benzadi

"The sea divides Africa from Europe. Yet the people who live in those lands need not be divided. I've lived in both places, and I know from experience we are more alike than we'd like to believe."
Rehan Khan

"If we focus on the inner world, which makes us all the same, then the outer world will not seem in such conflict. It will be enlivening, not dividing, enriching, not impoverishing, uniting, not damaging."
Donna Goddard

Cultural variation is infinite and undeniable. In the broadest context, the world is divided into collectivist and individualist social approaches. One best describes a focus on collectivist social methodologies as an Eastern honor-centric social system dedicated to "saving face" and preserving honor. The best description of individualist social approaches aligns with a Western truth-centric social structure dedicated to projecting honesty, whether it supports one's best interests. In both cultural contexts, integrity projects commonality and is manifest. The narrowest framework one could explore suggests that no two humans will share matching motivations or experiential knowledge sets. Therefore, any discussion about similarities and differences in ethics must include both ends of the continuum and avoid stereotyping.

Within the continuum, infinite numbers of social perspectives exist, far too many to explore here. However, doing a comparative exploration for clarity emphasizes how variance dictates differentiation despite all humans' biological similarities. Many of the differences align with ideological sociopolitical environments. Within the collectivist social context alone, one encounters communist/socialist (many), democratic/republic (only a few), and dictatorship/autocratic forms of government (among others). Acting for the welfare of the collective is expected and often mandated. Individualist social contexts tend to exist as forms of republics or democracies where members celebrate competition for an infinite number of definable limited resources as a social differentiator.

The ethics aligned with collectivist thinking requires sacrificing a portion of one's individuality in most existing paradigms. Anyone projecting self-interest over society's collective needs draws immediate attention and suffers reprisals from the state or other stakeholders within the definable commons. Expectations become the domain of the government. Suppression of individual choice dynamics is the norm, especially when they conflict with collective needs.

The ethics aligned with individualist thinking are much broader. The image of the "self-made man" dominates the conversation, although social stratification and one's starting point (based on one's level of affluence) create an uneven playing field. The socio-ethical norms explore weaknesses, exploit the findings to gain a competitive advantage, and take steps to sustain the achieved advantage. The marginalization of one's competition to self-elevate is the capstone of normalized behavior within individualistic cultures. Contemporary individualistic cultures actively embrace penetrating barriers and seeking personal growth as the quintessential holy grail pathway.

The distinct dichotomy of ethical differentiation between collectivist and individualist cultures is understandable. In many ways, how ethics manifest is a lagging indicator of overall social expectations. Collectivist norms align with teleological ethics firmly focused on social outcomes at the individual's expense, a form of ethics designed to ensure the "collective" is of primary importance.

However, teleological ethics become more discernible when the individual is marginalized, creating barriers to adopting deontological ethics. To communist governments, the ends become the only consideration, with the means ostensibly open to leadership exploitation. Other collectivist-aligned social constructs suffer from similar asymmetric power dynamics. This approach's artifacts mean a significant number of occupants within constrained individualist cultures view actions taken by the governments or leaders of collectivist societies as lacking compassion for their people.

From a reverse perspective, individualist cultures tend toward deontological ethics, with one outlier distinction. Competitive economics opens the door to weakening virtue ethics in the guise of pursuing profitability, which is a socially supported business version of the "ends justify the means" teleological perspective. In contemporary contexts, many business leaders view the "virtue" approach as sub-optimal when shareholder investors zealously reward competitors willing to explore ethical or marginal options to increase profitability.

The players project a "toe the line" ethical stance, but a "not caught is not guilty" perspective prevails. Moreover, seemingly unethical projections create public distrust of successful entrepreneurs when consumers must adhere to a standard not perceived as required of more affluent players.

The evident differences between collectivist and individualist cultures only scratch the surface of "not one world." There are distinct groups within cultures, starting with an easily identifiable majority (in most cases, not always, and not entropic), with many versions of minority and "other" defined groups to consider. Each, such as LGBTQ, or "Incels" (involuntary celibates), or economically-stratified within the same group, presents a multilayered worldview when ethics enter the dynamics. In vogue on today's book lists are multiple treatises on the culture wars and their social impact since, well, forever.

In the modern context of globalized and local players, teleological ethics has become the context of choice for all cultures, manifesting in different, often divergent ways. Members of all beliefs have marginalized deontological "virtue" ethics, making "doing the right thing regardless of cost" an archaic concept, which moves society to an "ends justify any means" mentality. Suppose most global consumers willingly forego virtuous thought processes for shallow, insignificant gains. Where does this leave people who believe in doing the right thing regardless of how it plays out? The answer may lie in critical thinking deep-dives into right versus wrong concepts combined with an underlying cross-cultural perspective.

"CRITICAL THINKING ABOUT RIGHT VERSUS WRONG"

*One morning, two monks were walking to a distant monastery
when they approached a swollen stream. Beside the water's edge was
an older woman trying to find enough courage to cross the rushing waters.
One of the monks picked her up and quickly crossed the stream,
while the other monk followed while frowning at his companion.
Once safely across, the compassionate monk set his passenger down,
bowed deeply, and started moving toward his destination.*

*The second monk admonished his action, "Why did you carry
her across when you know it is forbidden to interact with any woman?"*

*The first monk replied, "Why are you still anchored to the heavy burden
on your mind? I left the woman by the stream; you should do so also."*

*Sometimes a choice is just a choice, but right is invariably proven correct,
while wrong is consistently wrong.*

Buddy Thornton

*"Critical thinking is a learned process of deliberation, fact-checking,
and self-reflection used to comprehend and appropriately evaluate
information to decide what to believe or do."*

John V. Petrocelli

*"From what I can tell, most people are stuck in a developmental stage
before critical thinking, where social and psychological factors
are the ultimate reason for their ideas. Gaining popularity and social
acceptance are usually higher goals than figuring out the truth,
especially if the truth is unpopular."*

Steve Patterson

*"The human brain is an organ out of time. It stands as evolved
and best suited for daily life in the Pleistocene, yet here it is, having
to make do in a modern, high-tech, wired, and fast-changing world."*

Guy P. Harrison

*"Responsibility to yourself means refusing to let others do your thinking,
talking, and naming for you; it means learning to respect and use your
own brains and instincts; hence, grappling with hard work."*

Adrienne Rich

*"Philosophy ought to question the basic assumptions of the age.
Thinking through, critically and carefully, what most of us take
for granted is, I believe, the chief task of philosophy, and the task
that makes philosophy a worthwhile activity."*

Peter Singer

"Right versus Wrong" is not a simple process when extended
beyond classical "if-then" scenarios or applied to different
cultures with different personal values protocols. One specific cultural
context illustrates whether it is permissible to punish a woman for acts
men can do routinely. Driving is a privilege earned by any legal person
who can complete the necessary licensing protocols in many countries;
however, in some Middle Eastern countries, women are forbidden
to drive, and authorities punish them for the "crime." Depending
on the predominant cultural reality in many countries, society does
not perceive women as equal to their male counterparts by decree or

belief, sometimes by religious sanction, and sometimes by secular law. By Muslim ethics in many countries, women have only half of the legal standing of any male. The Muslim society subjugates women, condemning them to abide by the rule of men. Juxtaposed against this context, American women are "equal" by legal mandate; however, statistics show how the real-world reality of equality lacks substance in many settings.

In the monk story, who determines right versus wrong? The woman's perspective in the story would be the best choice for ethical purposes. Critically, depending on which character is one's focus, the act can be either right or wrong, with the only variables one should consider being the temporary nature of the action, how choice plays a part in the story, and whether violating a prohibition for doing good is acceptable behavior. One must consider contemporary contexts to arrive at an answer.

Minorities are "equal" under American law; again, the reality is far different from what is functionally supported based on a lack of access to equal education or resources and measurably indifferent treatment from legal and first-responder personnel. The premise, "If I am afforded equal protection under the Constitution, I should expect similar cultural results as my majority counterpart unconditionally," rarely occurs. Results-based equity or equality is not the reality in most, if not all, minority communities. Natural selection supports a broad distribution of talent across all cultures and demographic groupings, but "unproven ability and unequal access" to a wide-ranging array of development pathways (for a variety of reasons) is the context faced by all "at-risk" members of far too many identifiable sub-groups within the American cultural landscape.

Some contemporary contexts, such as Black Lives Matter and #MeToo, illustrate the disparity in the treatment of segments of the American population. In another unequal context, court decisions and choices made by judges minimizing penalties for male sexual predators once convicted further illuminate how "Right versus Wrong" has been subverted by the lack of deontological thinking. Another strong example is how unacceptably many people placed barriers to the investigation or established criminal charges in the long-term gymnastics scandal involving Dr. Nassar at Michigan State. The reluctance of involved parties and so-called bystander parties to act created a scenario where Nassar harmed hundreds of victims over decades. Society has visibly shifted concepts of ethical behavior from the role of predominance to a minimally functional requirement following the ideology of "only when expedient" or "only when unavoidable." (The Nassar scandal shall get further treatment in Section II, where the author explores the moral aspects of misaligned support.)

Within this environment of devalued ethics, how can anyone possibly know right from wrong? For example, the American legal system has constitutionally mandated rights, such as a speedy trial and qualified counsel, with a guarantee of universal representation in criminal contexts when a defendant cannot afford an attorney. The reality is entirely different. Less than 10 percent of criminal cases go to trial; in many jurisdictions, this shrinks to less than 5 percent. Most cases settle through the plea-bargaining process by design. If this balancing act of 10 percent "trial by jury" versus 90 percent "never reaches a jury trial" were to shift significantly toward 20 percent going to trial, the entire system would become inexorably backlogged and break.

The plea-bargaining process allows the system to continue unabated; the essential idea of "blind justice" suggests a projection of equality; however, reality supports the existence of unequal treatment of those involved, with statistics showing minorities receiving more severe judgments and sentences than their white counterparts for crimes of equal severity. When factoring for socioeconomic affluence, the disparity becomes magnified. Again, this suggests the process subverts the notion of "right versus wrong" based on asymmetric social equity, and unequal treatment has become the norm. Through the lens of critical thinking and focused in-depth analyses, the modern legal system, the oft-championed protector of social ethics, is broken at its core.

There are more examples available in today's world. With the change in the American administration in 2016, America shifted from the "give us your tired and poor" mentality to one of "zero tolerance of anyone dissimilar to us." This paradigm has many ethical and moral implications; however, focusing on the ethics of denying access to the immigration process by the Administration has created a global backwash intimating America has chosen "might is right" and isolationism over fundamental human rights. Moreover, the protocols are highly divisive with American citizens, so imagine how members of collectivist societies globally must process this shift in how American policy now treats potentially "at-risk" populations.

Imagine a world where the Sophist approach of "we must obey whoever is in power to survive" forces global citizens to shift gears with each leadership change. Most of the contemporary world exists in one form of this reality; however, America has politically side-stepped this context by maintaining its existence for over 240 years as a representative republic. The increasing use of decrees or proclamations to sidestep the constitution effectively eliminates or marginalizes the balance of power inherent to the American Constitution and potentially creates a scenario where ordinary citizens' rights are suppressed or disregarded. This text opens the debate on how ethics affect contemporary issues and projects a position extending from the author's stated purpose for the book: Undermined (or absent) ethics are the foundational underpinning of most social inequities and exacerbate social injustice across all populations. The problem is persistent, and proponents of positive social change should advance and support the need for exploring this question: "If current politics and policies marginalize ethics in contemporary America, what value has one life when inconsistent or absent consideration supports the disenfranchisement of basic rights?" Perhaps it is time to explore the foundational concept of the value of existence.

"VALUE OF ONE LIFE"

"Teach your children that a person is more valuable than any treasure found on this earth, teach them to love, teach them to sing and dance, teach them to be courageous, and tell them they will be victorious on anything they put their heart and mind to, teach them honesty, and never to give up hope."

Quetzal

"Human progress isn't measured by industry; it's measured by the value you put on a life."

Abhijit Naskar

How we should look at the value of one life:

"Many years ago, when I worked as a transfusion volunteer at a hospital, I got to know a little three-year-old girl suffering from a disease. The little girl needed blood from her five-year-old brother, who had miraculously survived the same ailment. The boy had developed the antibodies needed to combat the illness and was the only hope for his sister.

The doctor explained the situation to the little brother and asked if the boy would willingly give his sister his blood. I saw him hesitate for a moment before he took a deep breath and said, " Yes, I will do it if it will save my sister."

As the transfusion progressed, the little boy lay in bed next to his sister and smiled while observing the color returning to her cheeks. Then his face grew pale, and his smile faded. Finally, he looked up at the nurse beside him and asked with a trembling voice, "When will I start to die?" The young boy had misunderstood the doctor and thought he had to die to save his sick sister."

How should one perceive or question a child's wisdom or innocence?

Anonymous

The value of one life is an age-old debate transcendent of contemporary society. Without some ethical foundation, one's life loses context or meaning when considering "value." In Aristotle's time, the value perception of one individual life was attached to one's contextual citizenship. Most responsible citizens chose to adhere to deontological ethics to maximize the value construct, a concept the Greeks called *eudaimonia*. The only modern interpretation translates to "a life well-lived," which was to be an active participant in making life all around you worth living in the ancient world. Contemporary viewpoints, or axiology, focus on one's notion of self-worth instead of the social utility perspective of Aristotle's time.

The value of one life must stand against either a faith-based proposition or a decidedly secular counter proposition. Humans exist as a manifestation of the Creator in a religious context, creating a stewardship principle requiring each human to value life as a cherished gift. Indeed, the Christian Great Commandment sets a high bar for stewardship by requiring all humans to cherish their lives and the lives of others equally. In response to a question on the greatest commandment, Jesus answered thus, "***Love the Lord your God with all your heart, with all your soul, and with all your mind. This is the greatest and most important commandment. The second is like it: Love your neighbor as yourself. All the Law and the Prophets depend on these two commandments***" (Matthew 22:37-40). From the Great Commandment, one might say humanity needs to redefine the concept of "neighbor."

Christians recognize more than the Ten Commandments given to Moses. The actual total is 613 when considering the Old and New Testaments. Similarly, the Hebrew faith recognizes 613 "Thou shalt" references to follow as their laws. Other faith-based contexts have similar foundations; all focus on making life a gift to be cherished regardless of the "why."

The secular counter proposition flows from how society may value one's contributions when measured against the loss of those contributions. The secular viewpoint ignores values attributed to abstractions such as autonomy, personal choice, or any potential benefit derived from others' perspectives on one's behest. The current position also ignores the potential for intrinsic value acquired when one selflessly enhances another person's life. Hopefully, the author offers a humble premise, a viewpoint leading to copious amounts of social debate. The author's opinion centers on believing the secular counter proposition lacks ethical consideration. When explored deeply, the current normative position mirrors how many ancient societies failed to treat the "lesser" members of those societies with any level of personal consideration beyond their perceived utility to the ruling class.

The global protests emerging after the George Floyd debacle in Minneapolis (May 2020) exist as a shining example of humanity erupting angrily in response to a perceived lack of "value." When one acts to frame the racial injustice protests as a statement against existing perspectives of white privilege, police brutality, majority silence concerning entitlement, and the suppression of minorities across a vast amount of time, the collective voice of protesters becomes an outcry claiming social value (seen as equality and the dignity of existence without barriers) above all else.

Teleological ethics was most evident to the ancients when considering the stratified groups within this ancient society. Members of the army or navy were required to give their lives based on the royal decree and their commanders' whims and choices. In addition, beneath the military strata, ancient teleological thinking was also a problem for the enslaved people present in every society in the ancient world. Being on the wrong end of any conflict potentially moved one from being an ethically responsible citizen to becoming virtually worthless property instantly.

How does this evolve into a meaningful context in the contemporary world? In truth, modern thinking has not advanced as far as one might think or wish. Exploring current ethical value constructs requires two distinct "deep dives" into the context, one being through an extrinsic (outward-facing) social construct based on objective, observable principles. The other is an intrinsic personalized construct based on subjective, invisible ideologies within individuals, the same evolved precepts found in ethical behavior and morality, the eons-old concept known as altruistic reciprocity.

"THE ETHICAL ARTIFACTS OF ALTRUISTIC RECIPROCITY"

"The first stage of ignorance is 'illusion,' due to lack of exposure to reality. The second stage of ignorance is 'delusion,' or the refusal to acknowledge reality. The third stage of ignorance is the 'rejection of altruism.'"

Justin K. McFarlane Beau

"Perhaps the most legitimately dispiriting thing about reciprocal altruism is that it is a misnomer. Whereas with kin selection, the "goal" of our genes is to actually help another organism, with reciprocal altruism, the goal is that the organism is left under the impression that we've helped; the impression alone is enough to bring the reciprocation."

Robert Wright

"We are good to others only because we think that 'that' is, or will be, good for us."

Mokokoma Mokhonoana

"The measure of a human is sacrifice, the pleasure of a human is sacrifice, the treasure of a human is sacrifice."

Abhijit Naskar

"Altruism is not a moral or religious ideal, no matter what some people might tell you. It is an essential, biological part of who or what we are as a species."

Bill Nye

"The desire to help others is not necessarily incompatible with the desire to help oneself."

Khang Kijarro Nguyen

Any exploration of altruistic reciprocity must begin with foundational definitions, although they project an incomplete picture. If someone only considers the formal descriptions or normative usage, they will miss the underlying concepts that drive the behavior; thus, definitional ideologies beyond the two foundational contexts, altruism, and reciprocity, are required for optimal understanding. Here are nine applicable definitions:

Altruism: self-less concern for the well-being of others without expectations of receiving value or consideration for the act

Reciprocity: the practice of exchanging things with others for mutual benefit, privileges granted by one country, organization, group, or person to another

Self-interest: one's interest or advantage, primarily when pursued without regard for others

Group cohesion: unity or solidarity of a group, including the integration of the group for both social and task-related purposes

Group dynamics: system of behaviors and psychological processes occurring within a social group (intragroup dynamics) or between social groups (intergroup dynamics); the stages (life cycle) of group dynamics are Forming, Storming, Norming, Performing, and Adjourning

Predator: an animal that naturally preys on others; a person or group that ruthlessly exploits others

Prey: an animal that is hunted and killed by another for food; an intended victim of a predator

Banishment: the punishment of being sent away from a country or other place; the act of getting rid of something or someone unwanted

Ostracize: exclude from a society or group; exclude from an activity; give someone the cold shoulder

Other-interest: the concerns of anyone not defined as "oneself"

Altruistic reciprocity is the behavioral origin point of morality and ethical consideration, and this "ultimate consideration" concept has ancient roots. For example, humanity, specifically prehuman hominids, existed in a vicious predator-prey environment. Attempting to live alone or in minimized units during this period of human prehistory was hyper-hazardous and increased the likelihood of predation from animals or other hominids. Prehumans needed the relative safety of group dynamics to increase their probability of long-term survival, and the resulting group cohesion influenced the emergence of reciprocity.

Altruism (selfless consideration) was the priming act allowing cooperation to evolve. By synthesizing the need for group cohesion and altruism, more extensive group interaction became possible, and altruistic reciprocity became the glue holding everything together. Many different versions of group cohesion may have emerged over time, but all versions needed similar precepts and rules leading to optimized adoption and sustainability.

Based on archeological findings and theoretical modeling, modern humans now envision a typical prehuman environment with significant social norms. For example, individuals need to be hardy, capable of predation for survival or have some trait to offer those more capable individuals when lacking external self-competency, such as cooking, willingness to engage in procreation, or caregiving the younglings.

Furthermore, a social balance between hunters and other group members must have evolved and held sway for many millennia because this basic social dynamic can be observed across the globe and has been time-dated for more than a half-million years. How would this occur, and how did the behavior evolve into morality and ethical norms? Through reciprocity, or seeking mutual interests while setting aside competing interests.

Most theorists associate survival of the fittest with human prehistory, and they would be correct; however, how "fittest" is defined can be confusing. Altruistic reciprocity is the technical terminology for "tit-for-tat" contexts, an ever-present and notable social construct regardless of what historical period is considered. Inevitably, tit-for-tat only works when all stakeholders show equal consideration for outcomes while concurrently seeking a "balancing of the scales."

Furthermore, optimal cooperation requires "social fitness," an environment where all members perceive balance and equality as necessary artifacts leading to sustained survival. Based on the need for these foundational artifacts, survival of the fittest means survival of the socially most cooperative. So, what happens when cooperation is minimized or absent? A tad more foundation building needs to occur before tackling potentially adverse outcomes.

Let's shift to the concept of self-interest, a context most people assume is counterintuitive to prosocial behavior. At first blush, self-interest implies exploitation or manipulation for personal gain, a correct assumption if self-interest is taken to excess. However, add tit-for-tat to the equation, and self-interest quickly shifts.

A juxtaposed concept is "other-interest." At the extreme end of the self-interest continuum, guaranteeing "other-interest" becomes self-serving when one is required to balance the scales. When existential stress joins the picture, someone aligned with self-interest will go to great lengths to protect the other because doing so ensures self-interest is served, and tit-for-tat drives the bus. For validity, let's examine the "self versus other" interest continuum, which is the domain of competing or collective interest.

Most stories need the environment and cast defined for clarity; regardless of the who, when, or where within this theoretical enactment, the self versus other context applies. Any group must find, predate, and consume prey daily to survive in every potential scenario. By juxtaposing an optimal outcome with two suboptimal ones, enough data should present itself to demonstrate how the model works.

The optimal scenario shows hunters bringing sufficient prey back to the group for sustenance. Some hunters must have enjoyed great success; however, a significant percentage would return empty-handed. Not to worry, in the optimal model, the entire group would share in the bounty because of group cohesion and altruistic reciprocity. Unfortunately, "optimal" would be a rare occurrence.

The worst-case scenario would have the hunters come back en masse empty-handed; that failure would have disastrous outcomes, including starvation and loss of life. If the worst case occurred often enough, humanity would have perished; however, the human species is persistently ongoing. Therefore, despite knowing the worst case had to have transpired, abject failure was also rare. What about the scenario which occurred with significant regularity?

A continuum with optimal on one end and existential disaster on the other should have room for multiple variants of "average" outcomes. A few examples would be "plenty for all," but interlaced with confounds.

For example, what happens if a successful hunter chooses only to share with part of the group? What would the group do with a "free rider," someone who shirks responsibility for group cohesion? Finally, let's consider peering in a different direction; what happens to an injured hunter or member of the group? What is the compelling interest of the group?

Infinite confounds were possible given the harsh reality prehumans faced. Egoist issues, selfishness versus sharing, or various blends of the envy-jealousy context would be powerful, challenging confounds for the group to overcome. Given the harsh reality, an unforgiving environment, and how disrupting a balanced routine could lead to the worst-case scenario, options for re-establishing balance were minimal.

Anyone failing to comply with group needs became an outcast facing banishment or ostracizing, equating to a death sentence for the transgressor. The only sustainable, safe environment was within the group. Any day without a successful hunt, any situation where numerous predators limited one's options would reduce the potential for survival.

Whether or not they preferred to embrace altruism and reciprocity, every group member understood the need for group cohesion. Being an "in-group" member meant living long enough to procreate and potentially pass on one's genetics. Banishment eliminated one's options, so compliance with group dynamics led to early forms of universal positive regard for all survivors.

Human ethical traits emerged from this harsh reality, with non-compliance being unheard-of given the alternatives. Archeologists assert some form of the prehuman dynamic requiring altruistic reciprocity extended across 200,000 years or more. Let's explore the "why" of relative entropy, which acted as a cementing catalyst locking morals and ethics into the fabric of humanity.

Modern humans insist change is constant and inevitable, but why? What drives change? If nothing influences or stresses the social dynamic, nothing would ever change. Early prehumans had plenty of game to predate, migrated to water sources in sufficient numbers to ensure sustained viability for the species, and were only forced to relocate if conditions changed, which was rarely. The main driver of change was increased numbers, an artifact of the security provided by group cohesion.

Modern humans face new stressors based on a perception of global overcrowding, which artificially leads to a reactive change context in ever-decreasing time cycles, a dynamic the prehumans never faced. Long gone are abundant hunter-gatherer schemas; modernity has an over-abundance of sustenance based on technological advances, so the problem has shifted from local altruistic dynamics to finding ways to sustain the distribution of resources through global reciprocity.

When considering how any shortfall in the global supply chain creates artificial suboptimal distribution outcomes, is it doubtful whether adhering to ethical behavior and considerations has emerged as a primary need? Altruistic reciprocity has come full circle; ethical behavior is based on a compelling need for self-interest and other-interest in balance. Failures are easily identifiable in wars, the conflict scenarios where resources or access to resources is almost always the foundational culprit.

When taking a long view of ethics and morals, humanity has embedded proper behavior as an outgrowth of altruistic reciprocity. Genetically, survival of the fittest favored risk avoidance over risk tolerance, choosing cooperation and compliance over discord, the foundational elements leading humanity to its sustained existence. Those members of society who ignored the risks are identifiable as the selfish; the arrogant "watch this" types who perished needlessly or the banished, and those who tested the resolve of the group who preferred cohesion over turbulence. Ethics and its cousin morals were here to stay.

It is essential to embrace the sustained efficacy of ethical behavior, understand its role and relative importance to the past and the future, and consider how ethics drives relationships and group cohesion. Unfortunately, modernity has lost perspective on proper behavior; the following chapters will explore the extrinsic and intrinsic factors that must be understood to shift the failure in social attitudes about behavior to an optimal future based on reframed ethical worldviews.

Before moving on, reframe how ethical behavior aligns with self-interest in today's world. Of course, modern humans do not banish non-compliant members into extinction; however, would anyone choose unacceptable behavior if humanity still functioned as it did in that harsh environment? Being charitable is an ingrained human trait, a permanent part of the human psyche, and it takes a compelling reason for anyone to ignore the plight of others.

Understandably, each individual cannot possibly help every unfortunate soul they encounter, evidenced by the universal effect of cognitive dissonance combined with innate empathy, that feeling of regret one feels when they must bypass an opportunity to be someone's hero "at that moment." Thus, consider what empowerment might occur throughout humanity if every person made an effort to help one other daily. Just one per person, one for each of over seven billion people, is a considerable number; the tsunami of hope that this number of prosocial choices would create could change the trajectory of the species forever. Maybe doing just one good deed is impactful, so commit to one daily and let's start that wave of hope together.

Chapter Two

"ETHICS AS AN EXTRINSIC SOCIAL CONSTRUCT OF OBJECTIVITY"

Knowledge denotes the acceptance of "truth" about a fact. Knowledge without truism is opinion. Some truths are irrefutable, such as a triangle having no parallels. The human condition is mired in the fallacy of certitude since each human has a unique perspective about "truth. Social constructs, such as government, religion, etc., hinge on normative subjectivity, not objective reality.

Buddy Thornton

"Objectivity works to repel critics' attacks, like ethical pepper spray."

Brooke Gladstone

"No living creature can evolve and survive in the real world by processing information objectively, measured, and proportionately."

Rory Sutherland

Contemporary ethics exist as a foundational component of many schemas, although most people would have to peel back many layers of minutiae to find ethics in a recognizable form. Normalized behavior codes exist to form the basis for an overarching set of social rules, with the guidelines projecting as an identifiable social construct. The foundational principles have been expanded throughout human history, evolving through carefully considered "objective" truths, although truth in this context is a fallacious substitute for norms.

For example, throughout most Western societies, laws are part of a "living" system of governance functionally adapting to social needs and stress points through precedential considerations and limitations. "Has this happened before?" How was it decided in the past?" "Should past decisions evolve or hold sway in the context before the court?" The biggest problem for citizens embroiled in cases before any court is complexity, which usually requires participating parties to acquire legal representation. The cost burden of legal representation is a massive barrier to access for many, if not most, citizens within every jurisdiction.

Justice implies a philosophical path to social fairness; however, justice is a skewed morass for individuals because the legal system focuses on protecting society and the "State" and must operate within an economic model. Criminal cases allow defendants to retain free legal counsel when they cannot overcome the cost burden. The context of free counsel further reduces justice perceptions since research over many decades shows "public defender" representation is markedly substandard compared to the attorneys more affluent clients can afford. Social inequity has led to the current practice of plea-bargaining with a laundry list of artifacts, starting with constant pressure to avoid trial and coercing unsophisticated defendants to make poor decisions. Plea bargaining fails to project social equity into the system. Results suggest an ongoing and worsening impact on socioeconomically challenged parties. The projection, accurate or not, is that courts and the legal system have subverted equal ethical treatment and focused on a pursuit of expediency through limited access to trials.

Civil law gets further from ethical reality. For example, the legal system has rules blocking self-representation in all but rudimentary cases. Significantly socioeconomically challenged parties may gain a waiver of court fees; however, the requirement of legal representation combined with the complexity of many court hierarchies creates a deep psychological barrier many parties choose not to cross. Without getting deeper into the official schema, suffice to say, when a system creates barriers to access for any parties, affected parties should question the ethics inherent within the system's framework.

The bottom line? A party with greater affluence and means has a power advantage in most contexts. Consider, however, if the system claims to be as equitable or fair-minded as possible within the contemporary legal landscape, where does this leave those in society without apparent power? The only possible answer is "underserved or unserved by the system."

From a practical perspective, the system evolves slowly to ensure that whatever social equity may exist shall only be sustained or enlarged expeditiously. The slow pace of change projects continued inequity because the change is barely discernible. How does one find avenues to redress this inequity? One may discern a considerable amount of action potential to explore through ethics. Most of the action potential aligns with a need to utilize critical thinking skills on fairness and engage in worthwhile debate about requiring society to shift toward a more transparent, upright schema. Therefore, the aligned contexts depend on a blend of deontological and teleological ethics, as the following treatises shall explore.

"IN THE BEST INTEREST OF SOCIETY"

"A healthy social life is only found when, in the mirror of each soul, the whole community finds its reflection, and when, across the entire community, the virtue of each one is living."

Rudolf Steiner

"Forgiveness is unconditional, or it is not forgiveness. Forgiveness has the character of "in spite of" instead of "because."

Paul Tillich

"How do you measure one person's life against the greater good? Can it ever be the right thing to sacrifice an innocent person? And how do you know what the greater good really is?"

Amy Engel

"A compassionate way of life rooted in oneness and connectivity not only impacts your greater good, but it resonates out into the world, positively impacting the greater good for all."

Amy Miller

*I*n many ways, societal stakeholders interact with applied ethics from a lens of rights, interests, and "what's in it for me?" The lens explores one's perceived value and whether a choice will create one of many positive action potentials. By examining what society focuses on ethically, one may discern what constitutes one's best interests.

In most cultures, rights are objectively well-defined, although rights are not universal or considered equally across global populations. The concept of rights entitlement is highly differentiated across the global landscape and aligns with the type of governance enforced within a jurisdiction or nation. However, one may argue that whatever rights are present act as the catalyst for motivational approaches to the needs/wants paradigm, the essential pathway to overcoming inadequate conditions, regardless of social context. Within the hierarchy described by Maslow, rights serve as a foundational tool for climbing above the lower deficit needs rungs, enabling one to pursue the growth needs holding higher perceived values.

Rights align with society's view of how members overcome deficit needs, while interests are the vestibule of Maslow's hierarchy's higher rungs. When the mind is not focused on deficit needs, rights may or may not get in the way of a pathway to fulfilled interests. Luckily, one may set aside rights to facilitate individualized or collaborative efforts aligned with interests. Rights are permanent, at least in America, but permanence comes with conditionality. One may choose to exercise the rights given within the Constitution. One may alternately opt to ignore those rights out of hand for another path, and chiefly choices made not likely to interfere with another's rights. Society considers violating another person's rights egregious and always prompts a response. One may abdicate rights when appropriate, without fear of loss or reduction. What one may not do is deprive another person of their rights.

Rights are established within the social fabric of governance as a barrier to oppression and in support of social equity, if not equality. In other words, rights hinge on whether one chooses to exercise them and retain power and value, whether applied or not. Moreover, interests align with forms of motivation and an individual's action potential for fulfillment and derive their power from one's compelling desire to succeed. So, how do rights and interests align with applied ethics?

Consider for a moment several topics emerging as artifacts of the "Human Genome Project." Topics include extended aging as research acquires prevention pathways for numerous diseases, enhances a geneticist's potential to create designer babies as a genetic modification at the zygote level, or the emerging action potential to grow replacement organs through cloning from the original host. Each topic promises enormous outcome potential for humanity despite sharing one strong negative connotation: the possibility for abuses within the system aligned with access linked to socioeconomic affluence. Some points of reference are concerns voiced in research forums globally.

Human genetic engineering is fraught with a significant action potential, mainly with a negative slant. First, any engineering will offset natural human diversity from day one. Is it possible to characterize choosing traits artificially as "playing God?" Suppose only the wealthy have access to the genetic lottery, with "created" people functioning as means instead of ends via circumvention of random selection dynamics. How would the system remain inherently fair for society?

The business side shall follow a familiar script as new possibilities emerge through genome research. In the "designer baby market," children shall be treated as novel commodities. Early adopters will pay exorbitant fees to participate, and the price will only fall once the affluent consumers can no longer drive a market based on "assumed exclusivity." The next participant group, typically lagging "consumer-adopters," will play catch-up through compelling scenarios like the pursuit of entry into prestigious schools for their children. As the situations play out in an arena where one or two prior generations of enhanced genetics might create insurmountable socioeconomic barriers, the potential for in-fighting and conflict motivated by greed will emerge. The resulting artificial social construct will add the reality of genetic division to the laundry list of socioeconomic strata normalized people will only experience from afar. Consider "Naturals" versus "Gen-Rich" individuals. From an ethical perspective, this is a modified approach to eugenics, a failed and notably illegal social discourse. What can be conceptualized as a substantial benefit to humanity has more value if the emerging utility aligns with equitable distribution; however, the current reality will inevitably follow a predictable flawed business model.

From a different vector or ethical perspective and focusing on current end-of-life research, does potentially extending human lifespans create a real benefit? From a time perspective, the quantity of life never equates to or guarantees a corresponding optimal life quality. Assuming the current retirement schema prevails, not many people will be affluent enough to support themselves financially for an extra decade (or longer), increasing economic stress on an already overburdened elder care system. Shift the thinking to a different schema and set new retirement age expectations to sometime in the ninth decade of life, which has credibility once genomics applications enhance the context of active aging. Now, systemic stress takes on a whole new shape. A sidebar to a long beneficial life is the contemporary perception of how aging leads to reduced social or functional viability; however, emerging concepts aligned with genomics have a solid potential to overcome the inherent misconceptions of ageism biases. The question ultimately challenging humanity is, "Just because we can, is it in our best interest to follow this path?"

When a debate over what is in society's best interest occurs, the topic evolves based on who controls access to the seats at the debate table. Arguably, at no point in human history has the underserved, unserved, or defined minority groups been given or captured an equitable seat at the debate table, much less put enough pressure on the majority to gain fair access to functional equality. The business context of innovation, early adoption, normalization, to delayed adoption of innovation is proof enough.

Many late adopters only gain practical access to products and services once early adopters have already moved on to the next invention or technological marvel, which creates a cyclical feedback loop that guarantees that those with less affluence are always one functionality step behind every group of earlier adopters. "What's in It for Me?" is a power dynamic exploited by the affluent regardless of global location or culture unless the disadvantaged find and implement a practical path to earlier adoption leading to equity and equality. In simplest terms, the "haves" continually recreate social division by ignoring the benefit of uplifting everyone.

The system plays to the economic capacity to perform within each definable schema, a back door linked to teleological outcomes. The "ends may justify the means" when everyone enters the game; however, reality shows a different picture. Without functional access, the less affluent need not apply or hope to consider the possible options.

A deontological approach could only emerge if the wealthy adopted and implemented a philanthropic schema to ensure the masses would also benefit at the same level. Of course, one may always hope for enforceable equity throughout society. Still, no researcher can credibly demonstrate any point throughout history when the wealthy amongst humanity chose to address fairness equitably, which suggests the global community will keep on "keeping on," regardless of the potential harm existing within this emerging hot genomics topic. In no domain is inequity more evident than in the health care/self-care dynamic. Let's go there next.

"OVERCOMING DISEASES: THE CONTEMPORARY SOCIAL NORMS EFFECT"

"On November fourth, this pandemic will disappear since it was invented to destroy Trump's legacy." Unnamed Trumpian-October 2020 during the COVID-19 pandemic

"Each day, I receive a small card in my pocket; I carry with me my schedule. It shows the number of Americans who have been affected by or died from COVID-19. Today, we mark a truly grim, heartbreaking milestone: 500,071 dead. That's more Americans who have died in one year in this pandemic than in World War I, World War II, and the Vietnam war combined,"

US President Biden, February 2021

"The world is paralyzed, and humanity is in quarantine. It is strange symmetry that I was born in one pandemic and will die during another."

Isabel Allende

"I think a playbook on how to create fear in people's lives about a disease or variant. You must say it is scary, deadly, more transmissible, spreading rapidly, grows faster, and more dangerous than any variant or disease."

De philosopher DJ Kyos

"Burnout occurs when an individual has experienced prolonged demands, chronic stress, fatigue, a lack of support, and decreased satisfaction in what they are doing."

Asa Don Brown

Enhancing the future of humanity through genomics should be debated by policymakers from a perspective of enforceable all-inclusion. A "share one, share all" focal point on all-inclusion would create equitable action potential and serve all global citizens equally. From a governance position, enforced all-inclusion would mitigate or remove much of the potential for systemic abuse in "all processes aligning with genomics." From a similarly critical social equity and economic outlook, initial costs for blanket access would rapidly show an attractive long-term return on investment (ROI) as researchers flip the switch on multiple diseases. Enhanced medical genomics' social impact would shift the focus from an ambivalent, unbalanced universal healthcare plan to a future reality linked with less healthcare necessary over time as positive artifacts evolve and become viable. Universal healthcare would help mitigate the current imbalances in the health delivery system.

Socioeconomic stratification based on affluence may be acceptable when considering consumption choices aligned with varying degrees of disposable income; however, access to healthcare based on one's ability to pay should evolve toward open access instead of anchoring to economic capacity. Healthcare platforms structured to block access based on a purely economic model create an uneven playing field. Less fortunate or less capable wage earners (due to a litany of reasons, no judging allowed) suffer a disproportionate number of comorbidity issues, measurably more than their more affluent counterparts, usually due to limited appropriate healthcare options.

The current regulatory policy requires healthcare providers to give perfunctory service to everyone; however, vast differences in care levels still exist based on the current stratified social reality. From an ethics perspective, however, minimal emergency services are not at the heart of the social stratification question. Instead, the central ethical issue is how society perceives the value of one person's life and pushes the conversation directly into politics. So, why politics?

The ethical reality applies directly to the perceived value of one life, especially in a recognizable system focused on serving others based on social qualifiers. Today's policymakers often attempt to please their financial base first, their constituents second, and the overall society last. In the contemporary climate, many politicians take this context to an extreme, leading to division and a toxic outcome for those not their supporters. The reality of "contemporary, normative political discourse" suggests one life's value must align with how much support one gives a policymaker. Political parties and policymakers rigorously focus on sustaining power through reelection instead of "How may I ethically serve my constituents?" The opposing questions one should ask, "Where are the considerations for social equity and fairness?" or the retort, "Weren't you elected to serve?" have no place in today's seemingly unethical approach to politics.

By taking a page out of the deontological ethics worldview, the optimal path would be to serve the overall society first, constituents second, and enhanced financial support would emerge as positive artifacts occur, making the policymaker a social hero. The idea may be hard to sell in the contemporary climate, but a version of this ethical approach has historically served many people well. Before moving on, readers should research which historical people have stood as servant leaders to the masses by governing or providing constituents with consideration and even-handed ethical policies.

There are many topical areas with phenomenal potential for exploring current social realities while discussing the juxtaposition of disease and normative social effects. During the COVID-19 crisis, the best choice is to dive directly into how different factions perceive medical expertise and their rights in the American social landscape. COVID-19 is an emergent, rapidly evolving disease ravaging the entire planet, with billions of humans affected. Considering the realities linked to COVID-19, one might expect compliance with medical authority would be paramount. Still, many Americans choose to assert their right to select between compliance or non-compliance when considering expert medical advice. The mask or no-mask issue has become the biggest differentiator between rights advocates and medical conformists.

Primarily, one only needs to focus on genetically linked diseases, with age-related health issues a secondary concern; health experts assert these as the two most common comorbidity issues contributing to death via COVID-19. The microfocus would allow one to explore the potential for a broad range of ethical and unethical outcomes aligned with the social choice matrix. One must consider more issues in the medical landscape, such as the concept of herd immunity, which is somewhat viable if one is willing to suffer the inevitable loss of life while waiting for the social diffusion effect to occur. Or consider the emergence of possible vaccines and what percentage of the population would be prepared to jump in line to get the treatment. Because America is a freedom-based choice society, enforcing patriarchal governance rarely succeeds, and these topics will prove highly contentious.

Overcoming rigid "rights-based" thinking in free societies is foundational to mitigating any pandemic like COVID-19. In another section of the book, an exploration of rights versus interests should add perspective to the conversation about how humans may optimize their choices, especially in the subjective area of compliance with medical advice. First, however, let's focus on the process, then connect to one's potential rights perceptions.

For example, the laundry list of genetically linked diseases will theoretically shrink in proportion to the spending on genetic research focused on those diseases, but this will not be a short-term process. People have understood the truth about research ROI for decades; however, if a condition doesn't manifest as a specific daily stressful irritant in their sphere of influence, most people focus on their own lives and ignore the problem, assuming mitigation efforts are an issue for others to endure and overcome. While this viewpoint aligns with Maslow's deficit needs area, once one has entered the upper climes of Maslow's pyramid to pursue transcendence, one should explore how to achieve the spirit of Aristotle's conceptualization of eudaimonia for everyone within contemporary society.

Overcoming disease, one would think, should be universally supported across all societies, to significant effect. Unfortunately, artifacts of contemporary culture, namely commercialized research primarily in the pursuit of profit, mitigate or ignore many "trigger event" pathways to overcoming a disease. Changing the mindset from ROI to enhancing society's health prospects instead of pursuing profitability has escaped many policymakers who entertain Big Pharma lobbyists and sustain an entropic, ineffective economic model aligned with contemporary social norms.

Imagine a political reality where funds now spent on healthcare are shifted to many alternatives like infrastructure issues facing society. By preventing disease onset instead of reactively treating symptoms, the prevention of a single genetically linked disease would allow policymakers to invest billions of dollars in other areas. Billions! The trickle-down effect would change global social outcomes and lead to greater hope for humanity, although current political and economic entropy levels stand firmly in the way. For example, Big Pharma continually projects self-interest and profits as more important than broad social beneficence. The development of a one-dose cure-all for a disease traditionally needing decades of ongoing treatment has prompted one manufacturer to price the one-dose approach in the millions because they perceive the loss of sustainable profit and subsequently make an entitlement claim based on the lost ROI. The exorbitant price precludes all but the most affluent from the benefit and forces insurance carriers to make seemingly inhumane choices. Government oversight? Woefully absent and silent on the issue.

Beyond the genomics context, other disease paradigms exist. For example, one must confront emerging global crises like the previously mentioned COVID-19 pandemic of 2019-2020. As the contagion spreads across the planet, governments must face previously unheard-of choices about mitigating the projected loss of life. One artifact of mitigation efforts, namely, the disruption of economies, illustrates the reality of how socioeconomic factors impact society when evolving decision matrices create an environment of conflicting choices, creating a secondary crisis. From an ethical perspective, any decision could be perceptible as unethical or unsustainable, depending on which of the disasters affects one's reality the most. The essential portion of the debate circles back to one's perspective on life's value component.

Again, equitable consideration for the masses should exist in a perfect world, with a strong focus on innovative action potentials. The emphasis would precipitate the emergence of direct implementation paths based on social ideals aligned with the highest ethical standards imaginable. Choices like preserving life and livelihoods would drive every conversation. Instead, fractious statements about early pandemic mitigation decisions like total economic shutdowns have evolved into disputes around a "The cure should not be worse than the disease." mentality. Neither side of the debate wants to admit the sparsity of safe options on the horizon, much less optimal choices leaders could make.

The pandemic has given birth to some positive artifacts. A globalized approach or pursuit of universal distribution of curative agents such as the emerging vaccines, regardless of one's ability to pay, is supported by a "duty to perform" mandate from the world's governing bodies. The blanket approach to mitigation would seemingly endorse a paradigm shift focused on previously unheard-of inclusion dynamics. Suppose it proves to be a temporary one-time event. In that case, a paradigm shift in ethical health care inclusion will project or explain how actualized action potential on a global scale could change one's perception of one's value construct within one's primary socio-economic influential sphere. By reducing the efficacy of COVID-19, thereby diminishing one health care threat for all members of every global society, one would demonstrate the efficiency derived from the adoption of universal norms based on medical expertise and ethical considerations instead of choosing profits (or political outcomes) over beneficence.

"OVERCOMING SOCIOECONOMIC SPHERE OF INFLUENCE NORMS"

*"Individuals are not calculating automatons. Instead, people
are malleable and emotional actors whose decision-making is influenced
by contextual cues, local social networks, social norms, and shared
mental models. Individuals are social animals who are influenced
by social preferences, social networks, and social identities. It is essential
to understand that most of the decisions we take are hugely contextual.
Social network effects can amplify different types of behavior
(both good and bad). Influencing or nudging people to "think socially"
may prompt significant behavioral change."*

World Bank Development Report-2015

*"The people who are crazy enough to think they can change
the world are the ones who do."*

Rob Siltanen

*"Geniuses are always marginalized to one degree or another.
Someone wholly invested in the status quo is unlikely to disrupt it."*

Eric Weiner

*"I want to deconstruct the structural power of a system that marked me out
as different. I don't wish to be assimilated into the status quo; I want to be*

*liberated from all negative assumptions that my characteristics bring.
The onus is not on me to change. Instead, it's the world around me."*

Reni Eddo-Lodge

*"Meaningful, lasting change only happens when the pain
of the status quo finally outstrips the fear or the anticipated pain
of the change we seek."*

David Taylor-Klaus

*"That's what growth is all about. It doesn't come when things
are status quo. It happens only when something new is introduced,
forcing every integral part to adjust. This is a universal law
that can be applied on any level of life."*

Danny Dreyer

Defining the existing contemporary socioeconomic sphere of influence norms is an easy task in individualistic cultures. Everything hinges on one's level of affluence and access conduits leading to higher levels of wealth. The "ability journey" includes overcoming the entrenched barriers maintained by the current wealthy elite, a group of defined individuals who are not inclined to share. Consider how often affluent people engage in lengthy battles over current or future assets and opportunities to maintain their status, exposed recently when parents with means were caught resorting to cheating the system to access elite schools for their children. Projections of legacy entitlement are reliable indicators of how the system creates bottlenecks and barriers to success unless one is already at the "appropriate socioeconomic level" in various institutional gatekeepers' eyes.

Many stories exist to amplify the journey taken by individuals who have overcome systemic entropy. The fallacy is in the numbers, the percentage of people who overcome versus those who fail. Narratives often tell an "outlier-hero conquers barriers" story for a relative few.

The system shuts out the masses by limiting access to a microscopically small "educational Nirvana." Sliding sideways, access to better neighborhoods requires greater affluence, a factor often linked to innovative ideology leading to more wealth. The pathway exists, yet again, the system bottlenecks the path, and access depends on whom you know, or worse, whom you can impress. The truism here is that "naturally-occurring organic genetic diversity has spread intellect and genius throughout humanity, but today's social power conventions and elitist thinking block access to "functional" utility." Competition for the limited "elite" educational resources is a subjective norm many ascribe to, yet few enjoy. "Just the facts, folks."

Collectivist cultures also have their version of socioeconomic elitism, although most elitism hinges on historical factors traditionally proven to be quite intractable. Royals and their cohorts carefully guard the path to elitism in a monarchy. Dictatorships are commonly where power dynamics become entrenched through violence and fear. Communist cultures require one to act per the state's needs first, reducing the time for pursuing individual growth needs. The defining concept common to monarchies, dictatorships, and communist contexts is absolutism or despotism when governance aligns with only one correct course of action regardless of artifacts or social outcomes.

In emerging democracies (India, for example), historical, well-defined social stratification is entrenched and comes into conflict with today's authorities in a constant vortex of ideology. The governing wish to drive evolution to the new dynamic, while the established elite from the old dynamic will resist at a high cost. Change, although inevitable, will be slow in these environments. One artifact of the current power struggle in emergent nations is how the global migration pattern encourages those with enough affluence to escape the risk inherent to the conflicted social reality and move laterally into more favorable, thriving cultural climes, substituting dynamism for entropy.

The migration pattern has created two adverse effects globally while having comparatively little impact in India and many other similar social contexts. One may replace India in the equation with any number of collectivist countries, and the dynamic remains. First, those migrating are often the intellectual elite (the source of affluence and influence), which has the effect of tightening the bottlenecks existing in social environments where competition is already the norm, forcing more people to find alternative pathways to success in an increasingly scarce labor market. In less populated countries, the outbound migration of highly competent citizenry creates a capability shortfall, eventually hamstrings the remaining economy, forcing administrators to depend on costly outside resources. Second, the resulting dynamic for mitigating migration-driven job placement scarcity manifests as isolationism and nationalism as destination countries attempt to maintain an inward-looking economic base for their citizens.

Paternalized protectionism and xenophobic ideology are two factors driving the contemporary political climate in America circa late 2020, where most of the world's elite schools reside, making international students less than welcome. Indeed, the world's ultimate freedom-empowered economy remains a significant draw, which leads to a convoluted approach to inclusion and exclusion by academic institutions seeking to project transparent and inviting learning destinations despite the current divisive social discourse.

Ethically, the historical American ideal is to welcome less-fortunate souls, those who desire to improve their lives through the benefits our social dynamism offers through our socially mandated beneficence. "Give us your poor, your tired, your huddled masses" allowed America to grow through people motivated by the opportunity to achieve what was not a functional part of their homeland. Instead, the current Administration chooses to welcome the elitist global peers and students while attempting to reduce or restrict the American Dream for all others, including American social stakeholders defined as minorities.

At some point, the ethics involved are considered "irrelevant" based on pursuing paternalistic ideology. The ideal of American inclusion and generosity, allowing people to seek the "land of opportunity, the shining city on the hill," has been obscured or obfuscated, remaining hidden in the same file labeled, "Americans only, please, unless you are rich or hyper-talented."

Let's consider one highly relevant factor leading to how the socioeconomic fabric has become more stratified instead of giving rise to all-encompassing wealth. In an environment with varying cultural diversity levels, with visible differences present at some level universally, the broader context of knowledge aligned with diversity functions to drive growth. By limiting either cross-cultural or intracultural diversity in any way, entropy and division must occur. Consider two separate issues foundational to the context of progress versus entropy: genetic diversity and social diversity.

Through genetic diversity, humankind is evolving and gaining the ability to overcome many maladies society currently claims only exists in history books or laboratories. Assume the other end of the spectrum becomes the norm if affluence drives access to the genomics database. Over time, the genetic elite will subjugate the "norms" in what projects to become a cyclical return to eugenics, a discredited concept. Remember the Nazis? Consider the social divisiveness present in America today (2016-2020, for reference), and it mirrors the German landscape of the 1930s as Hitler came to power. The world debunked the claim of Third Reich superiority, although it took the death of over 100 million humans to make it happen. If memory serves, Hitler sought to end diversity through force. Humankind knows all too well how WW II turned out.

Now take contemporary social diversity. Limiting diversity via artificially constructed barriers creates haves and have-nots throughout society. The existing artificial constructs manifest as openly divisive silos of conflict aligned with inequality, and a sense of futility envelopes all groups who are not the defined elites. In contemporary America, this projects as white privilege and minority oppression. Beyond American borders, one quickly finds numerous conflicts where one group perceives itself as the social elite, often through social repression.

Americans rebuke those involved in global oppression while allowing insidious abuse to occur domestically. Examples of genocide or attempted genocide exist within every historical period, including the contemporary. Take, for example, Iran's insistence that they will eventually end the nation of Israel. Openly threatened genocide exists. Many global populations seek the destruction of other groups, including several entities who position themselves as the eventual annihilators of America in the future. Most people see the force projection as saber-rattling; however, there is always an element of truth in every statement born of hyperbole. The global dynamic supports the theory of how those in power perceive natural diversity as a threat to themselves. The threat perception exists based on in-group dynamics and how contemporary leaders utilize paternalism to suppress guaranteed or implied rights. The artifacts of continued or expanding diversity have the action potential to mitigate existing control dynamics and organically drive tangible power erosion linked to the elite, a reality the current Administration fears.

More than 3000 years ago, humans unilaterally accepted sophist thinking aligned with oppressive power dynamics. The ancients had not conceived democracies or republics, so sophist thinking was the norm. Fast forward to today, and one must consider how little has changed politically based on the current American Administration's preference for sophist philosophical approaches to power dynamics and society. Take the time to discern how many twists and turns humankind has taken to travel back 3000+ years in arrears socially and philosophically. Then, discuss the reality of sustained asymmetric power dynamics with peers and ask if this is ethically challenging for today's world.

One point for consideration as a starting point would be exploring how committed to change the greatest ancient minds must have been when considering the effects of sophist thinking. How they subsequently, and optimally, arrived at democracy to counteract individuals they perceived as social oppressors. How does the historical narrative compare to how checks and balances, once considered the primary differentiator making the Constitution unbreakable, now portrayed as minimized or absent by Constitutional scholars, are supposed to function in today's American political structure?

"CHALLENGING CONVERSATIONS DURING MULTICULTURAL INTERACTIONS"

*"Unity in diversity is the highest possible attainment of a civilization,
a testimony to the noblest possibilities of the human race.
This attainment is made possible through passionate concern
for choice in an atmosphere of social trust."*

Michael Novak

"Diversity is being invited to the party; inclusion is being asked to dance."

V Myers

*"The strength of my team is in its composition. Two are from Mongolia,
one is from Thailand, one is from Chicagoland, and one is from Texas. I'm
not sure, but they share one powerful commonality: a consistent work ethic
regardless of their origin story. Sounds like America to me."*

Buddy Thornton-June 2020

I am compelled to switch to the first person for this section. This departure from the ordinary discourse is apropos because the primes and triggers for this section are anecdotal, based on direct interaction and reflection of the social environment around me. Please attempt to embrace the emotions and empathy emerging from my telling.

As I watched, yet again, one of my neighbors move across the street to avoid any level of social exchange with another neighbor, one having a minority background, I could not help but to get angry. I know that "avoiding dissimilar others" is common in diverse neighborhoods like mine. Still, the stupidity of avoiding a neighbor is self-evident. Let me explain my position and offer a solution.

I am a middle-aged white academic who has focused his education on conflict and its artifacts in cross-culturally diverse environments. As such, I carry a broad, well-studied understanding of the effects of white privilege and how the American culture has evolved because of its influence and artifacts. I argue that white privilege is the main driving force for a generation of minorities who have chosen to stand against sustained barriers to equal opportunity and limited access to genuine, measurable social equality.

My neighbor crossing the street, a specific form of microaggression toward another person, exacerbates the problem. He makes this choice based on bias, stereotyping, and an expectation of conflict based on his perception of impending or sustained backlash against white privilege. I live in a diverse neighborhood by choice, not out of necessity, because I choose to embrace what makes our community strong and healthy. I seek the flavor of a full palate of cultural experiences, so my biased neighbor's actions insult my preference for being an engaging neighbor to a diverse group of people from many backgrounds and beliefs.

From my neighbor's perspective, he must avoid confrontation for safety. What he does not understand is the extended effect of his actions. By visibly and consciously avoiding interaction, he sustains the social barriers which have stained the American social culture for many decades. He says, "I want to continue embracing our differences, not our commonalities." He chooses to project hostility through avoidance. Through his poor choices and microaggressions, he actively says, "I do not want you here."

Minorities need to know they will be considered equals at every level, by thought and action, before considering discontinuing their fight for that equality. As a mediator, I am trained to identify power imbalance, then seek to mitigate the effects of that imbalance. The imbalance here stems from white privilege and many other forms of "privilege" and perceived entitlements, the results of which will not disappear in our lifetimes. However, we can CHOOSE to make a difference.

The first difficult conversation any person, white or minority, must have is an internal one. What expectations do we bring to the table? What anger do we need to conquer? Could it replace an expectation of inequality with the curiosity necessary to set social injustices aside? In my experience, cross-cultural conflict starts many years before it manifests at any given moment, a characteristic all groups share.

The majority, or the group currently in power, always ensures their advantage through privilege is sustainable, ever-present, and insidious. The asymmetric imbalance created by majority privilege encourages minority groups to vigorously seek pathways to overcoming the oppressive power in the environment. Social realities, such as racial and social injustice protests aligned with existing historical artifacts, demonstrate that social upheaval empowers potential change. Sadly, demands for change rarely manifest, and when a new group assumes power, that group immediately maneuvers to ensure sustainable control, repeating the dysfunctional cycle.

The answers to the previously asked questions offer clues to the only valid path forward. What expectations do we bring to the table? If we expect discord, anger, violence, or contempt from anyone, this is all we will look for in any exchange. The scientific terminology is confirmation bias. We want only to see what fits our mental projections. We will not see the numerous acts of kindness and positive regard, only any perceived slight that triggers our beliefs.

What anger do we need to conquer? First, people need to stop blaming others for the past. Our ancestors' choices about treating other groups, especially the negative behavior of people of majority-white descent, were appalling. Second, Americans need to recognize how untold generations of minorities were mistreated. Specifically, the descendants of the slave population have the right to hold and use anger about white privilege for some benefit, not through violence but through a well-conceived debate about achieving social equity and equality. Violence encourages sustained white privilege and the majority's "stubborn resolve" to possess power. Demonstrating the ability to set aside physical confrontation for meaningful open debate has been the message from Dr. Martin Luther King, Jr., Nelson Mandela (South African but a strong example of belief in dialogue), and other luminaries too numerous to list in this forum.

Is it possible to replace an expectation of inequality with the curiosity necessary to set the injustices aside? First, one must accept the statistical probability supported by research that every human, every group, and every distinctly different culture has positive attributes to offer the world at large. Then, instead of focusing on differences to support our biases, we should embrace differences with a level of curiosity that leads to the universal adoption of social amalgamation. Social amalgamation occurs when a diverse group adopts every culture's best attributes and creates a new or positively evolved social reality.

The white majority expects and embraces assimilation, a paradigm where all in-group members must be indistinct and homogeneous. By action and preference, assimilation meets the subconscious need to support confirmation bias within the white majority, and any ideology seeking heterogeneity is rejected. However, research demonstrates that contemporary social demographics are shifting to a context when the majority will be eclipsed by the minority population, projected by the mid-2040s, meaning the ability to assimilate will disappear over time.

Despite the Trump administration's efforts between early 2017 and early 2021, the American future belongs to a heterogeneous population with globalized ancestral roots. Heritage should be a positive talking point, race a descriptive attached to a positive self-image, and one's efforts should be recognized for their potential. Leaders need to focus on building a future based on the positive potential diversity embodies instead of division.

The negative artifacts linked to self-segregation and polarization represent a need for change at this "tipping-point" time for America. We are not a melting pot, not by a long shot. We are a patchwork quilt of distinct silos struggling for prominence within a vast tapestry. The time for social amalgamation is now. **There will be no social justice or inclusion until all society members embrace the tenets of racial justice, equality, and equity of purpose and opportunity.**

Americans can celebrate their uniqueness within the collective while knocking down the silos. The days of microaggressions and avoidant behavior need to become historical relics. Those who successfully set aside self-indulgent beliefs and anger for curiosity leading to dialogue with a broad, diverse audience are prosocial visionaries people I label "positive social change agents;" they shall be today's prophets and the best role models for tomorrow's leaders.

"RESPONSIBILITY AND ACCOUNTABILITY"

"Life is Messy. How one faces messy defines one's place within humanity, and one's right to exist as a member of our species. The only way to evolve, to overcome messy, is to traverse a multi-generational, cross-cultural journey where the primes, triggers, and action responses benefit everyone, not just those within our preferred in-group. Until we accept responsibility for doing this 'INCLUSION THING,' messy will continue to rule us all. We must accept accountability for yesterday's failures. Social choices made in the past, what came before, obviously have not worked. It is imperative for all people to change course, to choose to end messy!"

Buddy Thornton-2020

"The man who passes sentence should swing the sword. If you would take a man's life, you owe it to him to look into his eyes and hear his final words. And if you cannot bear to do that, then perhaps the man does not deserve to die."

George R.R. Martin

"You may believe you are responsible for your actions, but not for what you think. The truth is that you are responsible for what you think because it is only at this level that you can exercise choice. What you do comes from what you think. "

Marianne Williamson

*"A person may cause evil to others not only by his actions
but by his inaction, and in either case, he is justly accountable
to them for the injury."*

John Stuart Mill

*E*ntire volumes exist to allow exploration of the artifacts of responsibility and accountability. Examine and deliberate on the two concepts, including considering a "before and after" ethical treatment. The path starts with the simplistic notion that both models are the same or juxtaposed sides of the same coin. From an ethical perspective, responsibility requires critical thinking and planning aforethought based on one's choice to accept something. Accountability occupies the space requiring one to acknowledge one's contribution to an outcome, acceptable or not, based on ethical norms. As a before and after concept, the notion of responsibility and accountability becomes the flip-side, foundational framework of the rights and interests coin. If one wishes to sustain rights and simultaneously pursue interests, one must fulfill socially mandated behaviors aligned with an obligation. Without dipping into the concept of criminality and the legal system, one may explore how ethics innately drive social and behavioral norms regardless of culture or context when one is micro-focused on achieving interests capable of propelling one to desired outcomes.

Responsibility is a "duty to perform." The next segment shall explore aspects of the duty to perform; one must have prior knowledge of expectations and consequences of failure before acting to be effectively held to an applicable standard. All corporate officers, business managers, and employees know "standard operating procedures." Yet, how often do supervisors explain maximum versus minimum standards embedded within the measurable parameters? Is it an employee's responsibility to meet the minimum standard or strive for optimal results? If one "superstar" employee shines, does this "throw shade" on a minimal performer? Can both types of employees exist in the same environment? These are all deep-rooted questions about how to ethically consider where responsibility lies within one's sphere of influence.

Accountability requires understanding applicable standards and the consequences for success and failure as measured by those who set each standard. In most contexts, the ethical component lies between how an industry-standard is structured and whether authority figures actively support the standard. In other words, is the supervisor equitably applying the measure as written or explained or following a subjective interpretation of how the requirement has become normalized on a production floor? Will an employee accept an artificial construct in place of the defined standard, possibly an incongruent measure implemented by the supervisor? Many things fall under this umbrella, such as EEOC regulations, bullying, favoritism, and abuse claims, to name a few.

Consider a straightforward fact: Supervisors at all levels always expect maximal output and measure their response based on this reality, while employees may or may not see minimal throughput as acceptable performance. Which is right, ethically? Take the time to discuss standards and real-world applications with peers, and you shall grasp the reality of how application contexts are relative to the perceptual expectations about standards.

Now apply the before and after to a home environment. How often do parents involve their children in defining behavioral standards applicable to rewards or negative consequences? Is it possible to gain self-correction and adequate self-supervision from a child by including them in this process? Research shows that substantially fewer negative behaviors emerge when parents involve children in appropriate decision-making aligned with the children's age and demonstrated maturity.

Although the choice dynamics involved are part of another book, it is important to note how children learn ethical behavior from any authority figures in their environment, but only if they feel heard when they have concerns. Ask many teachers. They will tell you children will give the level of respect they internalize as being given to them.

"DUTY TO PERFORM-MANDATORY REPORTING"

Jesus said, "For judgment, I came into this world, that those who do not see may see, and that those who see may become blind." Some of the Pharisees near him heard this, and they said unto him, "Are we also blind?" Jesus answered, "If you were blind, you would have no guilt; now that you say, 'We see,' your guilt remains."

John 9:39-41

"Character is doing what you don't want to but know you should do."

Joyce Meyer

"Simple awareness is the seed of responsibility."

Jenny Odell

The duty to perform is a legal term in a contract requiring parties to agree to act based on the agreement's parameters. From a minimal ethical viewpoint, one's word is a contract. Based on both terminology and perspective, how does one measure an established duty to perform if the only standards are socially structured and not specific to a contract? The answer lies within the context of mandatory reporting. As the Scriptures eloquently state, to see (know through a lived experience) is to bear responsibility for oneself.

Most professional licensees must adhere to a "Code of Ethics" applicable to mandatory reporting. Teachers, doctors, mediators, attorneys, and psychologists are examples of mandatory reporters. What surprises non-mandatory reporters is how circumstances or context stand on their own merits. A competent professional must discern whether any singular event meets the standard requiring mandatory reporting or face censure or loss of license. Additionally, the Law of Unintended Consequences becomes a consideration. Will reporting have unforeseen adverse effects?

Is this an ethical problem? Unfortunately, street justice creates a social environment where many equate whistleblowers and mandatory reporters to "rats and snitches." Countless times, mandatory reporters are despised and denounced as the enemy when they have truly little control or choice in the matter before them based on their ethical reality.

Take the position of a client (or parent in school environments) who is asked to confide in a professional and expects confidentiality; assuming confidentiality applies, they may disclose acts requiring mandatory reporting. All intake forms include verbiage to notify all parties about compulsory, legally mandated reporting regulations. How many people take the time to read and discuss the details and parameters of a disclosure? Competent professionals handle this conversation upfront and reframe the barriers to comprehension until their client has an ample understanding of the risks inherent to the environment they face.

The duty to perform dynamics becomes the ultimate motivation test within risk aversion-risk tolerance contexts. Successful implementation of the duty parameters separates optimal-level professionals from the rest of the field. The palpable separation of optimal from normal competency levels supports the drive observers perceive when researching how top-level performers in any profession create their competitive advantage. In addition, peer reviews and constant feedback pressure recipients to be motivated and consistently seek higher skills and competency ranges through continuing education and training. So, where does one find the ability to drive self-motivation? To explore self-motivation in-depth contextually, one must turn to the intrinsic construct of ethics, which succeeds or fails based on one's level of motivation and self-appointed journey toward transcendence.

Chapter Three

ETHICS AS AN INTRINSIC CONSTRUCT OF SUBJECTIVITY

*"I am under obligation both to Greeks and to barbarians,
both to the wise and the foolish."*

Romans 1:14

*"Roberto Clemente was an outstanding young baseball player
in Peurto Rico, so good comparatively; major league scouts sought him out.
After an offer, young Roberto agreed to sign for $10,000, a reasonable
sum in his era. A few days later, he received an offer of $30,000
from another team. Roberto's father advised him to honor the first offer.
A promise made is a promise to be kept. Roberto went on to have
an exemplary career with the Pittsburgh Pirates. After dying in
a plane crash while trying to provide humanitarian aid to a devastated area,
Roberto Clemente became, and is still to this day, the only player ever
enshrined in the major league Baseball Hall of Fame without waiting
the mandated five years. If you ask anyone familiar with Roberto during
his lifetime, they would say he lived as he died, honorably."*

Major League Baseball Archives

*"When two things occur successively, we call them cause and effect
if we believe one event made the other happen. If we think one event*

is the response to the other, we call it a reaction. If we feel that the two incidents are not related, we call it a mere coincidence. If we think someone deserved what happened, we call it retribution or reward, depending on whether the event was negative or positive for the recipient. Finally, we call it an accident if we cannot find a reason for the two events occurring simultaneously or in close proximity. Therefore, how we explain coincidences depends on how we see the world. Is everything connected so that events create resonances like ripples across a net? Or do things merely co-occur, and we give meaning to these co-occurrences based on our belief system? Lieh-Tzu's answer: It's all in how you think."

— Liezi, Lieh-Tzu

"I tell my students, those concerned with the question of betrayal, that when it comes to memoir, there is no such thing as absolute truth, only a truth that is singularly their own. I say this not to release them from responsibility but to illuminate the subjectivity of our inner lives. One person's experience is not another's."

Dani Shapiro

How one meets an obligation is an exercise in synthesizing one's interpretation of social norms within one's defined quality world. Rights rarely enter the equation unless they are integral to one's interests. Prior explorations illustrate the permanent nature of one's rights and the flexible, evolving, often elusive nature of one's interests. Applying ethics to any fundamental process requires one to synthesize *Phronesis* (practical wisdom) and *logos* (logic) with either rights or interests (or both) into one's strategic path to ensure ethics are the underpinning of the strategy utilized to meet obligations. One must construct how ethics functions as an intrinsic personalized construct by exploring an expectation of duty fulfillment linked to one's motivation to act.

Are obligations voluntary or mandatory? From an objective viewpoint, commitments may emerge from either. When linked to subjectivity, both considerations exist as free choices. One of the most potent self-directed obligations is altruism, a deliberate choice of giving self-less concern for others' welfare without any expectation of reciprocity. Compare self-less generosity to the current projection of consideration based on how contracts function, a system based on negotiated mutuality between parties to the agreement.

Parties create contracts of all types, including considerations where parties agree to an obligation, with the broadest definable type of agreement binding the parties through promises within an honor system. A work contract is an implicit contract with the most substantial amount of global utility. One party, the employer, compensates the other party, the employee (or contractor, independent consultant, etc.), for engaging in, and completing, the required throughput. An employee always has the right to choose non-participation in productive utility, at which point they functionally make the work contract void. The now "ex-employee" renounced an obligation at a considerable cost.

How often does one hear, "I have to go to work" or "I must get this work completed?" The implied obligation appears to be mandatory, but it is not. If any theoretical "I have to…" context exists, it would be akin to indentured servitude or slavery, both socially inappropriate. With the perception that all obligations are voluntary, one may assert how both parties to an agreement (a contract) must receive consideration of value, or the legal context of an arrangement could not exist.

Consideration is a core tenet of all contracts. The principle is the foundational basis for a vast amount of "tort" law globally. Where do ethics enter the picture? Ethics is the first consideration. Enacting a contract without equal consideration is unethical because it potentially harms one of the parties. Many civil attorneys utilize artifacts from improperly structured arrangements based on inequitable terms to their clients' significant advantage.

Furthermore, legally defined harm is bound to subjectivity. Suppose a party wishes to "give away the farm." Exploring the steps leading to whether a party may accept or pursue an unbalanced agreement always starts with discerning motivation. One must keep asking why until every potential "why" about the scenario comes to light. Judges, attorneys, and mediators wrestle with the ethics involved in "do no harm" mandates, with the most challenging task being preventing a party from deliberate "self-harm." The struggle invariably relates to the subjectivity of motivation and how one makes choices. Once the subjective "why" becomes apparent, it may be objectively correct to allow a party to fulfill their self-mandated personal view of how an agreement plays out, regardless of the potential for sub-optimal outcomes. The whole world may think they are eccentric or crazy. Crazy is often permissible if the "why" makes sense first.

Business ethics is another exceedingly charged arena to explore. The entire field of corporate social responsibility wrestles with this question. Who is owed an ethical consideration from a broad stakeholder perspective, and when the answer becomes multiple parties, how does one quantify and prioritize the parties? Every scenario must stand as an independent construct and force decision-makers to learn to structure critical thinking-based solutions. Researchers and economics professionals view the ethical contexts thrust upon business scenarios as an optimal "subjectivity" petri dish for debate about stakeholder relevance compared to socially aligned outcomes.

The infinite realm of subjectivity concerning stakeholder relevance has artifacts to explore with a focus on ethics. Most individualized artifacts have a basis in one's worldview and how one defines "stakeholder," some align with social convention, while others emerge from misconceptions or biases. One incredibly unique type of focused bias, egocentric bias, is where the next deep dive begins.

"EGOCENTRIC BIAS"

"When authorities arrested a group of young men for assaulting a young woman in a park, one excuse given for the assault was, "She was an easy target, and I did not know her, so why should I care about her?""

NYPD-2020

"Egocentric bias occurs when people **fail to consider situations from other people's perspectives**. Egocentric bias has influenced ethical judgments to the point where people believe that self-interested outcomes are preferential and create an acceptable moral high ground."

Buddy Thornton

"To be profoundly dishonest, a person must have one of two qualities: either he is unscrupulously ambitious, or he is unswervingly egocentric. He must believe that for his ends to be served, all things and people can justifiably be shifted about, or that he is the center not only of his world but of the worlds which others inhabit."

Maya Angelou

"Henderson promoted an idea that we could all be the center of attention all the time. But if everyone is onstage, who's in the audience?"

Caroline Kepnes

"One of the biggest problems with the world today is that we have large groups of people who will accept whatever they hear on the grapevine just because it suits their worldview, not because it is 'actually' true or because they have evidence to support it. The really striking thing is that it would not take much effort to establish validity in most of these cases, but people prefer reassurance to research."

Neil deGrasse Tyson

"But I think that no matter how smart, people usually see what they're already looking for, that's all."

Veronica Roth

Egocentric bias tends to rely too heavily on one's perspective and leads to adopting a higher opinion of oneself than reality dictates. It appears to result from a psychological need to satisfy one's ego and opens a pathway to optimal memory consolidation. Research has shown that experiences, ideas, and beliefs are more easily recalled when they mimic or mirror one's outlook or worldview.

One perspective on egocentric bias emerges from Maslow's Hierarchy. Egocentric bias in the ethical arena aligns with supporting one's pursuit of deficit needs fulfillment before any other consideration. One should always make choices aligning with enhancing oneself while traversing a deficit-needs environment. Zero consideration or mental deliberation exists for others' needs until one achieves self-efficacy at some level above a self-defined deficiency, a reality crossing all social contexts. So, are egocentric choices dictated by environmental necessity? Yes, if the options emerge from an actual deficit needs context. Yes, holding to egocentric biases allows one to focus on goals aligned with achieving the perceived needs more effectively.

Consider the protests across America after George Floyd died in Minneapolis at the hands of an on-duty police officer, caught on video and sent out on social media across the globe, becoming viral within moments of the transmission. Mr. Floyd's demise was one in a long line of questionable actions by police officers across America. Hardened veteran peace officers became distressed by what they encountered and absorbed through the stark, relatively unfiltered narrative from social media and traditional news outlets. Social and racial injustice protests, a normative part of the American landscape, expanded the storyline by targeting the hyperbolic exposure of police brutality, leading to a rapid escalation of the protests.

A widespread perception of inadequate and uneven police interaction with minorities, essentially a deficit needs context, increased social reactions to a fever-laden pitch. The expansive response created an opportunity for exploitative and manipulative actions by parties seeking to disrupt the normalized social projection of discord. Perceptibly, external players on the periphery not identifiable as peaceful protagonists expanded the protests to include rioting and looting. Criminal greed drove a significant portion of the looting, encouraged to action by the divisive political environment and unmitigated, emergent opportunities.

Still, the root cause links back to a population mired in a needs-unfulfilled environment, fundamentally a perfect projection of Maslow's "deficit needs" continuum. Desperate people make bad choices, often for the right reasons and aligning with predictable theory. The egocentric words aligned with how one would describe people seeking to address the deficits, "No justice, No peace" and cries to defund the police, are foundational to their daily existence, not merely artifacts emerging from a snapshot event of racial violence.

Arguments abound surrounding the external issue of police brutality. One must explore how statistics show a significant number of wrong actions, both illegal and immoral in context, by a few bad actors in uniform. The protesters project this harsh depiction toward all police personnel instead of focusing solely on the bad actors. No matter where one stands within this debate, demanding an "all or nothing" decision matrix will never result in positive actions. The protesters, or their leadership, would better serve the community they represent through appropriate dialogue aimed at ethical outcomes.

Admittedly, mistrust is all parties' most significant hurdle to any movement forward. However, is it reasonable to remain intractable with demands? Rigid thinking never leads to progress. Instead, both sides should examine their options, starting with how to engage more effectively and with ethical principles in play, which would require a significant reduction in egocentrism. Therefore, the conversation circles back to how one's biases drive both acceptable and unacceptable choice paradigms.

Egocentric bias must be considered amoral and a normative part of human constructs unless actions are deemed illegal. Unlike cognitive bias, where one creates a subjective social viewpoint regardless of an overarching social discourse, irrationality, and illogical choice-making, egocentric bias is foundational to self-worth and self-indulgence synthesized with a concurrent form of universal positive regard from and for others. Plus, motivated social participants tend to gain competency aligned with cognitive bias suppression, a self-motivated factor involved directly with overcoming barriers while increasing social "fitness." How and when do cognitive bias suppression and a simultaneous expansion of egocentric focus occur?

Deontological ethics enters the equation at the demarcation line of fulfilled deficit needs and where growth opportunities become a focus. When one achieves each level of development within the hierarchy, increases in cognitive bias suppression occur. In ancient times and contemporary social environments, a person's pursuit of *eudaimonia* achievement becomes the overarching catalyst for optimal transcendence, often perceived as a solitary, subjectively personal pursuit.

Unless the perception of others is highly favorable, can one feel worthy? Mark Twain (the pen name of Samuel Clemens) wrote, "Man cannot be comfortable without self-approval." Twain intended the quote to focus on individuals and indicate how each human needs to embrace self-love as part of individualized specificity. Humankind, in its entirety, by extension, should embrace self-love as a foundational component of the "self."

Exploring and translating the evolution of Twain's thinking, one can extend the quote to "one cannot gain the approval of oneself without the correspondent perception one has the approval of others." One may dissect each rung of Maslow's evolved model from the viewpoint of gaining others' approval to increase self-worth until one reaches the pinnacle of Maslow's hierarchy. Reaching the zenith, defined in the new model as transcendence (Aristotle and Maslow's stated goal for all humans), would shift one's perspective of "needing affirmation from others" to the realization that one's actions stand as an unquestioned testament to eudaimonia based on one's self-chosen journey instead of any predetermined end goal, or the approval of others along the way.

At transcendence, humans live the whole experience of every step of the journey toward their end goal. As a result, they have gained the capacity to suppress egocentric bias and no longer need extrinsic affirmation. The manifestation further evolves Twain's quote to, "One must be comfortable in one's skin, and ignore the opinions of others."

Exploring and debating egocentric bias suppression as part of one's journey allows each reader to adapt the concept to reality. Subjectivity aligned with specificity reigns supreme, meaning right or wrong beyond one's interests does not exist within this debate. Instead, each participant creates the perception of truth based on their needs as defined within Maslow's model by exploring self-efficacy optimally.

Consider the following debate thoughts and restrictions to understand how one's egocentric bias may serve to cloud judgment above the Maslow demarcation line, but not below the line. First, everyone believes their reality is correct, leading to anchoring despite situations where they may be faced with significant proof otherwise. Two, the belief expands to think others should feel the same way or appear fundamentally flawed. Third, fundamental attribution errors (FAEs) emerge due to this faulty logic. "If I fail, factors outside my control are to blame; If others fail, they made errors" is one version of an FAE. The primary debate restrictions should be the reverse: a) flip the FAE to "If I fail, it is me; if others fail, the failure had an outside causative agent," and b) "If I am successful, who can I thank" as opposed to "if I fail, who can I blame."

Through reverse thinking, one gains a vastly different perspective on egocentric thinking. Consider habitual adherence to egotistic tendencies typically leads to enhanced action potentials for success while pursuing deficit needs. The evolving and often expanding worldview also opens the door to exploring ways to suppress any emerging negative inclinations once growth begins. The difficulty lies in finding balance within the concept while understanding why others need not agree.

While distinctly individualized by application and environmental context, the role of bias must always exist as a confounding agent during any effort to approach self-actualization or transcendence. (See Appendix C for a complete article on the subconscious, implicit, and explicit biases applicable to egocentric bias.)

"FINDING THE BEST __________"

"As I walked down the street, I couldn't help but notice the homeless gentleman on the corner. As a habit, I rarely carry money, so helping would only be through a proactive choice to engage. He looked so hungry; I asked, "Can I get you something to eat and drink?" His reply was just a nod. I expected him to dive right in when I returned with the meal. Boy, was I wrong! He ran a short distance to a stoop, gave the water to a small child, and shared his sandwich with her. I have since revised my definition of hero; he was truly that."

Buddy Thornton

"Before becoming an expert on anything, I must first become an expert on me."

Charles F. Glassman

"To conquer frustration, one must remain intensely focused on the outcome, not the obstacles."

T.F. Hodge

"Burning bridges behind you is understandable. It's the bridges before us that we burn, not realizing we may need to cross, that brings regret."

Anthony Liccione

"Is it fairer for everyone to have the same opportunities or the same outcomes? Equality of opportunity or equality of outcome? Is it fairer for decisions to be uniform or to embody an element of human empathy? Impartial justice or individual allowances? Is it fairer to let people know how decisions are made or to have an opaque system to prevent cheating? Transparency or security?"

Aileen Nielsen

"For any single decision, there are different ways the future could unfold; some better, some worse. When you make a decision, the decision makes certain paths possible (even if you don't know where they lead) and others impossible. The decision you make determines which set of outcomes are possible and how likely each of those outcomes is. But it doesn't determine which of that set of outcomes will actually happen."

Annie Duke

Complete the sentence, "I have to be the best at______________." Does the answer align with egocentric bias thinking? Now shift the sentence to, "I have to find the best ______________." Please attempt to answer both questions by aligning with social value constructs, not objective, physical possession.

Now, complete the sentence, "I must create the best ____________." One must shift to a creation-centric dynamic and anchor on social value constructs while suppressing or abandoning egocentric bias to arrive at an acceptable answer. Aristotle would have aligned his answers with servant leadership (answer to the first question), cultural environment (answer to the second question), and virtuous reality (answer to the third question). Why would Aristotle do this? He believed the path to transcendence could only be achieved by mutually benefiting others simultaneously with oneself. So, one must explore the context of "best" through that lens. When asked, many people give surprising answers to the questions.

Perceptions of optimal methods one may implement to conceptualize and utilize "best" subjectively are infinite. What is best for oneself? If one makes sacrifices for family, colleagues, or strangers when circumstances dictate, does the dynamic define the best possible portrayal of "oneself?" Is it best to allow others to take credit for positive outcomes while disregarding one's participation level? Perhaps it is best to enjoy the moment when others glance in your direction and acknowledge your support. In Aristotle's virtue society, the answer to these questions is a resounding yes. The silent hero should live an existence where intrinsic value reigns supreme, finding virtue in eschewing self-aggrandizement. So, why doesn't society experience this dynamic more often?

Circle back to the original question. Virtue is lacking because most people would answer the question with answers not aligned with social values. Comparison, the root of almost all conflict, has evolved into a hyper-competitive social environment where winning is paramount. Society deifies winning dynamics over fairness dynamics by celebrating the pursuit of victory at any cost. No matter the cost!

For example, politics is amplified competition. In a perfect world environment, candidates would debate the issues, inform the public of their competency, fact-check themselves first, and maintain a visible presence on the high social road. Unfortunately, the reality juxtaposes the muckraking and smearing campaigns of modern-day campaigns against any concept of virtue ethics. Modern political candidates fling themselves into the muck with innuendo attacks on their opponents, resort to half-truths (or no truths at all) and seek to obfuscate reality through misinformation. The normalized response to impassioned attacks between an incumbent and a challenger is to create half-truths or blatant falsehoods to misinform psychologically charged constituents who vote based on blind passion aligned with influential hyperbole. An honorable contest's possible virtue is absent; therefore, the ethics aligned with fairness and informed voting is not present during any modern American election. Candidates must create passionate followers instead of knowledgeable citizens if they wish to compete in the contemporary "false-flag" political environment.

Finding the best candidate to support as an individual becomes problematic when all examples of projected success emerge from unethical behavior instead of one's considerations of the day's actual social issues. Adhering to deontological ethics in a teleological landscape incites others to question your sanity. How often should virtuous individuals face "holier than thou" accusations or "do you think you are better than the rest of us?" Competitive dynamics and pursuit of winning regardless of potential cost or lost honor create a perverted sense of what society should desire or expect from a winning candidate. Arguably, contemporary society has undeniably devolved the process of electing officials at all levels into anarchy where the affluent can state something intangible into existence, leading to the current contemptible political savagery in evidence today.

Take a few moments and list how many questionable tactics you recognize from the 2018 mid-term elections and the dubious tactics discerned during the recently completed 2020 presidential campaign. Indeed, go deeper into regional politics and explore the shift from issues to character assassinations. One rarely discussed reality is the "why" of smear campaigns. Candidates will sink to incredibly minute ethical projection levels when campaigning because they fear (yes, fear) their lack of perspective on political issues or their ability to speak effectively about those issues.

Their political competency range is somehow lacking compared to their opponents. As a result, the candidates must rely on minimizing the image of their opponent instead of enhancing their persona and position. Subsequently, constituents focus on candidate image over substance, spread misinformation to influence voters, and ignore fact-checkers trying to control honesty levels and add transparency to the process.

Compare and discuss your list with those of others. The comparisons' predictable outcome should be illuminating and align with the punch line of an anecdote, "Never wrestle with pigs. You both get dirty, but the pigs enjoy it." Does a path back to reason exist? Not when most members of society prefer sensationalist drama over substantive dialogue.

So, does one assume the system must remain broken? No, one should not believe so, especially when one considers a fact: humans are the system. For example, when reframing the lead-in quotes, it should become apparent that unfettered variance controls both potential and outcome, so finding the best "anything" is tenuous in politics or real life.

The more humans strive for perfection, clarity about one fact emerges from the shadows. "Even if you do everything perfectly, you can still lose or fail." Therefore, instead of clinging to futile paths, humanity should pivot and explore the concept of socialized interaction through a lens of universal imperfection related to personalized constructs of subjectivity from within the system, asking: Are the imperfections part of the system or an embedded false construct? Might the answer lie in social or cultural relativity, where finding an optimal "thing" is utterly subjective?

"IT'S NOT THE SYSTEM!"

*"It's time, dear. Can you go to the store and get me the supplies
for this year's stockings?"*

*Every year, one lady makes stockings for a local first-grade at one
of the most impoverished schools in the area. She contacts the administrator,
gets permission to collect names from the teachers, and makes custom
hand-cut holiday stockings, one for every child. She even makes a few
extra to have on hand for newcomers who enroll before December each year.
Some of the kids will receive nothing else for the season.*

*She refuses to use her last name, preferring "Grandma Sharon."
Every year, after the students return to school in January, she gets
thank you cards from the students, her only reward. She has done this
for many years, since the 1990s.*

*No one asks, no one pays, and no one helps. People at her work believe she is
wasting her time and effort. Thank the good Lord; she disagrees. Sometimes,
you need to ignore the ordinary and do what is righteous, what's in your
heart. Ignore the system, ignore the naysayers, and do it!*

Buddy Thornton

*"Today, the network of relationships linking the human race to itself
and the rest of the biosphere is so complex that all aspects affect all others to
an extraordinary degree. Someone should study the whole system;*

however crudely, that must be done. No gluing together of partial studies
of a complex nonlinear system can give a good idea
of the behavior of the whole."

Murray Gell-Mann

"We can't get outside the aura. We're part of the aura.
We're here; we're now."

Don DeLillo

"A complex system that works is invariably found to have evolved
from a simple system that worked. The inverse proposition also
appears true: A complex system designed from scratch never works
and cannot be made to work. You have to start over, beginning with
a simple working system."

John Gall

Even though protests and voicing one's opinion is a historically normalized American tradition, most people in America believe one cannot buck the system, at least not successfully, and those who try are "out-of-control mavericks." Thank goodness people like Rosa Parks ignore the norm. Ms. Park's defiance of the day's social customs is a shining example of how the smallest unit of the system, one person, can influence change. However, were the social ills Ms. Parks brought to light addressed immediately or with any true expedience? No, they were not. As changes occurred over time, were the changes universal and achievable? Sadly, decades after her heroic stance, the equal rights enacted by governing bodies in response are still being debated, implemented by mandate but only marginally supported throughout society, and enforced with an unequal approach by authorities in many parts of the country.

Despite society's failure to universally embrace social equality as a "lived norm," the Rosa Parks example is uniquely suited to discussing one member's ability to influence change. Consider a beach anywhere in the world. One grain of sand can be irritating when it gets inside a shoe, yet it is impossible to discern individually in its natural environment. Ms. Parks became the grain of sand society needed to implement what became the Civil Rights Movement. By comparison, *Brown v. Board of Education-1954* did not move American society forward as effectively as Ms. Park's refusal to be treated as "less-than."

Any time one believes the system is intractable, the belief becomes a self-fulfilling prophecy. Prolonged change may occur slowly for many reasons, but social entropy due to limited systemic adoption of change tops the list. It only takes one brave soul to climb the mountain of systemic entropy and shake its foundations to initiate an avalanche of change for social benefit. God bless and keep those who engage in this challenge, especially in today's social environment.

Another excellent example of the "one grain of sand" is Cesar Chavez, the migrant farmworker who challenged a highly exploitative system and won. Mr. Chavez took the path of garnering support by seeking non-violent means to expose the corrupt system. The success of Mr. Chavez's vision hinged on his ability to portray how inequity projected at one person steadfastly is inherently unethical. Once his vision became manifest, Mr. Chavez expanded the projected foundational unfairness to an entire class of people. Many people perceive Rosa Parks and Cesar Chavez as social heroes throughout society because they chose to be positive social change agents, at least in the author's opinion.

What does this mean for ethics and the system? President US Grant said (misattributed to President Abraham Lincoln), "The best way to get a bad law repealed is to enforce it vigorously." In the modern social media environment, Grant's vision has influenced a shift to vigorous exposure of many injustices to the masses. If social media had been a factor for Rosa Parks or Cesar Chavez, their path to success would have been much shorter, if occurring at all.

Social media leverages the concept of "we are the system" to significant effect in most cases, although abuses due to misinformation and outright lying are always possible. One should explore and understand any issue before embracing a cause, a process social media usurps by projecting as the ultimate authority over knowledge. Before moving beyond system theory, take the time to debate how social media positively influences the masses. One must remain mindful of the inward-looking proclamation, "we are the system," while engaging in the debate. Any criticism would, therefore, be aimed at oneself as much as anyone.

"GOLDEN RULE OF ETHICS"

36 "Teacher, which is the greatest commandment in the Law?"
37 Jesus replied: " 'Love the Lord your God with all your heart
and with all your soul and with all your mind.' 38 This is the first
and greatest commandment. 39 And the second is like it:
'Love your neighbor as yourself.' 40 All the Law and the Prophets
hang on these two commandments."

Matthew 22:36-40 of the Christian Bible

"I have something that I call my Golden Rule. It goes like this:
'Do unto others twenty-five percent better than you expect them
to do unto you.' The twenty-five percent is for error."

Linus Pauling

"We mistreat others not because we don't understand how people
should be treated but because we don't consider them people."

Michael Austin

"The Golden rule is if we asked for more and negotiated
with more confidence, we would get more."

Abhishek Ratna

Based on the second of the two Great Commandments, with versions present across most human belief systems, is a universal axiom, "Do unto others as they do unto you." The derivative most Westerners call the "Golden Rule" is inherently shortsighted and incomplete when viewed through an ethical lens. An ethically aligned, universal positive regard version would be "Treat others as you would have them treat you, regardless of how they treat you."

Most professional codes of ethics take a much simpler, direct approach, focusing on the existing axiom, "Do no harm." For example, an attorney must represent a client with optimal consideration and competence based on the Law but owes an opponent a "due consideration" approach which depends on adherence to their code of professional ethics. In plain language, the requirement means the attorney must avoid deliberate deception as a tactic. In criminal cases, for example, discovery must be shared within the framework of the case. Having professional codes of ethics as a foundation, one may expand the "do no harm" context into an applicable "Golden Rule of Ethics."

The rule extends from Aristotle's *eudaimonia*, which implies that if one has the right to seek a life well-lived, all people deserve the same consideration. A secondary factor is the concept of servant leadership when one aims to ensure a projection of how to achieve eudaimonia through optimal modeling and mentoring. Here is an example of one thought on the Golden Rule of Ethics, constructed based on how the projection of the "self" extends to others equally:

> *"One deserves a well-lived life when one has extended all efforts to ensure others may achieve the same end through dignity and social equity while not harming any person or group of persons."*

Arguably, one could discern infinite versions of a "well-lived" life. Two examples are an "enviable" existence or an "admirable" one, both having a well-lived context, but the dichotomy opens the potential for a broad interpretation. One should debate with peers whether one worldview should hold sway over another, but one should also define limitations to the debate. First, one's individualized choice theory applies, meaning one only has control over oneself and actions independent of all other persons. Second, the first measure is always not to harm. Third, it is not inherently possible to achieve Eudaimonia based on social equity if anyone within one's sphere of influence lacks the same possibility due to asymmetric concepts of fairness. In every instance where the ethics debate has honestly occurred, the consensus achieved led to vast amounts of introspection and heightened self-awareness of how one treats others.

What are the ramifications of having or not having a debate on how to create a "well-lived" life founded on ethics? First, the golden rule lacks meaning without intentional implementation and consistent application. Implementation requires participants with significant motivation to engage in self-control and effective collaboration with like-minded others, a type of impetus found at the top of Maslow's hierarchy where one seeks transcendence. Transcendence aligns with a willingness to help others along one's journey through acts of benevolence. Examine this point from a position of "what is the value of an achievement without the ability to share one's joy of accomplishment," not through gloating or condescension, but as someone who knows a journey well-traveled depends on the efforts of many others along the path. The examination requires exploring two complementary tasks, perspective-taking and perspective-making.

"PERSPECTIVE-TAKING AND PERSPECTIVE-MAKING"

"Often, it isn't the mountains ahead that wear you out; it's the little pebble in your shoe."

Muhammad Ali

"Men are disturbed not by the things that happen but by their opinion of the things that happen."

Epictetus

"Reject your sense of injury, and the injury itself disappears."

Marcus Aurelius

"There are no facts, only interpretations."

Friedrich Nietzsche

"Some people see the glass half full. Others see it half empty. I see a glass twice as big as it needs to be."

George Carlin

"Most misunderstandings in the world could be avoided if people would simply take the time to ask, "What else could this mean?"

Shannon L. Alder

$\mathcal{M}$ost contemporary academics can adequately define perspective-taking. The concept is integral to all learning environments. Perspective-taking is a thorough exploration of all facets of a topic intentionally focused on utilizing or exploiting the knowledge gained. In most corporate environments, attaining goals enhances a sustainable competitive advantage, while individuals use perspective-taking to advance their personal goals.

Perspective-making, on the other hand, is where leaders thrive. Most perspective-aligned quotes, such as the lead-in quotes from three historical figures, attempt to project perspective-making and allow others to create a subjective perspective based on similar reference points in their quality world. The concept emerges from an optimal perspective-taking context where focused individuals discern innovative ways to overcome barriers and reach "blue ocean environments" where competition is no longer considered. Steve Jobs was such a leader. Tablets and smartphones are the direct results of Jobs' vision of what society would need, followed by an unrelenting pursuit of making the public buy into the concept. Perspective-making creates and influences the future, while perspective-taking explores, considers, then embraces the here and now.

From an ethics perspective, accepting the here and now supports the "rightness" of contemporary norms. However, acceptance works in multiple ways, making it possible, sometimes necessary, to utilize an ethical approach to understand the "wrongness" embedded in existing social contexts. As stated earlier in the book, perspective-taking aligns with teleological processes and "the ends justify the means" thinking. Is it possible to align teleological processes with the golden rule of ethics?

Adhering to the golden rule requires a shift toward deontological ethics and expanded adoption of universal positive regard for others, requiring the existence of an army of perspective makers. Imagine the emergence of servant leaders across many fields and cultures, creating a perspective of the reality of infinite approaches to Eudaimonia, which, in turn, influences others to consider the needs of others instead of seeking to exploit them. Exploring the concept would cut across several areas, covering business and personal ethics in various contexts.

Circling back to Maslow's Hierarchy further delineates perspective from both sides of the coin. Deontological ethics cannot function well when people struggle to meet basic needs. Virtually all forms of ethics become meaningless in existential contexts. Survival becomes the only focus. As servant leaders, authentic leaders must embrace the struggle many people endure based on their insufficient capacity to access resources tied to scarcity. Leaders should reduce the deficit needs by focusing on increasing access to resources or creating optimal paths to acquiring resources versus today's reality.

Navigating Maslow's motivational hierarchy is more likely to occur when societal leadership supports ethical approaches to deficit needs. Servant leaders are more likely to create and sustain action potential for encompassing choices designed to enhance most humans' lives on the planet while simultaneously driving growth environments. In contrast, in his treatise Ethical Considerations, Tollefson refers to most humans as "sheep." Tollefson quotes several positions on "Egoism" and suggests humans are sheep due to their inherently "herd-mentality" negative focus on insecurity. Elevated to prominence by his encouraging worldview on applied motivation, Maslow becomes the counterpoint, where humans seek pathways over, under, or around barriers, supporting the servant leadership paradigm.

Tollefson focuses on insight and reflection, an attribute Tollefson asserts manifests in a small percentage of people, while Maslow expands upon a strong point Tollefson misses. People who find themselves mired in a "needs" context cannot afford to waste time reflecting or exploiting potentially valuable insights. One may agree with the view espoused by Tollefson, suggesting that most humans are incapable of reflection and meaningful insight creation; however, one should color the belief with a broad brush of perspective. Limited resources, limited access, and reduced success models are the foundational causes leading to the shortfall.

How does one create a new dynamic within the space between Tollefson's negativity and Maslow's action potential linked to human motivation? Again, one must shift toward virtue ethics adapted to the contemporary social environment. Shifting shall not be easy since it will require building a framework where soft skills outperform hard skills as a value construct. Adherence to virtue-oriented value orientations must become a socially acceptable concept through a deontological application.

The perspective continuum has occupied the fabric of American social discourse for many decades. For example, how perspective impacts disadvantaged populations is explored in many forms. For example, one forum where individual perspectives project how social change and entropy exist simultaneously is pop culture. Very few people over sixty can deny the impact of the civil rights protests and how worldviews changed in the 1960s. But, upon deeper introspection, have they changed that much?

Consider a movie from the era, *Watermelon Man* from 1970, with Godfrey Cambridge as the headliner. The socially relevant comedy portrayed a bigoted white man who became a black man overnight, with predictable foibles related to how white privilege and a harsh awakening drove the central figure to turn to an extremist group bent on forcing change. Being openly racially biased and subsequently living inside the proverbial flip-side symbolizes how and why racial and social injustices endure, perhaps because too few individuals can see the world from an external or juxtaposed lens. The movie could be re-imagined today with almost no change and still be relevant to current social discord issues. (See Appendix C for a complete article on perspective-making, perspective-taking, and projection of context.)

"LOCAL TO GLOBAL" AND "GLOBAL TO LOCAL"

*"A boy was standing on a beach tossing starfish back into the water.
When his father told him his action would never matter when the beach
held thousands of starfish he could not possibly save, the boy replied,
"It matters to this one, and this one, and this one…"*

*"It is widely said "Think globally, act locally"… well,
the disaster happens when people do the opposite."*

Sameh Elsayed

*"The sun rises, the sun falls, the wind blows, and the birds sing
no matter where you are. These are experiences that unite us all;
something we can all enjoy together."*

Melanie Charlene

*"As a global community, we face a choice. Do we want migration
to be a source of prosperity and international solidarity
or a byword for inhumanity and social friction?"*

Antonio Guterres

The concept of a continuum stretching from local (and quasi-local) to global and vice-versa is an idea linked to Maslow's hierarchy in several unique ways. One, migration patterns are unpredictable and based primarily on people seeking an environment where they may climb above the deficit needs section of the hierarchy by changing their opportunity landscape. Two, migration's unpredictability stems from various motivations observers discerned through interaction with the migrants, whether voluntarily relocating or as involuntary refugees.

Voluntary migrants seek an environment where they may simultaneously reduce risk while maintaining their identity. Conversely, forced populations seek survival despite all potential costs. The migration patterns create varying stress levels in a global system already struggling with limited resources and equitable distribution of the resources present throughout society.

When considering the relative scarcity of resources, one should envision natural and developed resources as "linked" to applications and processes designed to overcome needs, such as nutrition, housing, or jobs. Once a person sorts out and emerges from the deficit needs puzzle, the contemporary knowledge economy offers infinite possibilities for exploitation focused on gaining a personal advantage at considerable expense to others. The barrier most often encountered is access to innovation, which cycles back to why migration creates an opportunity for oppressed groups of people.

Understanding applied ethics in a fluid environment, such as in countries where significantly relevant numbers of migrants gather, requires exploring the fluid environment from two perspectives, the one held by the refugees and the one owned by the original occupants or citizens. How should an entitled citizen view incoming refugees? Should the refugees be considered interlopers who overburden available resources, becoming an existential threat? Should the refugees be perceived as victims seeking relief from their abandoned environment? On the other hand, how should a refugee view their new situation? Is the climate resource-rich enough to provide sustenance? Are the entitled citizens sympathetic or resistant to the refugee's presence?

Environments limited to in-country migratory patterns, which tend to be either rural to urban or urban to suburban logistically, induce the same existential questions. Human groups tend to be tribally possessive of what they collectively have, and sharing can become contentious. The newcomers may exhibit needed skills, immediately contribute to an environment, and still be considered a threat in a limited resource context. The current knowledge economy mitigates this to a point.

The best way to view how migration affects people would require a resource perspective. If enough resources are available, sharing is both profitable and ethical. If resources are stressed and become scarce, the entitled citizens act to reduce sharing and protect self-interests. Whether the reduction to access, usually a local phenomenon, leads to conflict is where the ethics of equitable distribution becomes a debate. Global (broad-based) interests do not matter from the locals' perspective. At this point, incoming migrants are decidedly a threat.

The reverse effect occurs when incoming migrants can increase throughput. In contemporary urban contexts, city officials use various enticements to attract outside companies to relocate and expand the local resource base. Migrating populaces bring a consumption pattern, and well-established cities can exploit consumption favorably. Even declining cities like Detroit, where a burgeoning migrant refugee population has settled and begun to thrive, may reverse tax-base shortfalls by synergistically welcoming the refugees.

Arguably, the ethics of exploitation have both positive and negative connotations. Examine the concepts by answering the earlier questions. Do the incoming migrants overburden available resources and assume the label of "interlopers?" Perhaps they also bring value and adapt to the environment by increasing commerce with their presence. Hence, a rising tide lifts all ships. Yes, they are victims in most cases, afraid of what they may find, but acquiring the ability to set aside victimology through a willingness to risk much by escaping an untenable situation is indicative of resolve on a previously unheard-of scale regardless of what precipitated their migration.

Local to global or global to local is mainly a perspective issue. The original occupants may enhance their ethical position through perspective-making by projecting, "We want you here, but only as producing neighbors, not exploiting newcomers." The migrants can increase sympathy for their plight through perspective-making and modeling good behavior. "We are willing participants who eagerly engage in the process of becoming welcome neighbors and productive citizens."

Aristotle arguably described how virtue ethics apply to the equitable treatment of others. Providing dignity, a welcoming environment, and a willingness to engage are essential to eudaimonia, requiring adherence to fair treatment and uplifting the less fortunate through collaborative processes. In Aristotle's era, this was limited to citizens, with little consideration for enslaved people beyond their utility. If Aristotle peered across time and interacted with the contemporary world, his first consideration beyond personal needs would be "How goes the normative interaction between common men today?" One might support a position suggesting Aristotle would be appalled at what he would discern about social behavior within modernity. So, one should answer Aristotle's question by looking at it first within a local context, followed by exploring more global approaches.

The fractious social environment of "America 2020" mired in the COVID-19 crisis finds half of the country approaching "others" from an empathetic, open position of willingness to share. The other half seeks individualized "Me First" preferences, some rights-based, some focusing on saving lives, some concentrating on preserving wealth and sustainability, and some extending to influencing or expanding the existence of a conflict with Americans who aren't "just like me." Ethical approaches are limited to a teleological process of seeking ends satisfactory to whichever group one identifies with, regardless of the means utilized while getting the job done. Any global worldview emerging in the local environment becomes colored with "what's in it for me" thinking and whether the worldview advances one's cause. Aristotle would say this is the ultimate display of selfishness and contempt for all others.

On a global scale, the projection of "America first" with isolationist tendencies creates barriers to cooperation and collaboration. Regardless of how a group is defined, all humans seek the path of "least resistance" to their interests. Contemporary America counter-intuitively projects a challenging track for accomplishing virtually all cooperative efforts. Admittedly, the global effect shifts with each new Administration, so change is never a new concept. Still, America's reality from 2016 through 2021 (thus far) is a projection of a distinctive Sophist image of "might is right" from the ancient world's pre-ethos era. Deontological virtues are absent. The historically significant absence of social virtues creates an environment where "stratified" social division is "quasi-acceptable" locally and globally; unfortunately, fair or acceptable is not a consideration.

When high levels of contention or division are present socially, people tend to shrink back into a deficit needs mentality. Heightened perspective-taking levels influence how people measure risk when faced with a media onslaught of "us versus them" dynamics, which further reduces the deficit needs context to the mitigation of existential fear. The top of Maslow's hierarchy becomes invisible, hidden by a cloud of doubt and hostility.

One needs to leverage the power of deontological, "virtuous to a fault" ethical processes to overcome the fear-based divisiveness in today's social environment, whether locally or globally. Of course, one would have to be naïve to think all divisive discourse can be solved this way. Consider the Hebrew-Arab conflict, already several millennia old with no conceptual ending. Do you think any approach will work in their context? However, the norm for most humans globally is "find a way to get along with your neighbor first" or "go along to get along," so it is reasonable to start there and expand one's definition of neighbor, starting with how one perceives social stratification and one's sphere of influence.

"CHANGE ONLY OCCURS WHEN COMPELLING REASONS EXIST"

*"Everything that can be counted does not necessarily count;
everything that counts cannot necessarily be counted."*

Albert Einstein

*"The only thing a person can do is keep moving forward. Take that
big leap forward without hesitation, without once looking back.
Simply forget the past and forge toward the future."*

Alyson Noel

*"Sometimes, it takes an overwhelming breakdown
to have an undeniable breakthrough."*

Unknown

"The great secret of passion is an emotionally compelling purpose."

Robin Sharma

"Teaching kids to count is fine, but teaching them what counts is best."

Bob Talbert

Everyone has heard the mantra, "Change is Inevitable." Well, not so fast. Humans despise change. Genetically, humans are predisposed to seeking comfort in familiarity and embracing order above entropy unless threatened. Fact. Not much debate. Most humans are complacent, comfortable right where they are, and only embrace change when enticed to seek some "thing" or forced to avoid an unpleasant outcome. Given the normative human aversion to change, how challenging would one's sphere of influence need to appear to drive change dynamics? Overcoming entropy takes significant energy and resolve, implying the threat must be genuine.

Most Americans don't know (or won't acknowledge) that most of the global population rarely goes beyond the horizon from their birthplace. The lack of knowledge about migration patterns confounds one's perspective on the social entanglement inherent to local-global interaction. Limited migration is due to an embedded form of group social risk aversion. So, let's unpack the "why" of social change, not historically, but within the contemporary world, if the context is factual about humans and their aversion to change, especially given we know, "Change is inevitable."

The world is perceptibly separated into two very different paradigms when considering social change: a) highly opportunistic environments and b) limited opportunity environments. Yet, although differentiated, many of these paradigms exist within the same global geo-point when one considers variants of the two worldview attributes and how humans perceive their unique version of SWOT (strengths, weaknesses, opportunities, and threats).

The most critical characteristics are found on the continuum of risk perception based on risk-aversion or risk-tolerance and how one views dynamic or entropic choices. First, one must accurately comprehend the risk of accepting challenges while seeking positive change. A crucial second attribute is a developing self-awareness trait that aligns with intrinsic motivation to thrive regardless of all other factors. Combining perceived risk-perception and motive leads one directly to SWOT with its action potential for utility when making choices.

In highly opportunistic environments, enterprising or determined individuals find many paths to their goals. Consider this friendly environment as a large tree. There is one trunk where commonality exists, so everyone must get up to the canopy by conquering their basic needs similarly. Once in the tree's crown, there are endless paths to the top of the tree, most with little to no resistance to choices. Competition may place barriers to success for less competent people, but everyone eventually settles in at a personally happy place.

Only those who are affluent, privileged in some fashion (legacy or favorable attributes), or highly gifted intellectually may pass into the canopy in limited opportunity environments. All others are stuck at the base of the trunk. The only options for the less fortunate are to overcome challenges or find another tree.

One might understand how contemporary migration has evolved in local and global patterns by synthesizing the optimal and sub-optimal concepts; humans genetically change-avoidant are forced to accept change's inevitability, often with suboptimal outcomes. Migration patterns within countries show two realities; those with means or who can acquire means will migrate from a depressed socioeconomic area to one with possibilities. Those who fail to meet that threshold will remain mired in squalor and poverty due to lacking opportunities.

Between countries, barriers to this process exist, now more than ever in global history. Most migration is tied to existential fear, such as avoiding cartel violence, gang violence, or being a war refugee. Those with affluence or acquired means can escape and pursue a better life; those without access or opportunity to escape become victims of their circumstances. None of this is new; it is a rinse and repeat of human history and only covers voluntary migration. The alternate form, forced migration, drives participants to create an entirely different change dynamic with few optimal outcomes.

Chapter Four

APPLIED CONTEMPORARY ETHICS

*"With the truth, all given facts harmonize; with what is false,
the truth soon hits a wrong note."*

Aristotle, The Nicomachean Ethics

*"Virtue lies in our power, and similarly so does vice; because where it
is in our power to act, it is also in our power not to act…"*

Aristotle, The Nicomachean Ethics

*"How can a man know what is good or best for him and yet chronically
fail to act upon his knowledge?"*

Aristotle

*"There may be times when we are powerless to prevent injustice,
but there must never be a time when we fail to protest."*

Elie Wiesel

*"Until he extends the circle of his compassion to all living things,
man will not himself find peace."*

Albert Schweitzer

"The law of evolution is that the strongest survives!" '
Yes, and the strongest, in the existence of any social species,
are those who are most social. In human terms, most ethical.
There is no strength to be gained from hurting
one another, only weakness."

Ursula K. Le Guin

*E*xploring applied ethics is genuinely a personal journey each reader must take. Learning and retaining knowledge, delving into how one encounters, engages with, and understands essential facts and values associated with learning, is a subjective, highly individualized pursuit. Exploiting the acquired knowledge and creating value is a purposeful quest focusing on the utility one derives from the action potential of one's acquired knowledge as it applies to one's specific sphere of influence. Ethical ideology is a universal concept with many possible perspectives, and the exploration of ethics has traversed all of human history. Every ethically-aligned application depends on one's sphere of influence, one's worldview (rigid or adaptive), and one's motivation to act in either of two ways: through narrow self-interest or broad social-interest focus. One links to deontology, while the other links to teleology.

One's sphere of influence occupies two domains, each with action potential for reaching Maslow's transcendence. The first is local to global, meaning one seeks to apply a micro-perspective of one's worldview and project it as a generalization applicable to global contexts. The second is the reverse, global to local, meaning one attaches one's broad worldview concepts (individualist aligned or collectivist aligned) and tries to make sense of the ethics normative to one's immediate needs or growth pursuits.

First, consider Bronfenbrenner's Ecological Systems Theory and add a lens of omnidirectionally where humans pass seamlessly between the multiple ecological environments. Then, apply individualized motivation to the model and choose whether a micro to macro context supports the transcendence drive. Perhaps a macro-to-micro context induces optimal results instead?

Both paths potentially traverse some meaningful social concepts and constructs, such as in-group and out-group action potential, how and why self-segregation and social stratification endures, the conceptualization of rights versus interests, and risk-tolerance versus risk-aversion. Consistent or optimal answers are debatable since every social stakeholder embraces differing perspectives based on "taking" or "making" choices and acting on one's motivations. The best way to explore these concepts is at the foundation, where the "me-to-us-to-others" continuum exists; by labeling the continuum with relatable terminology, with me being "local," us being "quasi-local," and others being "global." (See Appendix C for a complete article on perspective.)

"IN-GROUP TO OUT-GROUP" AND "SELF-SEGREGATED STRATIFICATION"

"The paradox of the modern age, I realized, is that we live in a world that is closely integrated in some ways but fragmented in others. Shocks are increasingly contagious. But we continue to behave and think in tiny silos."

Gillian Tett

"A tribe is a group of people connected to each other, connected to a leader, and connected to an idea. For millions of years, human beings have been part of one tribe or another. A group needs only two things to be a tribe: a shared interest and a way to communicate."

Seth Godin

"A team is where a boy can prove his courage. A gang is where a coward goes to hide."

Mickey Mantle

"The tribe often thinks the visionary has turned his back on them. When, in fact, the visionary has turned his face to the future."

Ray A. Davis

*"The reality is that there are no successful loners in the history
of social evolution. Being a solo survivalist is arduous
and inefficient. Survival has only been accomplished in groups."*

Billy Baker

*"Public acceptance will never replace self-love. Nor will group
membership add, create, or dictate your value."*

Tiffany L. Jackson

"A single voice cannot make a choir. A single tree cannot make a forest."

Ron Lizzi

*H*ow one defines "neighbor" is at the heart of In-group and out-group descriptive labeling dynamics. In one context, a neighbor is someone within one's sphere of influence without regard to social relevance. Yet, as written in the New Testament of the Christian Bible, the second part of the Great Commandment explicitly states, "one must love thy neighbor as thyself" without defining how one decides who is or is not a neighbor. Perhaps more evolved but still entropic, modern neighbor concepts require a more nuanced understanding based on easily measurable parameters.

Proximity is the primary criterion, and interaction levels within a defined bounded proximity context enter the picture as the secondary criteria. However, in today's digital social media world, organic concepts of proximity need to expand to include digital commons. Aligned with defining who should be a neighbor, one should discern how one perceives whether someone is a member of an in-group or out-group. Identifying "in or out" depends on how the primes present in one's early developmental stages influence one's worldview. A "prime" in this context is an embedded thought aligned with the subconscious or implicit biases supporting and motivating how humans respond to others' actions. Primes are more relevant to one's moral perspective;

however, they connect to how one creates self-identity; therefore, they are an anchor concept for in-group and out-group dynamics.

Many possible types of "in-groups" exist. An in-group may be family, but how does one define a family? Is it biological, or does a broader social context determine family membership? An in-group could be those with significantly similar social norms, social values, stakeholder interests, religious beliefs, shared experiential knowledge, or almost any other recognizable shared trait. For example, team members, a military platoon, a band, a gang, or a business unit are in-groups. Over many centuries, members of certain religious groups have been socially identified by "brother" or "sister," which bridges how family and in-group have become a blurry concept.

Understanding a member of an "out-group" is much simpler. Anyone not inclusive to an in-group is defined as an out-group member. In contemporary contexts, social primes have created an environment where the demarcation line between in-group and out-group is in sharp focus. How does the razor-sharp focus manifest, and how does ethics play a role or influence social outcomes based on the intense focus?

Throughout human history, identifying whether someone was "in or out" was a question of survival. For this reason, one of the manifest human traits is the ability to make this determination rapidly. Survival of the fittest was never about who was the strongest or the fastest; fitness was and still is about who functions optimally within one's sphere of influence. Discerning "in or out" in context is the human equivalent of understanding and protecting one's ability to be one of the fittest through risk management or how to become an accepted member of a specific group for safety reasons. In an exploration of a survival concept in a frequent contemporary "in or out" context, where being an "out" may often have deadly consequences, understanding one's identity is critical within the day-to-day reality of gang membership.

Gangs have a closed membership mentality. Invitations and initiation rites are often blood-in/blood-out (or never-out). Non-members, anyone not identifiable as a member for any reason, are automatically a threat. Now, take the gang mentality to a closed environment like a prison, and one can easily understand the level of risk anyone who chooses not to be a member must endure. No matter how one may envision the in-group mentality, gang membership is the most recognizable in-group in the contemporary sense.

Ethically, it is hard to defend anyone's choice of becoming a gang member, with one caveat. At-risk underserved or unserved social outcasts, those members of society who believe zero opportunities exist for climbing out of their deficit needs social environment, are drawn to the "family" context of the gang in-group. When presented with perceptibly insurmountable barriers, humans will find and choose a path offering promise, whether those paths lead to behaviors society deems illegal or unacceptable or not.

The question becomes, "Is gang membership an inevitable outcome for many at-risk persons in urban areas where gangs thrive?" From the gang membership perspective, is membership tied to existential factors? If one can answer yes to either or both, does society need to continue castigating gangs, or should there be a more significant effort to reduce gang membership's likelihood by creating an environment with more opportunities for alternate choices?

Perhaps community leaders should focus on a restorative justice approach with action potential for shifting gang activities from crime to a productive social enterprise. Remember, genetic distribution suggests nature spreads intelligence and competency evenly throughout every social group; the only significant differentiating factor is whether an opportunity exists for all groups to leverage the existing intellect, and many gang members would embrace becoming socially relevant as opposed to being considered a social outcast if they perceived a viable path leading to success.

The outcry of most at-risk groups aligns with a lack of opportunity. Minority-based or socioeconomically depressed populations seek validation as social equals, asking or demanding consideration and access to equitable paths leading to success. The resulting clamor is the factual foundation for virtually all negative social primes exhibited by these groups, most recently projected by angry participants during the George Floyd protests. Historically, the majority has viewed lack of opportunity through the lens of legally mandated equal opportunity, meaning the majority only needs to suggest equal opportunity exists. Functional social equity aligned with practical means of enforcing or embracing equality in the real world does not exist.

Research supports a social imbalance created and sustained by in-group/out-group dynamics. The social inequality stems from fundamental attribution error and how perspective-taking influences consideration. Members of an in-group hesitate to give any level of attention to an out-group member, which is most evident in how the majority treats all minority out-groups. From 1865, the end of the American Civil War, across the decades since, through the Civil Rights movement of the 1960s, gradual shifts in the lawful approach to majority-minority interaction and the most visible artifact, real opportunity, have softened the rhetoric of discrimination; however, discrimination based on dysfunctional in-group/out-group dynamics endure and is the basis for the multigenerational primes driving racial discord and injustice.

An in-depth examination of two dynamic concepts influencing in-group/out-group dysfunction shall illuminate the fallacy of equality through the power of perspective. The two ideas of expectations and entitlements require understanding motivated action potential as the most instrumental component of a prime extending from bias. Both concepts function as foundational influencers for whether a prime takes shape during one's developmental years.

Expectations are two-fold, with positive and negative affectations. Parents and other caregivers build momentum through expectations, particularly caregivers labeled as teachers, coaches, or mentors. Participants may embrace others' expectations and make them part of their life goals, which is fantastic when done voluntarily, and not-so-great when pressed to feel obligated to pursue expectations intended to satisfy someone else's vision of their perfect scenario. The expectation dynamic invariably becomes an outcome-deficient success-failure continuum, which leads to questions about the underlying why of one's motivation.

Entitlements are also two-fold, with one type centered on affluence and the other type centered on accessibility versus exclusion. First, people with wealth and influence tend (many outliers to this characterization are possible, so no stereotyping is allowed here) to project a sense of entitlement, a normative practice of entitlement extending across many generations. The glass ceiling effect is one example of how affluent parents (and most other wealthy society members) support and defend entitlement, often through legacy contexts.

Defining how entitlement functions could take another entire book, so a base definition must do, a description aligned with both sides of the ethical discussion about entitlements. The most functional is "a belief one inherently deserves privileges or favorable treatment which may be limited to those of similar existence or trait." For example, a club or private entity membership is limited to those affluent enough to belong or to those invited by existing members. By extending the model, seeking membership may be limited in scope based on the current group's entitlement perspective. One glaring instance for decades was Augusta National Golf Club, a bastion of exclusive male entitlement. Systemically, within highly affluent circles, implicit access versus exclusion exists; however, entitlement's perceived benefits have a flip side.

Minority groups legally hold the same rights entitlement as any majority group based on the Constitution in America. The crucible where expectations and entitlements clash hardest is the intersection where an individual may challenge the concept of entitlements received or not received based on their anticipation of inclusion based on existing legal mandates. The practical barrier of unrequited entitlements is the junction of place and time when privilege takes precedent, usually seen as "white privilege," which is well-known and understood by all minorities who perceive limited access throughout society.

The cruelest barriers to affluence exist to deny equal opportunity due to inequities seen in the unfair application of hard-won equality. A gatekeeper mentality exists to limit access to the masses, and entitlements remain elusive to many, especially minorities. The "expectation" of limited access to "entitlements" is how minorities perceive and define white privilege. Because the misguided perception of privilege being upended would irreparably disrupt the power status quo, the concept of white privilege is an ethical minefield many majority whites refuse to acknowledge.

Any social group enduring discrimination is wrong at every level and context. Social or racial injustice is morally and ethically wrong; bigotry is an appalling choice; unacknowledged bias is the universal prime for sustained inequity, and perpetuating the ongoing systemic injustice by remaining silent is contemptible. By comparison, Aristotle never addressed the widespread cultural bias or mistreatment of others because slavery and social stratification were the ancient world's norms, and democracy was the domain of "citizens." Ample evidence suggests one's race was glaringly absent from consideration throughout the ancient world. If forced to extend eudaimonia to every social stratum, Aristotle would have been hard-pressed to conceptualize how the lower classes of his era would sustain any approach to transcendent happiness, and he would have asserted one's social class was a function of circumstance, not of race.

The contemporary world, especially the America of stated equality for all, has struggled to navigate or answer this puzzle. Unlike throughout the ancient world, the context now includes race and heritage. One visible artifact of the problem is how negative primes pass from an older generation to a younger generation in every social group through habituation aligned with the tenets of self-segregated stratification. Okay, that's a mouthful. Human groups, mainly minority-centric groups, perpetuate a silo mentality by passing explicit-biased stories from generation to generation, which is problematic when the stories are suboptimal tales of woe.

Unfortunately, the problem is perpetuated by all groups at all socioeconomic levels, with virtually every group clinging to a silo mentality focused on preserving some form of social identity. Negative primes, the intrinsic mindset which influences socially derived explicit biases, are present as barriers to overcoming inflexible in-group thinking. Positive primes exist; however, the flexible mental approach seeking inclusion is rare compared to the vast number of people anchored by negative primes. One artifact linked to negative mindsets aligning with primes is self-segregated stratification, also called the "silo effect," mentioned earlier, mainly in response to perceived threat environments. The isolation effect of self-segregation perpetuates differentiation and social entropy.

Perceived social threats are catalysts or trigger events exacerbating racial and cross-cultural strife, especially in the social reality of 2016-2020, a period many academics label one of divisiveness caused by the

Administration's never stated but easily discerned goal of American social disruption. The purpose is not to say whether self-segregation is warranted, but the primary artifact emerging from the silo effect is "a failure to communicate" across social groups. The silo approach exists within the contemporary social context, mainly as a primary defense mechanism supported by racial isolationists. Psychological silos shield participants against the constant negativity emerging from frictions inherent to the broader social reality.

Outliers exist despite negative primes. Dyadic personal cross-cultural relationships from all contexts are an expanding phenomenon globally and have been for several centuries. Many luminaries and social experts, including President Obama before he left office, noted that the world population is becoming more homogeneous (in Obama's words, browner or non-white). Demographic projections show America evolving into a minority-majority nation where no racial group will have a majority by the mid-2040s. Non-whites and other minority factions will have the ability to cooperatively create a majority power dynamic if they choose to join ranks and act together.

The impending demographic shift brings us back to in-group and out-group contexts. Thus far, minority groups have maintained their self-segregation preference, preferring to act in "selfish self-interest" and not as a collective group. The lack of minority group cohesion weakens every minority group's power, limiting collaborative alliances and preventing positive social change.

If explored expeditiously, the situation could lend itself to empowerment and social uplifting within the entire minority block. Servant leaders must emerge with the mindset of reducing all entropic in-group/ out-group dynamics. The ethics involved would begin to merge with moralistic approaches to one's fellow man. Ethically, as a population, Americans need to increase inclusion centered on consideration for others regardless of their race or ethnicity. Inevitably, socially designed or not, warranted or not, the wall supporting self-segregation and rigid in-group/out-group dynamics will eventually come apart, a reality projected as a vessel leading to all groups' betterment. So, where do we begin? One approach would be to explore how rights manifest in myriad ways across a continuum leading to positive and negative outcomes within a population and discovering as a nation the "power of interests."

"RIGHTS VERSUS INTERESTS-HOW DO WE KNOW-HOW DO WE DECIDE?"

*"We talk a lot about individual rights, but Americans are very willing
to give up individual rights if it means property values
will be protected, and so on."*

R.D. Kaplan

*"Democracy is not freedom. Democracy is two wolves and a lamb voting
on what to eat for lunch. Freedom comes from the recognition
of certain rights which may not be taken, not even by a 99% vote."*

Marvin Simkin

*"Undoubtedly, interests carry such egomania and greed that denies and even
disgraces laws, rules, resolutions, reports, rights, equality, justice, and peace."*

E Sehgal

*"It's not hard to decide what you want your life to be about.
What's hard, she said, is figuring out what you're willing to give up
to do the things you really care about."*

Shauna Niequist

*"If you want to discover the true character of a person, you have only to
observe what they are passionate about."*

Shannon L. Alder

"They said love is fleeting, so we hung on to it through thick and thin.
They said marriage is about compromise, so we made it about equality.
They said jobs exist to pay bills, so we made up one we enjoyed.
They said you need to settle for a mediocre life, so we made it
about chasing the extraordinary."

Savi Munjal

Americans learn their Constitutionally mandated rights early in life, although they also gain a perspective about those rights' social expression. The broad perspective about how rights manifest creates contentious debates, and a significant portion of the population arrives at poorly structured rights contexts. For example, one could debate each person's level of understanding and belief in whether an equitable distribution of "rights" occurs.

Beyond the context of enduring Constitutional rights, one should consider a broad spectrum of human rights, especially when exploring social and behavioral ethics based on those rights. The primary conceptual thought should always be, "Rights exist for our universal basic needs and protection, and one may set aside personal or group rights if and when they disrupt the pursuit of interests; however, they may never be lost or abridged, only set aside as a matter of personal convenience, and this applies to all."

A secondary boundary exists within rights most people fail to acknowledge. Rights are permanent, and exercising those rights is optional: "Our rights end at any point where we interfere with the rights of any other." People must understand that rights are not sacrosanct; they are an optimal choice dynamic with considerations. Before moving into the "interests" domain, consider how rights enhance or obfuscate human existence.

Interests are a subjective part of one's human existence. Earlier in the text, an explanation of competing interests laid the groundwork for the current discourse on the rights-interests continuum. Interests often project as being counter to the manifestation of rights, a mistaken perception held by many "rights-obsessive" stakeholders. For example, a homeowner has the right of "quiet enjoyment of his domicile," which he may set aside to operate a "bed and breakfast style business" or hold a block party. The homeowner's interests may run afoul of his neighbor's right to the same quiet enjoyment; therefore, he needs to get permission from others by asking them to set aside their rights temporarily in consideration of his needs. Pursuing interests does not remove or reduce the rights of anyone; the pursuit only takes precedent temporarily.

In mediation, competent professional mediators navigate getting all participants to the "interests" side of the equation, often when asymmetric power imbalances exist between the parties based on exercised rights. Once interests align and rights are appropriately addressed, agreements usually follow. However, how does one know when to protect guaranteed rights or pursue personal or group interests, not solely during a negotiation or mediation process, but in general? The answer lies in how one perceives the obligation to practice the ethical treatment of others, which one must examine through the lens of a relativistic local-global continuum.

Rights are artifacts within the governance domain on the one hand and universal human rights in general. What happens when a conflict exists between the two types of rights, guaranteed or normative? What happens when people spend most of their lives in global areas where governance or social strife conditions limit rights and create incentives for oppressed people to escape an environment of limited existence? Do humans have a fundamental right to seek increased viability by pursuing interests, by migrating to places where growth potential is more evident than the finite existence left behind?

In the case of limited universal human rights contexts, upheaval or rebellion emerges, followed by an inevitable migration away from the perception or reality of burdensome deficit needs to where conditions offer growth and safety. The level of rights available in many global contexts is vastly different from the everyday freedoms Americans enjoy. Asymmetric observance of fundamental rights is a normalized but frustrating artifact for most global citizens. Given how rights should align with essential human value constructs universally but often fail in that duty, current realities negatively influence the natural continuum of rights versus interests, with interests occupying more of the overall global actuality based upon a severe lack of observable rights.

In local (domestic as opposed to international in scope) contexts, the division between rights and interests becomes blurrier. An inherently equal diffusion of civil liberties at the micro-level should be present when and where governance is consistent, whether fairly applied or defended by authority figures. Interests always align with individual motivation; interests are ever-present but challenging to measure on a broad scale due to their subjective nature. In American society, personal interests become entangled with rights as many believe, rightly or wrongly, that their expressed choices should be equated to rights and defended as entitlements.

At a macro-level, the effect of one's abrogation of rights tends to wane as the effect of pursuing one's interests begins to flourish, and the pursuit of interests aligns with one significant factor, the opportunity to achieve one's stated or implied goals based on one's preferred choices, which constantly intertwine with one's interests. The primary argument or debate is whether or how authority figures enforce rights within American society's contextual fabric. The core tenet of the discussion centers on the opportunity level given to disparate groups outside the majority in-group. With the foundation laid, here is where one inserts ethical principles into the equation.

Normative contemporary philosophy depends on whether all humans are equal in value or social worth, both morally and ethically.

The practical value component extends into a spectrum based on multivariate criteria and may contain an infinite number of variables aligned with perspective-taking or perspective-making. Exploring the possibilities may take two paths. One path is based on teleological ethics inherent to preferred outcomes serving intrinsic interests regardless of whether others incur costs. The other approach is based on deontological ethics attached to preferred results aligning with the acquisition of extrinsic social needs while preserving or enhancing social equity.

Therefore, the relevance of the ethical discourse on rights and interests depends on artifacts aligning with opportunity. But unfortunately, no consistent metric exists for determining equity or equality of opportunity within humanity's social fabric across cultures, even if one explores within subcultures of identifiable domestic groups or sub-groups, mainly due to cultural relativity.

Therefore, one's default position should be to measure every ethical discourse based on individual interests aligned with fulfilling the journey through Maslow's hierarchy. Achieving transcendence is comparable to Aristotle's eudaimonia for every human, a significant consideration that connotes interests must occupy a higher rung than rights in virtually all scenarios. However, overarching potential confounds exist.

Is it ever possible to remain ethical if one does not attempt to obtain equal opportunity for all humans through acts focusing on non-maleficence? Do individual interests support ignoring a broader social imperative? Conversely, should someone allow the existing social conditions to place barriers before compelling interests?

One argument from teleological thinking suggests how protecting one's interests is ethically based on one's perception of scarcity, such as when "available opportunity" is considered a limited resource, such as during a crisis like the COVID-19 pandemic. However, in this context, any discernment of opportunity scarcity is faulty thinking since normalized insights surrounding available opportunity, especially in the era of knowledge-based economies, is a subjective concept with infinite pathways and action potential.

Despite opportunity levels becoming increasingly unbounded and limitless, numerous barriers still exist. Moreover, defined approaches to endless possibilities aligned with opportunity are often inaccessible to many groups for various reasons. Therefore, withholding or limiting access to any other group's potential opportunity context is fundamentally unethical because it denies them a path to eudaimonia stemming from inconsistent deontological virtue ethics.

Coming full circle, where does this leave rights versus interests? Rights shall always exist; the only consideration is whether one sets them aside to reduce barriers or increase the action potential for achieving one's interest pursuits. In addition, one cannot abridge or limit others' rights unless exercising those rights abridges any other person's rights.

When one extends the concept of rights and interests to their maximum potential, a demarcation line of one's rights versus another's becomes the foundational bar of legal limits and the basis for tort law, which the author shall not explore here. Finally, interests, being inherently subjective and universally viable as a pursuit, are bound to the same limitations as rights when considering personal boundaries.

Understanding how rights and interests interact won't change one essential factor. A significant portion of the population will never pivot from their ideological position on their guaranteed rights, and that anchored position will always generate conflict and challenging conversations. In addition, the rights/interest debate is hardly the only compelling issue with sustained conflict. Socially relevant topics abound; therefore, an exploration of social discord based on ethical considerations follows.

"IS INCLUSION ONE BIRTHPLACE OF CONTENTIOUS CONVERSATIONS?"

"We could learn a lot from crayons: Some are sharp, Some are pretty, Some are dull, Some have weird names, and are all different colors, But they all have to live in the same box."

Author Unknown

"What if all the trees were oaks? How plain the world would seem; No maple syrup, banana splits, And how would orange juice be? Wouldn't it be a boring place, If all the people were the same; Just one color, only one language, Just one family name!

~But~

If the forest were the world, And all the people were the trees; Palm and pine, bamboo and willow, Live and grow in harmony. Aren't you glad, my good friend, Different though we be; We are here for each other; I learn from you, and you from me."

Author Unknown

"Sailors do not learn to sail on smooth waters."

Ancient African Proverb

"Diversity happens; inclusion is a choice."

Harjeet Khanduja

*"Moving from childhood to adulthood; that's not growing up.
Moving from selfishness to selflessness, that's growing up. Moving from
I to We, that's growing up. Moving from my culture, my country,
my religion, to our cultures, our countries, our religions, that's growing up."*

Abhijit Naskar

*"Equality is the planning committee. Diversity is being invited
to the party. Inclusion is being invited to the dance.
Belonging is choosing a song!"*

— Aisha Thomas

As difficult conversations go, most Americans, but minority Americans specifically, will identify acceptance and inclusion as a hot topic. As globalization becomes embedded into humanity's fabric, free society nations like America need to evolve and embrace acceptance and inclusion as a social norm. The academic and employment arenas are the two most recognizable social environments where acceptance and inclusion levels exhibit measurable disparity.

For several decades, one requirement in many academic or corporate campus environments has been the inevitable "tolerance training session," now labeled diversity, equity, and inclusion (DEI) training. Early on, trainers and administrators touted tolerance education as the optimal path for keeping organizational culture moving toward an acceptable environment for all stakeholders. Unfortunately, however, the name denotes the problem with this perspective: a widespread insistence on "tolerance" instead of acceptance. DEI is also problematic as a label, mainly because C-suite level leaders fail to conceptualize equity in ways compatible with their staff or human capital.

When discussing this topic with tolerance or DEI trainers, most practitioners state how and why the normative labeling (which hasn't evolved with societal needs) doesn't fit their group interaction reality.

These well-meaning professionals project their craft as being focused on increasing harmony and enhancing corporate culture. One only needs to open the floor for debate in diverse groups to see their beliefs' fallacy. So, let's unpack the perception of tolerance training from a modern-day minority perspective, which many trainers avoid because it exposes an aversion hidden in their expertise, the crutch of political correctness.

Minorities embrace political correctness (PC) for one main reason. PC fits the decades-long narrative of avoiding any form of speech or behavior that creates disharmony based solely on perception. The artifacts of PC have become weaponized to silence hate speech and blatant bigotry, obviously a good result, but have also given minorities a tool to shift any instance of perceived racism into an attack built directly on the perception, with or without substance. The resulting "harmony" in the workplace is fundamentally anchored on fear of reprisal, causing all people within the organization to function in a dishonest, silence-based environment of "tolerance" or "inclusion" at all costs. Where exactly should one search for sincere and sustainable inclusion supported by tolerance experts?

Simply put, tolerance education, in contemporary contexts based on PC, discourages interaction. Why? All humans, when interacting, will encounter some level of conflict as a natural occurrence. When the inevitable occurs, one or both parties make choices based on a "backing down to fit in without losing one's place" mentality. From a real-world perspective, this is embracing the avoidance of interaction or lying by omission. No matter which may be correct, since both are bad for institutional culture, regardless of the type of setting, the embedded insistence on PC reduces interaction, which, in turn, impedes productivity and throughput. Everyone loses.

Americans have become comfortable avoiding challenging or tough conversations. Citizens become complacent to a point where the avoidance enlarges conflict by forcing issues to linger and become lagging indicators of cultural failure. For example, lack of communication between management and employees means claims of EEOC violations based on perceived slights and microaggressions are rampant. From one viewpoint, where there is smoke, there is often fire.

Admittedly, some individuals discriminate against virtually anything or anyone they see as different for nefarious reasons, projecting their targets as inferior in some way. The need for hate crime and discrimination laws is obvious. However, shameful exploitation of those laws while pursuing a cause has also risen to dangerous levels, creating a divisive culture. If your worldview is one where any perception of a slight means you can rebuke another human as a bigot, factual or not, tough conversations are significantly absent.

That absence is an admission that tolerance and DEI programs fail to address social needs effectively. Human capital functioning in scenarios completely absent of honesty is a critical existential failure for any entity. Consider the existing dynamic, where participants avoid a meaningful conversation by making a claim, then steer clear of the other party entirely, hoping to give long legs to their stated perspective of the contentious situation. The result of avoidance is an underlying form of "culture wars."

At the other end of the spectrum lies a plausible answer. Encourage interaction as the only viable option. Instead of tolerance education, create a cultural environment where people utilize ombudspersons or mediators to have tough conversations when direct communication is tenuous. Instead of focusing on avoidance and disciplinary processes, learn to seek inclusion and understanding through meaningful engagement.

Life is messy. There must always be a place for disharmony leading to debate. For thousands of years, social evolution has only occurred when conflicted parties choose to end the fighting long enough to realize everyone is the same, just living in slightly different contexts. In our enlightened (we hope) contemporary era, what would be wrong with accepting different perspectives as having the right to coexist? "I like blue; you like red, okay, let's move on..."

By the way, the majority loves tolerance training regardless of what political pundits say. Whether stated or not, it extends from the concept of "white privilege." By getting the minorities in the academic or work environment to ensure everyone is making pleasant (or guns are a-blazing in constant conflict), the majority can continue tolerating their presence instead of enlarging every group's social equity universally. Wow! What is wrong with this picture? It avoids the tough conversations, yet again, and implies tolerance is an acceptable norm. It also suggests why more progressive programs will never be implemented. The minimum "tolerance" is preferred.

Cultural competency is quickly replacing the "tolerance" context in institutions and organizations willing to go beyond PC limitations and admit tolerance training is ineffective while becoming obsolete. Inclusion depends on a willingness to embrace the right of equal consideration for all people, all students, and all co-workers, not just tolerance. No, it doesn't force anyone to go beyond what should already be happening within the environment. Instead, it removes psychological barriers and allows everyone to be more honest and transparent. In a divisive, historically self-segregated silo mentality country, you probably think, "this guy is nuts."

To be culturally competent, one must be willing to explore other cultures. That doesn't mean one must embrace different cultures. Still, one must pursue increased understanding, especially of the similarities present within all global cultures, which leads one to see and feel the presence of "humanness" in others. A form of honesty emerges as one's level of awareness rises to a degree of comfortable familiarity, which allows those pesky tough conversations to emerge and evolve.

Debate, even arguments, won't create existential or irrational fear because understanding leads to sharing and caring about others at a visceral level. Notice that no one is required to embrace unwanted discomfort; however, experiencing someone else's reality shifts one's perspective and worldview measurably and consistently over time. Everyone who participates, and I explicitly mean everyone not radicalized or pathological, changes when they see what cross-cultural experts see, that everyone is the same.

Tough conversations are infinitely present throughout society, dependent on each person's unique perspective on their environment, so trying to digress into examples is a waste of everyone's time. From a leadership position, choosing to be a servant-leader willing to delve into the inclusion arena is optimal. Debating "what" tough conversations are in your sphere of influence is a great place to start. Focusing on finding similarities over differences; exploring explicit and implicit differences so misguided perspectives can evolve, invariably, people find themselves more inclusive as they work through the process.

Remember, these are tough conversations. Accept some conflict as being natural along the way. If you find yourself getting too emotional for the discussion, take a break to decompress, but never give up your chair at the table, and never accept a less-than-optimal outcome. Building an organizational culture that works today and into the future is well worth the effort.

An appropriate ending for this section is an anecdotal story about a conversation several years ago, explicitly focused on "tough conversations," a crucial narrative to add to your coping library. The lesson contained within comes from universal positive regard.

The question: "Why work so hard to be inclusive? Why care about others when we all face the same struggle every day? As the majority, shouldn't my perspective be paramount?"

The answer: "Life is Messy. How one deals with messy defines one's place within humanity, and one's right to exist as a member of our species. The only way to evolve, to overcome messy, is to traverse a multi-generational, cross-cultural journey where the primes, triggers, and action responses benefit everyone, not just those within our preferred in-group. Until we all do this "thing," messy will continue to rule us all. Social choices made in the past, what came before, obviously have not worked. Therefore, it is imperative for all people to change course, to choose to end messy!"

"THE ETHICAL VECTORS OF SOCIAL SCAFFOLDING"

*"Your thoughts construct patterns like scaffolding in your mind.
You are really etching chemical patterns. In most cases, people get
stuck in those patterns, just like grooves in a record, and they never
get out of them."*

Steve Jobs

*"When all the scaffolding is removed, it is our integrity that both defines us
and identifies us. Men of integrity are like the Rock of Gibraltar, steadfast
and immovable; men without it are like the shifting sands on the Sahara
Desert, tossed to and fro by every variant wind of life."*

Tad R. Callister

*"The story is everything, so it always begins with a story. Research is
a kind of scaffolding built underneath the story as I go along. My enjoyment
level varies, but in general, I'm writing about topics I find interesting,
so I can't gripe too much."*

Neal Stephenson

*"Thus, physics, chemistry, biology, anthropology, sociology, history,
and the arts all interpenetrate each other and cohere if considered
as a single convergent study. The physical studies scaffold our understanding
of the life sciences, which scaffold our understanding of the human sciences,*

which scaffold the humanities, which scaffold the arts:
and here we stand. What then is the totality? What do we call it?
Can there be a study of the totality? Do history, philosophy,
cosmology, science, and literature each claim to constitute the totality,
an unexpandable horizon beyond which we cannot think? Could a strong
discipline be defined as one that has a vision of totality and claims
to encompass all the rest? And are they all wrong to do so?"

Kim Stanley Robinson

"We must recognize that we have a great inheritance in our possession,
which represents the prolonged achievement of the centuries;
that there is not one of our simple uncounted rights today for which
better men than we are have not died on the scaffold or the battlefield.
We have not only a great treasure; we have a great cause.
Are we taking every measure within our power to defend that cause?"

Winston Churchill

"The real scaffolding of racism is institutions that are so fully entwined
with prejudice that to change them would require overhauling entire systems,
entire ways of life. When keeping Black and brown people marginalized
literally elevates white people, as they use our backs as stairs,
why would they want us to stand up?"

Luvvie Ajayi

"You can't build the bridge of trust with the scaffolding of lies
and underhand deals."

Ian Paisley

Social scaffolding is everywhere and every "when." The universal support system can be a crutch preventing progress or a safety net allowing improvement until social optimization occurs. So, if social scaffolding is a harsh binary, what drives outcomes? Research is "fuzzy" on the topic, primarily due to qualitative processes which depend on sample pool self-reports. Therefore, exploring social scaffolding is subjective, relatively undefined, and becomes a potentially contentious journey of discovery.

In engineering or mathematical terms, vectors are defined as "real" (definable) or "complex" (undefinable). In social scaffolding, vectors are abstractions attempting to delineate and support social processes, although organic variance creates confounds within the construct. A secondary consideration is the complexity of any social paradigm. If experts assert infinite numbers of potential vectors intersect in social environments, finding effective scaffolds that optimize social processes within the complexity should be challenging. However, one expert turned scaffolding into a digestible concept.

Many field professionals view Vygotsky's Social Scaffolding Theory as too simplistic; however, the simplicity allows the theory to sustain efficacy across many social environments. As a result, virtually every modern learning environment leverages Vygotsky's model. Subsequently, the following exploration will give readers insight into the power of his vision despite his uncomplicated approach to learning.

Let's explore some of Vygotsky's key terminology, starting with labeling and definitions:

> Zones of proximal development (ZPD): a space where learners demonstrate competency absent external influences, then develop through more knowledgeable others, and an "as yet unattainable" future knowledge growth area

> Differentiated learning: Learning focused on leveraging individual student's ZPD, ideal in smaller classrooms

> Scaffolding shift: The model of "I do; We do; You do" modifications pivoting learning engagement from a teacher-centric model to a student-centric model

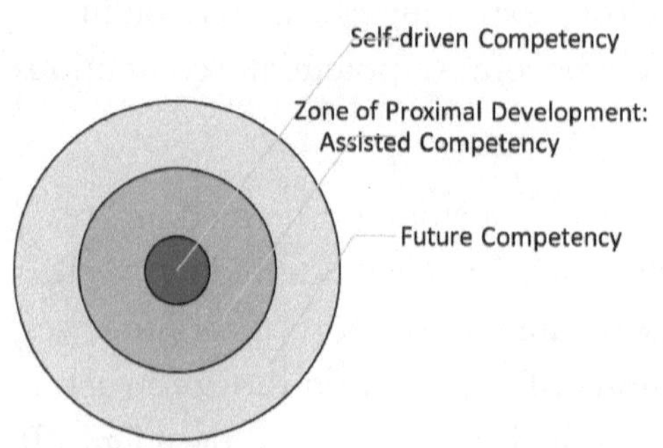

More Knowledgeable Other (MKO): the person providing the scaffolding who can be a teacher, another student, or an external source agent

Scaffolding model: The steps for optimizing Vygotsky's model, which are preparation, pre-test, teacher modeling, teacher/student/group interactive learning, independent student optimization, post-test, rinse and repeat with a new focus

Based on his original terminology, it should be apparent that Vygotsky's Theory was focused on educational environments. However, over time, the utility of his model allowed practitioners in every field to leverage ZPDs and MKOs. Therefore, let's traverse two areas where Vygotsky optimizes the process.

Sports specificity requires all athletes to learn their skillset through MKOs, more commonly labeled "coaches." Analytics from decades of statistics show how optimal coaching creates a competitive advantage for athletes accessing their sphere of influence. The competition for access to top-tier coaching is a well-known fact.

The medical field requires iterative learning after someone graduates from medical school through a process labeled "internship and residency." Asserting optimal medical competency cannot occur until the iterative process is completed successfully, and advanced field access extends the mentoring process through a "one-on-one" specialized teaching modality. For example, neurosurgeons take more than a decade to reach optimal competency.

The examples are strikingly similar, reinforcing the efficacy of educational scaffolding. Next, however, one must shift to "social scaffolding" to gain novel perspectives on how Vygotsky benefits society. For example, how would optimized utility occur in global cultures when relativity asserts itself as a confound? The answer is surprisingly simple, similar to his model.

How does anyone determine who the MKO is within their environment? Regardless of position or status, the MKO is the person with the highest knowledge and experiential competency in the group at hand. All settings share the commonality of hierarchy, from inexperienced to transcendent stakeholders; therefore, the "MKO" is present in each, and anyone may function as an MKO at some point. Consider the following scenario:

A company hires someone to fill a position, then hires another two weeks later. The first employee, benefitting from two weeks of seniority, is an MKO for the newbie. The "person with the most experience" factor influences the labeling in this context. So let's pivot to a multi-vectored, bi-directional MKO scenario.

A hiring manager brings on board a twenty-year veteran with considerable industry knowledge. Simultaneously, another candidate is hired with impressive academic standing who is abreast of the most current industry standards. The veteran is the MKO when discussions of field application are required, while the intellectual is the MKO when discussing relevant standards. In addition, the hiring manager is the MKO for both when talking about benefits or company policy.

The power inherent to Vygotsky's model is broad application. Establishing a ZPD for individuals offers clarity and directionality for the teacher or mentor. Understanding the iterative nature of the model allows students to focus on learning in a unique student-centric environment with scaffolding when necessary while driving toward self-competency. So, when or how do ethics or social scaffolding become applicable in this model?

One must explore the self-interest aspect inherent to prosocial behavior. More knowledgeable others diffuse higher knowledge to mentees primarily to drive mentee development. Any enhancement is a social gain; therefore, the MKO provides a prosocial service to society by increasing overall competency, which leads to self-efficacy. But does development stop there?

Embedded in any process are rules, boundaries, and standards. Learning "how" to complete a task doesn't end until limitations, confounds, and allowances are included. Ethically, it would be unacceptable to forego including the complexity of the multi-vectored job or task descriptions regardless of context.

Let's pivot to purely social considerations, such as how to enhance cultural interactions or relational engagement. The MKO in the social sphere is the "role model" exhibiting optimal prosocial competency. The ethical vectors become multi-faceted and relative to the local or immediate environment. For example, hiring someone who becomes the first out-group member in an organization would potentially lead to microaggressions and conflict without the buffering effect of a competent MKO experienced in cross-cultural group dynamics.

From specific contexts to the broader aspects of society, MKOs play a vital role in social enhancements leading to optimal group dynamics. The only goal of social scaffolding is to mitigate discord between members of that society. Additional benefits are possible; however, they are ancillary to the primary purpose of sustained peace. Vygotsky's Theory is instrumental globally when appropriately implemented due to the MKO effect on stakeholders.

"ASSIMILATION, ACCULTURATION, AND SOCIAL AMALGAMATION"

"The question of the stranger in a society which estranges everybody from it while forcing everybody to assimilate their alienation takes cover under dubious and sinister masks."

Norman Manea

"The seed of cultural harmony lies not in the culture you are born in but in recognition of the sweetness of other cultures."

Abhijit Naskar

"If you want to be relevant only in your household, then you only need to know the things that are important in your house, and if you want to be relevant in your neighborhood, you need to know what's important in your neighborhood. The same thing applies to your city, state, and country. If you want to be relevant to the entire world, program the computer known as your brain with all kinds of information from everywhere to prepare yourself."

Ben Carson

I think that's the beauty of life. We're this collection of moments, this collection of experiences that we've had, or little tics that we've stolen from other people; it's like we're this amalgamation of all of that."

Frank Iero

*B*ased on the impending demographic shift predicted by demographic research, emerging societal interest aligns with how to move through assimilation, acculturation, and social amalgamation. Many authors have described America as a melting pot society; however, exploring self-segregated stratification suggests America presents as a patchwork quilt as a more accurate social projection. For decades, conservatives and liberals have debated how to navigate the artifacts of shifting and evolving demographics. The most ethical (and practical) path to resolving the debate resides in how each social group perceives the pros and cons of assimilation and its two cousin concepts.

The three-legged stool of social inclusion is a textbook example of how perspective-taking and perspective-making influence in-group/out-group dynamics and the concept of belonging. The majority utilizes perspective-making to project the optimal path for inclusion within assimilation. The core projection connotes that one must blend in seamlessly or become invisible as an individual if one wishes to attain the goal of in-group inclusion, which increases the opportunity to achieve Maslow's transcendent stage. If not for an obvious process shortcoming, assimilation could be a worthy goal; however, the identified deficiency encourages division instead of inclusion.

The primary precept of assimilation requires social invisibility. How does a person of color achieve invisibility? In America, any color other than majority-white is immediately identifiable as an outlier to the majority. White privilege stems from the unconscious extension of assimilation and how the majority anchors on required invisibility aligned with inclusion. How does a member of a non-white minority group achieve practical assimilation? Several centuries of forced or attempted assimilation (see thousands of stories about indigenous peoples globally) overwhelmingly demonstrate that functional assimilation is untenable. Here is where the debate shifts to tolerance, education, and acculturation. (See Appendix C for a complete article on assimilation.)

Acculturation requires acceptance of difference, not tolerance of difference. Modern contexts of tolerance education suggest one should "tolerate" the inclusion of those members of society dissimilar to oneself, regardless of appearance or trait expression. The legal exclusions preventing one from acting on personal bias aligned with another person's race, color, national origin, biological sex trait, gender choice, or religion are examples of social differentiation often explored in tolerance education. The tolerance expectation projects how one must not discriminate, which is the minimum standard of social inclusion; however, the minimum rarely infers and does not require explicit inclusion, only blocks explicit exclusion.

In a functional approach to acculturation, one would seek inclusion within the new environment or in-group while maintaining a stable connection to one's cultural roots. An underlying ethical component would be the widespread acceptance of the contexts of acculturation by the majority. New social members are working to achieve inclusion, but the new players wish to honor the historical artifacts found within their cultural past. The concept sounds achievable, but the majority adherence to assimilation remains a barrier to acculturation, leading to sub-optimal results. (See Appendix C for a complete article on acculturation.)

Culturally inclusive social amalgamation, a broader concept, adds several components to assimilation and acculturation, making social amalgamation the new "optimal" path to social inclusion. There are two ways to establish extant amalgamation. The first requires a deep dive into cultural appropriation (often referred to as misappropriation as the only recognized, viable context). The other requires increasing social awareness of embedded amalgamation as it exists within contemporary social norms.

Hairstyles, food preparation, and clothing choices have taken center stage as the target of social media negativity based on a flawed concept inherent to cultural appropriation. Minority students beat a white student for choosing to adopt a hairstyle most often observed in black culture. The defense offered for the beating was that "the white student made an unacceptable choice based on misappropriation of an artifact of another culture." Likewise, social media participants castigated a white teen for wearing a gown design based on an eastern cultural context and utilized the same weak defense for their actions.

Further research demonstrated how this gown design had first been appropriated from European origins during the colonial period, subsequently becoming fashionable throughout the Forbidden Kingdom, making any claim of cultural misappropriation a fallacy. Similarly, social media pundits challenged a food establishment for copying a favorite Southeast Asian sandwich. Each of these protests ignores the existence of certain cultural norms already present across all global cultures.

People worldwide wear blue jeans (denim if you prefer). People make food choices that include entrees from diverse origins; restaurants tout international cuisine options as a differentiator, all distinct forms of embedded social amalgamation, contexts vital to every major city in America for decades. Clothing, regardless of design origin, is sold on the open market. Claims of cultural misappropriation focus on two factors; both elements conveniently ignore personal choice and the concept of intent. One issue insists a majority member should ask a defined minority group member's permission before appropriating an artifact from the minority's cultural past or present. The second issue aligns with a well-established historical perspective; misappropriation aligning with many global cultures is a historically accurate negative artifact of global colonialism, which should be acknowledged as a validated factor within the debate.

Both arguments stem from primes intentionally focused on creating conflict. One should set aside any consideration of affront since social norms aligned with the ubiquitous cultural adoption of many "other cultural artifacts" are present and ongoing, not emergent, in all defined global societies. Personal choice replaces rights with interests, absent any legal mandate to criminalize cultural appropriation. Any current or future legal considerations toward criminalizing cultural misappropriation will encounter significant resistance to efforts focused on proving intent to harm members of the culture in question. Claims of harm do not equate to actual harm, and psychological damage based on being insulted by someone else's actions has proven extremely difficult to prove in court.

Cultural appropriation is not solely a majority artifact. Members of every socioeconomic stratum and cultural background adopt artifacts from a broad palette of available personal choices. What to wear, what to eat, and what to prefer are all subjective choices. So why is it only misappropriation when the majority exercises this choice dynamic?

The typical claim implies the majority violates the tenets of cultural appropriation due to an unhealthy adherence to habituated historical colonialist entitlements. Arguably, the truth is much simpler and more believable. People like what they like and generally ignore cultural considerations suggesting impropriety. Globalization has lowered barriers to innocent types of appropriation. Is it ethically problematic to exercise a choice of preference unless one intends to incite another person or group's anger? Most of the claims made, sometimes well-intended but often to instigate racial discord, are disingenuous because of the continuing discourse on why or how social or racial injustice stems from white privilege. In the current divisive climate, the move to mitigate weak or false claims supports the need to shift away from any focus on assimilation or acculturation and pivot toward social amalgamation. Everything should be acceptable across the cultural choice palette.

Granted, one can cherry-pick ethically inappropriate scenarios, such as any circumstance where the motivation behind appropriation may be portrayed as an insult or an attempt to exploit differentiation by the majority at the expense of the minority. Cherry-picking usually emerges from someone's agenda focused on demeaning another's cultural choices through an exposition of righteous indignation for misguided, shallow reasons. Fortunately, the overuse of isolated tropes creates negative action potential, invalidating the claim and the claimant. Finding examples of misappropriation indicates negative personal choices more than any overall social indictment of the majority. How might one discern the truism inherent to normalized appropriation?

Embedded social amalgamation is everywhere. The "patchwork quilting" effect is observable in every city in America. Names of streets, parks, and subdivisions traverse many cultures. Food emporiums from every culture line the streets and give people a broad array of consumption choices without worrying about cultural appropriation. Social amalgamation is a blending of all global cultures. Assimilation and acculturation should become less the norm when people increase their awareness of how blended American society has already become. President Obama was verbalizing his observations of American reality with his characterization of America's future linked to the "browning" demographic. (See Appendix C for a complete article on social amalgamation.)

"COOPERATION-COMPETITION-COOPETITION-COLLABORATION ETHICS"

"I would like to see anyone, prophet, king, or God, convince a thousand cats to do the "same thing" at the "same time."

Neil Gaiman

"That word is 'willing.' It's an attitude and spirit of cooperation that should permeate our conversations. It's like a palm tree by the ocean that endures the greatest winds because it knows how to bend gracefully. "

Stephen Kendrick

"You don't have to expect perfection of any man, but certainly expect a strong sense of "We're in this together" to know if the relationship is on solid ground."

Samara O'Shea

"We have since come to the full realization of the important part that cooperation plays in strategic situations, and how good strategy must appropriately mix competition and cooperation (coopetition)."

Avinash K. Dixit

"Collaboration is the essence of life. The wind, bees, and flowers work together to spread the pollen."

Amit Ray

What is more challenging or contentious than "intense competition?" Through practical application, competition permeates the fabric of all social contexts, existing in individualist and collectivist cultures. Further, most competition is benign, anchors to the pecking order, and produces measurable outcomes that resolve within a framework of rules. Plus, alternate forms of competition stretch how ethics influence society. So let's define competition and its extended artifacts, cooperation, coopetition, and collaboration to kick off an exploration of this challenging concept:

> Competition: the activity or condition of competing; an event or contest in which people compete; the person or people with whom one is competing, especially in a commercial or sporting arena; the opposition; interaction between organisms, populations, or species in which birth, growth, and death depend on gaining a share of a limited environmental resource

> Collaboration: the action of working with someone to produce or create something; the act of working in concert with others to complete a task or reach a goal

> Cooperation: the process of working together to the same end; assistance, especially by ready compliance with requests

> Coopetition: collaboration between competitors in the hope of mutually beneficial results, generally, but not always, in a business environment

When competition is the topic, most people think of sports contexts or business rivalries. But, ostensibly, these forms are minimal comparatively. Instead, think of the origins of competition, a sustained pursuit of scarce resources that is timeless. In addition, humans have been fierce competitors for eons, notable examples being wars;

however, the Romans had their gladiators, the Greeks their Olympic games, and numerous sporting events occurred in every culture.

The bottom line on the overarching domain of competition for resources has always been how to serve the greater good while feeding the intrinsic desire to be competitive. What is the value construct attached to the outcome being sought? Notice outcome has been substituted for resource in the modern conception of scarcity acquisition.

Although pockets of limited natural resources still exist, globalized food distribution is in its glory days, supply chain challenges align with natural disasters more than human hostility, and competitive organic contexts are rare. Instead, humanity now creates artificial competitive scenarios where individuals or groups seek intangible value constructs like awards and championships.

Neurally, competing for tangible or intangible is indistinguishable. For example, research shows why gambling for $5 is the same as $5,000 to the brain. In addition, extending the study further, the brain cannot discern the difference between acquiring existential resources and artificially-created rewards. But, let's not stop there. Is in-fighting while pursuing the most significant annual bonus any different than banging heads for the local bragging rights at the bowling lanes? Neurologically speaking, no, there is no discernible difference.

From an abstract perspective, competition is an extension of play. As children develop, they journey through several stages of "play." For example, early levels typically exhibit stinginess, refusal to share, arguing, and anchored win-lose dynamics. As children mature while developing, their concept of play changes, becoming more intense. The "why" is emergent competition.

When play shifts, adhering to rules confounds outright winning unless one's skillset creates a competitive advantage. Immature players turn to deception or cheating to overcome someone else's superior skills. The moment innocent play becomes a more intense concern with winning an imperative, ethics joins the conversation. As competition intensifies, the other artifacts, collaboration, cooperation, and coopetition, emerge.

Ethical considerations ensure fair play and undisputable outcomes in theory. But unfortunately, real-world application or adherence to rules falls short of expectations, which leads to coping mechanisms and attempts to insert balance into the asymmetric reality. Those coping mechanisms evolved into the emergent trio of competition artifacts.

For ethical purposes, cooperation and collaboration are "lock-step" concepts. Cooperation is a passive choice where one competitor allows another to act unchecked. On the other hand, collaboration is an active construct where a competitor may facilitate the competency of another, making collaboration a higher-tier relational concept.

Coopetition takes collaboration to the next rung. By aligning with a competitor, sharing proprietary concepts, or enabling on some level, competitors utilize coopetition to intensify results, leading to innovative processes or optimal outcomes a single competitor may find challenging. Essentially, this is sharing in the glory while serving the neurological need to compete.

Is it possible to circumvent ethics while competing? Yes, of course. Cheating is the ultimate form of competing at all costs; it removes dignity from a competitor's efforts, win or lose, and diminishes victory by inserting losing respect or honor into the matrix. The environment or context is immaterial. Cheating to win or to level the playing field regardless of the outcome is always frowned upon by participants and stakeholders alike. For example, codes of ethical conduct dissuade professionals from acting outside the lines in every conceivable field of endeavor.

Understanding power dynamics apply to the competition matrix, assisting stakeholders in their efforts to gain or sustain a competitive balance. The trio of subordinate concepts functions as balancing act coping mechanisms, with each having a specific purpose within the matrix. Determining which choice is optimally applicable requires a fundamental shift in how someone views competition.

The transcendent reward for any competitor is the journey, not the outcome. Winning over weaker competitors is a shallow victory and makes a competitor lose their "edge" over time. The ultimate performers, the superstars in any field, embed an ethical approach into their mindset for a self-serving reason; being an honorable competitor has more intrinsic value than winning at all costs, making winning ancillary to sustaining dignity within the journey.

Some people take an opposing viewpoint to the principled approach. For example, "If you aren't cheating, you aren't trying hard enough" is an oft-repeated mantra. However, statements like this rarely pass through the lips of top-shelf competitors. The message should be clear. Honor and glory are earned through fair play, win or lose. Ethical competitors should be the role models, not the "win at all costs" group, and the next section addresses the lane markers that separate dignified, ethical participants from all others.

"THE CODES OF ETHICS IN PROFESSIONS AND WHAT THEY ENTAIL"

*"A code of ethics cannot be developed overnight by edict or official pronouncement. It is developed by years of practice and performance of duty according to high ethical standards. **It must be self-policing.** Without such a code, a professional soldier or a group soon loses identity and effectiveness. Once we know our job, have a genuine code of ethics, and maintain unquestioned personal integrity, we have met the first and most demanding challenge of leadership."*

Silas L. Copeland

"A choice is the root of all morality. Without choice, one can have no moral code. In a vacuum bereft of alternatives, there can be no values. And without values, there can be no reason for a code of ethics. What gives our lives meaning is which alternatives we choose. If we have no options, if we can take but one path, we are by definition slaves."

Dave Galanter

"The only way to truly be protected at all times is to claim your 'personal power' with the highest code of ethics and responsibility. If you are centered in this type of power, the power of the universe supports you, and no one and nothing can defeat you."

Christopher Penczak

"Elder Mediation is a dynamic field of practice growing and developing in different jurisdictions worldwide. The EMIN Code of Ethics (the Code) has been and continues to be, informed by the knowledge and experience of mediators, individuals, and organizations working with aging issues in different jurisdictions and cultures. In these challenging times, there is a great need for skilled, person-centered support for individuals, families, and care providers to constructively address issues and concerns to enhance the quality of life and wellness of the older person(s) while respecting the needs of each participant." (Description of the EMIN professional code for global mediators)

Margaret Bouchier 2021

*M*any people are confused about professional codes of conduct or ethics. Silas L. Copeland sums up the reality, the "essence" of what a code of ethics should be regardless of one's field of endeavor. In addition, he opens the door to exploring what codes of ethics imply, a duty for the oath-takers, and the relevance to all stakeholders. However, understanding the codes becomes optimal through engaging with and understanding concepts embedded within any code of ethics.

Professional codes of ethics impact society in ways laws never will for one critical reason. Adhering to one's word to peers is an intrinsically motivated choice, making the oath an intensely powerful tool for self-compliance. As Copeland asserted, self-policing is a differentiator. In addition, all codes include essential ideology. First, all must define the scope of behavior covered within the code, describe the behaviors and expectations under consideration, explain the field's guiding principles, and unequivocally state the professional conduct, including responsibility and accountability.

Scope of behavior can include "within the lines" and "outside the lines" boundaries. For example, criminal behavior, claims of moral turpitude, or other choices which may diminish society's perception of the overall field can be outlined within a code of ethics. Every section of a code encompasses acceptable versus unacceptable behavior; therefore, the base code is a "moral code" defining individual behavior, while the overarching code is an ethical one defining the interaction of professionals with other practitioners and stakeholders, such as clients, staff, and vendors.

The power inherent within a code of ethics is derived from group communities of practice members agreeing to abide by the code. For example, in many instances, provisions for disciplinary action applicable to violators are absent or reactionary, giving membership latitude to self-police based on novel circumstances. Potentially losing the respect or support of professional peers is a credible barrier for most practitioners and creates a compelling interest for sustained compliance.

This section aimed to increase social awareness of the lengths professionals must traverse to maintain their credentials and good standing. For example, many governing bodies attach code compliance to licensing renewal, and for a good reason. Renewing licenses of "bad actors" would weaken any professional community. In addition, accreditation usually requires belonging within a group bound by a code. Unfortunately, codes of ethics are not ubiquitous in more professions, leading to an excellent question: Why not?

One potential reason is the underlying social image of specific professions. For example, Hollywood and comedians often characterize attorneys as unethical, which creates a social stigma. Likewise, most people who interact with mediators think they are only for divorce or business conflicts, which is true of a segment of mediators; however, most conflict professionals can handle multiple forms of mediation, so they lose business due to fallacious stereotyping. Perhaps more professionals need to tout their code of ethics and the bounded reality they work within to offset the negative branding issue.

A professional code of ethics does not guarantee the practitioner is in compliance; however, extended time in service, the body of work, and the need to sustain ethical behavior regardless of the code existing are evidentiary, indicating that a specific professional is trustworthy and is maintaining standards or market mechanics would have ended the professional's business lifecycle already. Therefore, consider the code of ethics as an affirmation tool for consumers and look beyond stereotyping when engaging with professionals.

"RISK-TOLERANCE TO RISK-AVERSION"

*"In school, we learn that mistakes are bad, and we are punished
for making them. Yet, if you look at how humans are designed to learn,
we learn by making mistakes. We learn to walk by falling.
If we never fell, we would never walk."*

Robert T. Kiyosaki

"A ship is safe in harbor, but that's not what ships are for."

John A. Shedd

*"Take risks! That is what life is really about. We must pursue
our happiness. Nobody has ever lived our lives; there are no guidelines.
Trust your instincts. Accept nothing but the best. But then also look
for it carefully. Don't allow it to slip between your fingers.
Sometimes, good things come to us in such a quiet fashion. And nothing
comes complete. It is what we make of whatever we encounter
that determines the outcome. What we choose to see, what we choose
to save, and what we choose to remember. Never forget that
all the love in your life is there, inside you, always."*

Linda Olsson

*"If you are afraid to take a chance, take one anyway. What you don't do
can create the same regrets as the mistakes you make."*

Iyanla Vanzant

*"Since that day, there is nothing anyone could ever say
to convince me that one person cannot change a nation.
One person can do unbelievable things. All it takes is
"that one person" who's willing to risk everything to make it happen."*

Sam Childers

*"The more we love, the more we lose. The more we lose, the more we learn.
The more we learn, the more we love. It comes full circle. Life is the school;
love is the lesson. We cannot lose."*

Kate McGahan

*"To live a life of excellence, you must take risks. You will have to step
into new territory and climb new mountains. If you're up to something
as big as you are, it will be scary. If it feels perfectly safe, you are probably
underachieving. To leave your mark in the world, you will have to stand
someplace you've never been willing to stand before. And you will have
to have the courage to aspire to excellence."*

Debbie Ford

"To win without risk is to triumph without glory."

Pierre Corneille

One factor that aligns with the pursuit of interests is the concept of risk. As previously mentioned, one's interests are subjective, existing with few limits beyond one's imagination. Humans are genetically inclined to overcome Maslow's needs paradigm and will take any path to achievement. Once needs are met, one enters Maslow's conceptualized pyramid growth portion, and interests come into play. With few limitations on how humans perceive interests, one tends to seek interest viability through decision trees. These decision trees function based on one's risk-tolerance level or risk-aversion, with "risk" being another context centering on personal choice.

Consider this example of how risk links to decision-making. George and Andy are competing for a supply contract with a lucrative client. Although both run comparable businesses, they request a quote (RFQ) with differing risk tolerance levels. Risk tolerance in this context has many variables; however, for simplicity, one variable shall be utilized to measure their differences, which is how long each is willing to extend account receivables. George offers a five percent discount on his invoices within thirty days, while Andy extends a ten percent discount to be paid on his invoices within fifteen days. Andy is more risk-averse than George regardless of all other factors since he seeks to shorten his payment cycle significantly more than George. Both owners are interested in the contract; however, one is willing to forego higher profits for faster cash flow.

From a personal perspective, all potential risks should be perceived as a fundamental consideration, even when the risks only function as limiting factors. When the measurable potential for peril is equal between two options, it ceases to be a factor. For instance, two women approach the risk inherent to sexual activity based on their risk tolerance level. One has multiple partners but utilizes a pharmacological approach to birth prevention and gets tested regularly for sexually transmitted diseases (STDs). The other also has multiple partners; however, she insists on condoms and tests less frequently for STDs. Both women exhibit risk-averse behavioral artifacts and take measures to limit risk.

Parents approach the school transportation dynamic with a broad perspective on risk-tolerance versus risk-aversion. Some parents escort their children to and from school buses, others transport them to and from the campus, and others allow their children free-range. Depending on the magnitude of criminal activity in the local environment, each is risk-free when the parents make a context-appropriate choice. However, one needs to exercise basic math to understand how parents routinely over-estimate the risk inherent to getting their offspring safely to and from the school environment. The author wholeheartedly agrees that any parent's choice of refusing to accept any level of risk is essential based on their conceptualized individual rights; the author only seeks to illustrate the risk-aversion fallacies utilized to make a parenting choice.

Consider a typical American subdivision with an average set of neighborhood schools. The neighborhood has 1800+ homes where 2700+ children must attend various local elementary, middle, and high schools. With 95 percent attendance, this would mean over 5200 trips to and from schools daily. In mathematic terms, almost a million trips to and from the schools in this one medium-level school environment occur annually. Unfortunately, the statistics juxtapose and contradict actual documented cases of a substantially elevated risk environment manifesting in a specific school district, an over-stated risk dynamic utilized as a justification for many parenting choices about offsetting one risk variable, predators.

The risk overstatement becomes meaningless to the family of any child who comes to harm, which circles back to the worth of one life; however, understanding the fallacious math involved in making the risk assessment creases one's awareness of a need to do enough critical analysis before validating choices based on risk. To emphasize the supremacy of parental choice, especially where danger may be present or possible, one must always consider the likelihood of some parents refusing to accept any risk level, which is certainly their right based on individual choice dynamics. Alternatively, the math does not support castigating those parents who choose to take higher risks in this school context, especially when "free-range" parenting is a stated factor.

Another parenting debate surrounds attending school during the current COVID-19 crisis. More variables exist within this contentious debate, such as multigenerational households with high-risk family members or households that must accept the higher risks associated with the disease due to the need to sustain livelihoods. Any acceptable solution must be multi-layered and give unconditional regard for every parent's right to make subjective choices.

Exploring risk means one must open up to the upside of challenging scenarios, not solely anchor on the ambiguity or downside; a habitual issue for many people. Several lead-in quotes touch on the positive artifacts, such as Pierre Corneille's assertion about how victory absent compelling opponents would lack a sense of accomplishment. Professional athletes and extreme sports enthusiasts thrive in environments where failing incentivizes optimal outcomes. Anyone can think of stories when an extreme risk-taker succeeds or fails; both results make for spectacular tales.

A variation of the risk continuum is central to a regulatory focus concept. Humans allow a preference for risk-tolerance to traverse one of two paths based on whether seeking pleasure or avoiding displeasure is their core preference. Risk-takers are prone to extraversion and exploring newness, while risk-avoiders prefer introversion and the comfort of familiarity. Viewpoints about risk would create a scatter plot on any graph. An ethical approach to risk should ensure all risk choices are personal and not subject to adverse judgment from others. No one has the right to force perceived danger upon another person.

Risk creates some novel dynamics as it manifests. Therefore, one needs to break down risk scenarios in a specific way. "Danger is real; fear is optional" expresses the ultimate risk-tolerance versus risk-avoidance choice matrix. Fortunately, human evolution has created a biological imperative where the "fight-flight-fear-freeze" response overrides choice when danger overwhelms someone.

Therefore, learning to navigate the space between auto-responses and the choice matrix must be intentional. Let's explore one arena where optimizing the choice matrix creates competency regardless of the field or topic involved; the space labeled tough conversations-tough choices.

"TOUGH CONVERSATION-TOUGH CHOICES"

*"You're not learning anything unless you're having
the difficult conversations."*
Gwyneth Paltrow

*"I don't ever want to humiliate a human being, and I don't want
the fear of being humiliated to participate in my thoughts."*
Caroline Myss

*"Difficult conversations are always uncomfortable. But with
the right person, you can have those conversations."*
Gina LaManna

*"The single most important thing is to shift one's internal stance from
"I understand" to "Help me understand." Everything else follows from that.
Remind yourself that if you think you already understand how someone feels
or what they are trying to say, it is a delusion. Remember a time
when you were sure you were right and then discovered one little fact
that changed everything? There is always more to learn."*
Douglas Stone

*"No matter how good you get at reframing, the 'single' most important rule
about managing the interaction is this: You can't move the conversation in
a more positive direction until the other person feels heard and understood.*

And they won't feel heard and understood until you've listened. When the other person becomes highly emotional, listen and acknowledge. When they say their version of the story is the only version that makes sense, paraphrase what you're hearing and ask them some questions about why they think this. If they level accusations against you, before defending yourself, try to understand their view. Whenever you feel overwhelmed or unsure how to proceed, remember that it is always a good time to listen."

Douglas Stone

"The point is this: difficult conversations are seldom about getting the facts right. They are about conflicting perceptions, interpretations, and values."

Douglas Stone

"Even if a conversation is difficult, we must still be loving, gentle, decent, honest, moral, honorable, virtuous, and full of integrity."

Delores James

"I love when conversations and energies just flow. Not forced, not coerced, just present."

Dau Voire

"Every challenging conversation begins within oneself."

Buddy Thornton

From Klein and Winnicott to Bowlby, psychologists have examined human development through a critical lens of "what makes what." Without getting into the science, working through challenging conversations begins where the psychologists' observations take the confounding context of the "tough conversations-tough choices" topic. Until humans reach the developmental phase where multiple concepts are conceptualized about "others," conflict scenarios are disjointed and unpredictable, always originating within the "self."

Therefore, let's begin the exploration of how the experts arrived at their conclusion by listing some of the pertinent "other concepts":

Agency: action or intervention, especially such as to produce a particular effect; a thing or person that acts to produce an outcome

Attachment theory: the system that guides us in our patterns and habits of forming and maintaining relationships based on Bowlby's research and his reframing of earlier developmental psychologists' theories

Reality/Unreality Internalization: reality is the world or the state of things as they exist, as opposed to an idealistic or notional idea of them; unreality is the quality of being imaginary or illusory; internalization is the process of making attitudes or behavior part of one's nature by learning or unconscious assimilation; when synthesized, reality/unreality internalization is the process of accepting how people can be tangible and simultaneously hold abstract artifacts within

Grief Cycle: the stages one endures as a response to intense, sometimes overwhelming emotions for people, regardless of whether their sadness stems from the loss of a loved one or from a terminal diagnosis they or someone they love have received, among an infinite number of other less compelling reasons

Coping Heuristics: methods acquired through learning, training, or optimized strategic utilization of essential processes to mitigate or avoid confounding artifacts

Order and Chaos-The Dao in Us: The balance between acceptable and unacceptable with a truism that nothing can be entirely at one end of any behavioral continuum

What makes any "tough" context, tangible or intangible, challenging? Tough conversations-tough choices (TC Squared) create a formidable amount of apprehension in those facing this crucial relationship domain. The "challenging" dynamic emerges because proper or improper resolution can enhance or destroy one's social efficacy, a dynamic that allows forward-facing fear to discourage engagement.

According to developmental theorists, difficult conversations originate with confusion within the self. Therefore, before attempting to hold a difficult conversation with an "other," it is essential to have a basic resolution that leads to some position to offer during that discussion, which requires a first step, the "self" exploring, then reducing intrinsic confounding. Please note that no mention was made that the point one provides must be accurate; it must open the doorway to an engaging conversation seeking resolution by consensus, which requires vulnerability and accepting the possibility of being wrong. Does that sound easy?

How often do people endure sleepless nights struggling with some compelling issue, some with an extrinsic conflict basis, some with an internal struggle to resolve a dilemma, and others with conflicting interests regardless of context? There are infinite societal artifacts or vectors that one could potentially label "tough" or "challenging." No attempt shall be made to isolate one possibility over another; therefore, let's honor the ubiquitous nature of this concern.

Instead of seeking environments where conflicted souls traverse, attempt to arrive at an abstract place where "challenging" does not exist. Can't conceptualize many? Organically, conflict scenarios emerge anywhere or any "when" people engage in activities or conversations. What does this universal reality suggest for finding space where "challenging" is absent? Discovery may be blocked; why not explore "creating" conflict-free space?

When the confound is internal, one of several self-limiting behaviors occurs. The first possibility is insufficient information to clarify one's position; however, lacking information is rarely the case in this digital information-abundant environment. A more likely secondary limitation is more plausible, the existence of misinformation or disinformation, with side orders of bias and doubt. Finally, all forms of limiting behavior originate in the self, diffuse outwardly, altering and confounding every dynamic encountered until the problematic issue is resolved through self-work or outside collaboration. Therefore, understanding agency, the ability to create an effect or outcome, is the first step to addressing the challenging conversation scenario.

Can you make an optimal choice in a sub-optimal environment? Despite variance creating barriers, an optimal outcome is still possible but unlikely. From examples like parent-teen conflict to elder domain conflict, people must endure navigating "tough" conversations, and arriving at sustainable consensus is rare without volumes of hard work or intervention by an external conflict expert. Therefore, starting the exploration of how and why human "agency" works should provide clues and an eventual roadmap to resolution.

Regardless of the challenge, the agency is confounded by the bias effect embedded in the reality/unreality internalization process. Humans anchor on personal choices and opinions and give little consideration to whether their preferences are tangible or abstractions. Guess what? To the human brain, real or imaginary makes no difference when facing stress. The chemical response is similar in hypothetical and substantive scenarios. The magnitude of stress is not a factor; the only artifact pertinent to seeking resolution is whether fear is present.

When the fear response is triggered, the higher brain functions are blocked, meaning executive decisions and critical thinking are off-line. Often labeled the fight-flight-fright-freeze response, the amygdala's rudimentary response to existential threats must resolve before anyone may engage in challenging conversations. Although the amygdala functions along evolutionary embedded pathways, coping mechanisms can be utilized to offset the fear and permit one to regain control.

This exploration focuses on the "why" of choice failure and the "how" of getting choice right, not establishing coping mechanisms. That exploration follows. The study of primes, triggers, action potential, self-awareness, self-control, other autonomy, and the importance of "I" statements focused on one's contribution to a scenario is critical to choice optimization. For example, choosing and accepting an "I" focal point versus a "you" declaration focused on projecting blame or shame toward others during conflict resolution creates a roadmap and clarity. The aim is to explore and engage with the foundational knowledge that opens your future to the "best version of you" during trying scenarios, not to seek avoidance while blaming others.

Most people, especially in contemporary terms, find vulnerability and self-awareness problematic. It is easier to blame, shame, or judge others, but doing any of these creates confounds, not answers. Therefore, a better option must exist, and it does.

Developing an internalized locus of control (LOC) is the first step. Clarity about self-contribution and forgiveness aligning with vulnerability are the two components that push LOC to an optimal place where addressing challenging conversations, the first "tough" in conflict resolution under duress, is possible. Therefore, until someone conquers fear, then activates LOC properly, getting beyond the first step won't happen.

For some, successfully navigating the first step can become inspirational; for others, a sense of "getting beyond fear" manifests into a life-changing lesson. Both artifacts lead to the passage beyond the conversation and take one to the boundary of the choice matrix. "Here" is when humans can become superstars or abject failures. What does that harsh binary encompass?

Someone got to a place where they engaged with an adversary or held a crucial conversation with a loved one, but they failed to understand that gaining traction was only half the battle. Perhaps, but not always, enough clarity emerged from the "tough" conversation to shrink future options to one or only several acceptable choices for all stakeholders. Making a choice is a defining artifact for whether one traversed the "TC Squared" process optimally.

What makes an "optimal" choice? Unfortunately, that answer is unique for everyone facing this dynamic. Should the outcome be self-serving or considered for the greater good? Based on altruistic reciprocity, can a choice do both? Regardless, any option must resolve the foundational conflict that created the challenge.

A secondary confound is the "Law of Unintended Consequences." Worrying about how others peripheral to the challenge might be impacted has derailed or prevented conversations. If the goal is honesty, there are often no optimal outcomes available when participants cast a wide net. From a prosocial perspective, hesitation before engaging is beneficial because it adds often-overlooked dimensionality to the mix, broadening the conversation and allowing for more thoughtful solutions.

The "order and chaos" in all human engagement is the final artifact to consider. Critical thinking should hold dominion over opinion or fact when involved in a TC Squared interaction. Why would factual data take a back seat to vital considerations aligned with critical thinking? All environments and all actions within an environment contain some Daoist duality. Therefore, all stakeholders must explore the potential "enhancements and confounds" within their solutions to the conflict. Failing to consider all potential vectors is how unintended consequences creep into the process, and no one needs extra stress adding to the challenge.

The most significant benefit to traversing any TC Squared context is future competency. First, research and analytics suggest how successfully resolving a challenging issue embeds self-confidence that future events will have similar positive outcomes for participants. Second, the time required to enter conflict resolution shrinks dramatically because the "unknown" gets out of the picture.

Failing to accept self-contributions to contentious relationship challenging scenarios is the primary barrier creating TC Squared moments, but fear is a close second. Keep in mind that all humans endure the fear of the unknown. The coping mantra for approaching fear is thus: "Danger is real regardless of its origin, but fear is optional." Sometimes, fear saves people from danger, so fear should be respected. However, embrace the existence of fear and work diligently to understand it so fear can be coped with appropriately, which is the key to not letting fear dominate oneself.

Coping with the tangible aspects of TC Squared scenarios requires a template of sorts, self-driven and non-prescriptive, based on the need for vulnerability and finding a calm demeanor from which to approach others. For example, how someone might disarm an adversary is a frequent "primacy question" to answer. According to ralph Kilmann, the architect of the TKI conflict index, there are five conflict resolution possibilities or modes: competing, accommodating, avoiding, collaborating, and compromising. In addition, Kilmann asserts that all five forms intertwine with assertiveness or cooperativeness as an underlying agent.

However, the conflict coping domain focuses on resolution over prevention. Ideally, prosocial approaches to reduce or remove conflict potential would precede any form of conflict resolution or management. Unfortunately, challenging dialogue is often accompanied by the dissonance emerging from developing or ongoing disputes, making proactive approaches untenable. So what are the critical takeaways from the TC Squared conversation?

One, "tough" is only present because someone dwells on a future event instead of approaching it head-on. Two, using a "when-then" approach optimizes the mitigation process. "When" the "other" is stuck on a position, "then" the best option is to agree with the other's premise, "then" offer alternate viewpoints after getting permission to expand the conversation. Finally, having a contingency "when-then" trajectory designed for multiple scenarios allows one to reduce the fear preceding any challenging task, so work diligently to expand the skill set suggested here.

"When-then" leverages the three soft approaches from the TKI, accommodating, collaborating, and compromising, and removes the contentious aura of competing or avoiding. With "when-then," one coping mechanism with multiple vectors and outcomes potentials, challenging becomes manageable. Wasn't that the goal?

"A LYING SOCIETY?"

"Lying has long been a part of everyday life. We couldn't get through the day without being deceptive."

Leonard Saxe, Ph.D.

"You save your big lies for the person that you're closest to."

Bella DePaulo, Ph.D.

"The ubiquity of lying is a problem, but would we want to will away all of our lies? Let's be honest." (The Paradox of Social Lying)

Allison Kornet

"There is no sickness worse for me than words that to be kind must lie."

Aeschylus

"Sometimes we tell white lies to hide an embarrassing truth about ourselves or avoid offending others for telling the truth about them. It's a conciliatory white lie, albeit not necessary, that reveals the modest and gentler sides of our humanity."

Danny Castillones Sillada

"Today, I bent the truth to be kind, and I have no regret, for I am far surer of what is kind than I am of what is true."

Robert Brault

*C*onflating risk is an example of how contemporary society embraces popular opinion instead of validated data constructs or expert advice, consequently making false assertions. Estimates vary; however, sociologists infer that humans make between 40-200 false statements daily. Many lies align with social expectations and the reduction of conflict. One prominent falsehood is the "Good to see you; I'll call you later" blow-off that softens the distance between ex-acquaintances. "You are looking lovely today" is another, especially when the compliment recipient knows it is factually incorrect, regardless of the sincerity involved. There is an ethical artifact to social lying dynamics, making the social practice acceptable in many contexts, which is how society perceives increased civility. Reasonable, or not, fair, or not, the convenient lie remains a permanent fixture in one's daily existence.

A contemporary example of falsehoods attached to innuendo exists within the political environment. The omission of facts or the inclusion of only points aligned with one candidate's position is commonplace. From a purely analytical viewpoint linked to the existing unethical behavior, voters should not elect any candidate. Constituents expect the barrage of negativity inherent to modern politics; however, the decision tree should align more with a candidate's positions and whether the candidate's stated intent aligns with a constituent's interests instead of making decisions based on emotions tied to half-truths or outright lies.

Most of the "lying society" contexts explored thus far within contemporary applied ethics have led readers to what the author believes is the most significant indication of malicious intent in existence within the early 21st century's social norms. How one treats another has been shifted from honesty in most forms to pragmatic political correctness (PC) and a requirement to withhold thoughts or beliefs potentially offensive to another.

One must always understand the First Amendment's tenets in all contexts, such as not yelling "fire" in a crowded theater or not using racial epithets of any kind; however, PC goes far beyond practicality when people use their interpretation of PC to attack others. The debate on PC and all aspects of PC's context becomes a natural expansion of the "lying society" conversation. In straightforward language, society requires everyone to bury their perception of truth and lie to appease others.

One should never doubt that social truth-bending keeps etiquette front and center. However, the blatant truth is that PC is a social pariah of incredible magnitude. Of course, this concept could be fantastic if PC were kept within its acceptable boundaries, but let's be honest.

PC is the ultimate gaslighting context, a "damned if you do, damned if you don't" social nightmare. Aeschylus was correct about using words to be kind that are insincere, and he lived over two millennia ago. But unfortunately, humanity, particularly over-sensitive people who anchor on victimology, never learned that lesson.

There is zero value in forcing someone else to lie to make yourself comfortable. That is the essence of PC. So someone wins, but someone AND SOCIETY lose and lose badly. From an ethical perspective, PC damages everyone's self-image.

Demanding sensitivity and false projection where meaningful conversations would serve a socially optimal purpose are abhorrent. The fact that PC has remained a "thing" for this long needs to be discussed. That's why we are going there next. The lying, socially deceptive practice needs to stop.

"POLITICAL CORRECTNESS CONTEXTS/ ANTECEDENTS/ARTIFACTS"

"I take no issue with the new cancel culture; it acts to obliterate that which is judgemental and must surely end by canceling itself."

Anthony P. Mauro, Sr

"It is a form of generational narcissism to change texts to suit one's own needs."

Luke Timothy Johnson

"Democracy was supposed to champion freedom of speech, and yet the simple rules of table decorum could clamp down on the rights their forefathers had fought and died for."

E.A. Bucchianeri

"You're not allowed to call them dinosaurs anymore. It's speciesist. You have to call them pre-petroleum persons."

Terry Pratchett

"An elementary school student asked me the NOT politically correct question, "Is an idiot smarter than a moron?" I had to Google it because I was afraid to respond in today's PC society and didn't want to offend him, his parents, or anyone else. Here's what I found:

Technically, a moron is more intelligent than an idiot. An imbecile is also more intelligent than an idiot. Although, today, the words are considered insulting and derogatory. Before the 1960s, they were widely used as actual psychology terms associated with intelligence on an IQ test. IQ of A) 00-25-Idiot, B)26-50-Imbecile, and C)51-70-Moron

Explaining all this to a nine-year-old with an IQ of 130 made me feel like society has turned all adults into one of the above, myself included. When I told him that I was afraid to say it openly, the nine-year-old said, "Adults are idiots!"

Ray Palla

Ah, political correctness (PC), the ultimate socialized, required falsification of self-projection. It becomes socially unacceptable if one says what is in one's thoughts in front of another who may (not always) take offense. PC stems from how some segments of society, through threats of actions in the court systems or from a social media "bully pulpit," align with forcing the majority to exhibit deference for others' feelings, mainly through consideration toward all minority-defined group member's emotional sensitivities.

By forcing majority compliance with PC, some outlier questions emerge. The practice projects how it is politically correct for one African-American to use the "N" word to characterize another black person because it is within a quasi-acceptable social construct based on the defined group's choices and norms. However, suppose a white majority member crosses this social boundary. In that case, African-Americans will view the act as improper majority-specific power exploitation and a socially unacceptable choice leading to immediate conflict.

However, PC loses validity in all contexts when it does not equally apply to all persons' sensitivities, majority or minority. For example, consider the supposition that it is inappropriate for a white majority member to make an utterance or speak a thought with action potential for harming a minority group member, a premise most people would agree with automatically. For social equity to exist, the opposite should be correct, but it is not, and many minorities state the inverse should not be valid based on a fallacious position. If equality is the ultimate goal, a bidirectional expression of dignity and respect must be present within the social environment. For this reason alone, one should explore the context of PC and expand the discourse to include a broad continuum of PC contextual factors.

PC has clear antecedents, all emerging from negative historical contexts aligned with colonialism and the mistreatment of indigenous populations or those who endured slavery because of forced migration. The racial and historical injustice argument persists because many majority-defined social groups seek to sustain institutionalized white privilege covertly. These sustained efforts have projected the perception of "less than" labeling on all other groups. Up to and including the historical emergence of implied, then socially mandated PC, the majority has been slow to adopt an acceptable level of consideration for minority groups. Of course, outliers to the perception exist, but the typical characterization remains "systemic racial inequality" or "institutionalized racism." PC has an innocent origin story, but the current reality has shifted away from any semblance of humble beginnings.

Thinking shifted when PC became an overarching social focus, but in unexpected contexts. Seemingly overnight, the majority-white population had a concept they could embrace. "Why?" you might ask? Because PC does not force the white majority to explicitly support an intentional form of inclusion, only to project an absence of exclusion by "voicing" insincere pleasantries. PC becomes a double-edged sword when minorities adapt to PC and clamor for immediate redress when someone violates PC. Of course, the outcry may induce a degree of projected consideration; however, the majority can continue to hide real inclusion and practice institutional exclusion behind the PC wall; they can sustain dominance and endure deflecting criticism and counter the complaints insidiously.

This viewpoint of PC is not window dressing. If one digs deeper, it becomes an exercise in whether one should "tell the simplest of social truths," only with broad societal repercussions. Minorities, especially the black population who have suffered immeasurable harm for centuries at the hands of their white majority oppressors, are quick to embrace a context designed to insulate and protect themselves. Unfortunately, the same PC system allows the white majority to interject, "You have PC," insinuating the PC context makes up for other systemic shortfalls. The truth remains one of inequality and inequity based on a sustained (thus far in history) limited opportunity environment in exchange for PC. The asymmetric trade-off is the self-limiting legacy of the broadest antecedent stemming from PC. The abysmal compromise between groups creates a bi-directional barrier to progress. The PC foundation allows and often compels lying by omission, not to forget the implications of intentional deflection from the truth. Plus, PC ignores the possibility of multiple realities simultaneously signifying honesty.

A second artifact attributed to PC is the regression of critical thinking on diversity or cultural inclusion. The perception of PC violations on campuses triggers a form of primed latent anger, which normalized functional PC serves to suppress. The expression of hidden outrage on college campuses manifests as protests and orchestrated reactions designed to further the return to PC since it is the comfort zone preferred by minorities. Often loud or violent, the responses get plenty of media attention while fostering the white majority's hidden interests. The majority thinking is, "If minorities focus on PC, they will ignore other issues." An in-depth exploration of the shifts in observable social upheaval caused by PC reactions will reveal how often protesters achieve minimal substantial progress through their actions. So, what would be the optimal approach if overt responses and ample social media coverage have not moved the needle?

Minority leadership often pivots to old, tired arguments, functionally creating boundaries to meaningful change. One example is the oft-voiced demand for reparations. Undoubtedly, one must consider the history of social repression. If reparations could benefit the original victims, a physical impossibility, they would gain widespread support for ethical and moral reasons. Yes, subsequent generations have been disenfranchised and dismissed as social outcasts. Arguably, the current descendants of those victims suffer immeasurable harm due to past injustices' residual effects. For example, systemic harm's existence forces modern-day young minorities to endure a starting point disadvantage attributable to systemic white privilege in many social environments. Sadly, seeking restitution through reparation has zero legal context, which places the action potential for redress through recompense firmly in the domain of social beneficence and requires the majority to approve whatever they deem appropriate. Reparations only move forward if the majority chooses to act with altruistic intentionality, which rarely occurs. Here, the point focuses on whether embedded action potentially delays real social progress based on arguments with substantial moral value but no legal substance. Consider instead how any viable concept of actual reparations should include institutionally embraced inclusion and vast amounts of investments or grants focused on making members of the minority population equity partners in humanity's future.

The debate about PC is a subjective exercise in entropy, a colossal waste of social energy. Admittedly, PC does reduce conflict in many environments temporarily; however, anchored PC's trigger effect, which potentially leads to a cascade of protest activities, only restarts the wasteful pursuit cycle. The best example of an optimal approach starts with openness and curiosity about others and leads to better, ethically aligned outcomes across all cultures.

"UNCONDITIONAL EQUAL CONSIDERATION-INTENTIONAL POSITIVE REGARD"

*"When you criticize me, I intuitively dig in to defend myself;
however, when you accept me as I am, I am suddenly willing to change."*

Carl Rogers

*"So, how do you do Unconditional Positive Regard — especially as a parent
or teacher/mentor/caregiver? First, smile. Second, let your child (student)
know their choices and mistakes are separate from them as a person (i.e., you
love your child or student, but you may not love their behavior). Third, show
understanding of their emotions. Counselors say that 'emotions are neither
right nor wrong.' Finally, put yourself in their shoes. Remember the times
you've felt the way they do. Remember what it's like to be an irrational kid,
moody teenager, or frustrated adult.*

*Remember that God is the only real Judge. God offers absolute
forgiveness unconditionally: "as far as the east is from the west,
so far has he removed our transgressions from us."(Psalm 103:12).
"One should remember God loves us despite our imperfections."*

Buddy Thornton

*"In a million years of falling off, humans never realized that maybe
the pedestal isn't made for their kind."*

Adeel Ahmed Khan

"Being considerate of others will take your children further in life than any college degree."

Marian Wright Edelman

"We must delight in each other, make others conditions our own, rejoice together, mourn together, labor and suffer together, always having before our eyes our commission and community in work, our community as members of the same body."

John Winthrop

People from all cultures and socioeconomic groups can extend curiosity and infinite consideration for others. Does this happen often? Unfortunately, no. In an ideal context, unlimited choices aligning with "unconditional equal consideration" would be a positive social trait. "Unconditional" supports how the explicit or implicit characteristics of a recipient of the consideration would be immaterial. Equal and equitable for the same reason. The existence of genuine regard would make existing PC as practiced throughout society obsolete as a concept. Consider the following statement:

"If actions extended toward others in public become the equivalent of similar actions taken in private or in the absence of potential observers, then those intentional actions should become a habitual norm based on one's level of intentional veracity."

Is it possible for people to embrace how important being ethically consistent in all environments influences creating a shift in how social norms function? First, consistency across contexts forces one to abandon primes emerging from biases contrary to normative social discourse. Also, incomplete information evolves into a known quantity or a perceived trait by extending and embracing curiosity about others, mitigating any latent fears of differentiation. Finally, without any viable distress from perceived differentiation, the concept of intentional positive regard for others has action potential for becoming the social norm, and pejorative worldviews should disappear over time.

Optimal methods for understanding intentional positive regard are available; however, one must explore an ethical environment from both ends of the relationship spectrum. The relationship context returns consideration to the customary norms of the public-private-solitary statement earlier in this section. Start by conceptualizing a relationship within a dyad.

The dyadic relationship is the central component for all agreements, the focal point of all negotiations, and drives social existence universally. Marriage counselors unequivocally state how and why long-term marriages and partnerships are fundamentally sustainable based on each partner giving the other intentional positive regard. In modern contexts, any sustained long-term relationship depends on absolute equal consideration. Passions may wane as youthful exuberance diminishes; living to make the life of another a blessing is, by its endearing and enduring nature, a choice aligned with being "intentionally unconditional" and non-judgmental. So, what about outside the realm of intimate relationships?

In multinational organizational environments, team members find themselves working in cross-cultural contexts. The dynamic increases the knowledge base but has the action potential for conflict if two or more team members have historically conflicted backgrounds. As familiarity increases through functional interaction, the action potential for conflict diminishes proportionally to the level of sustainable collaboration. What often starts as minimal consideration for "others" based on differentiation evolves into a thriving professional practice community. From any perspective, a developed sense of equal significance and intentional positive regard becomes the basis for inclusion by mitigating existing negative social primes by reducing bias.

"SOCIAL INFLUENCE AND OPTIMAL OUTCOMES"

"Some of the most important decisions I have made might well have never been made, or might have been very different, if it hadn't been for the influence of the people in my life. We all need mentors."

Tony Clark

"A teacher affects eternity. He can never tell where his influence stops."

Henry Adams

"The key to successful leadership is influence, not authority."

Ken Blanchard

"The greatest witness we can give another is grace. Showing mercy and grace is a privilege. Do you have the capacity to exhibit this?"

Kelly Markey

"Effectively wielding personal influence implies that you are in the energy transfer business. Your ability to transport your audience into emotional, spiritual, physical, and mental energy states through your actions and message is the context from which all your ideas are judged."

Kurian Mathew Tharakan

"The moon must be willing to illuminate a world that it doesn't live in, with a light that it didn't create, from a place that no one wants to visit. So, therefore, to change life on earth, maybe we need to be more like the moon."

Craig D. Lounsbrough

"I can name every teacher whose class I attended from first through sixth grade and each teacher who influenced my life since, through today. Besides my spouse and immediate family members, the teachers in my life count the most!"

Buddy Thornton

Influence and persuasion from past eras have evolved into the powerful social media conduits of the contemporary world. The impact of any form of influence depends on access to digital platforms and creating reactions. With the emergence of social media influencers and the ubiquitous nature of microscopic attention spans, research and impact have taken center stage in how positive social change agents develop and deliver content, drive change, and shape the fabric of the future social enterprise across all societies. The artifacts from current influencer research stand as the foundation of future ethical standards for social evolution.

The position and relevance of how "influence" impacts society allows leaders and advocates for change to synthesize optimal approaches and programs. The limited complexity and identifiable simplicity of how human responses to persuasive efforts exist across all groups are significant to the research; however, it would be more accurate to portray the limited choice context as the "why" optimization can occur across multiple learning platforms.

Regardless of the source, responses to every type of influence occupy only three potential outcome paradigms. The reactions evolve into conflict, compliance, or commitment. If one chose to build a "response to influence continuum" with a fourth category for balance, the fourth category would be an avoidance of conflict absent compliance or commitment. In simpler terms, one responds to influence (or attempts to exploit or control another) by walking away, arguing, going along to get along, or embracing some envisionment of a benefit. Depending on personal choice dynamics, each option may achieve optimal outcomes.

There are sub-influencers, artifacts driving motivation, and all attached to how one approaches the choices available in the moment. Does one feel attracted to intentional focus embedded in the influence context? Is the allure minimal or full-bore? If one assumes the topic is social injustice (or any of many available hot topics), are the rational responses tied to the extremes with minimal consideration for the moderate middle? Depending on the authenticity of the issue, perhaps one with considerable social outcome weight, would one shift or expand the magnitude of one's potential response? Here, while approaching the conclusion of how to structure ethical choices, one can openly explore how humanity makes decisions based on reactivity to influence synthesized with each person's worldview's uniqueness. Will the unique nature of one's perspective be normative or a social outlier? Remember that both are equally acceptable within the contemporary ethics domain.

Reaching either end of the continuum requires one to hold a specific perspective with significant magnitude, which should be labeled a "compelling interest." The influencer's task, without exception, is to find what induces a compelling argument for or against the topic on hand. The toolkit for task completion includes the power dynamics of leveraged risk versus attraction, appealing to recognized forms of authority, providing strong exemplars of social proof or disproof, and finding the balance point where reciprocation and altruism support the compelling interest.

An argument can be made that reciprocation is the foundation of human social discourse, quite a fancy way to portray ongoing relationship dynamics. In commerce, within dyadic entanglements, within any schema where bargaining leading to social equity is the optimal outcome, reciprocation, more accurately reciprocal altruism leading to balanced conclusions, has existed since humankind emerged from pre-history. The reason? Social debt compels humans to seek compensation while avoiding the adverse psychological "drag effects" of owing anyone anything. Every form of contract is based on reciprocation at some level. The current discourse on social and racial injustice anchors the argument on a desire for equity and equality based on optimal reciprocity.

Influencers exploit the human need to belong or fit into a whole greater than oneself. The social proof context utilizes peer pressure and desired in-group inclusion while manipulating the psychological effect of the "fear of missing out" (FOMO) phenomenon. The artifacts bind the regulatory focus effect to measurably shortened attention spans, often leading people to make hasty, regrettable decisions. The catalyst cementing the influence dynamic is confirmation bias and misunderstandings about how one should utilize risk avoidance to limit sunk costs. The proof is self-evident. How often would someone openly admit to bad choices or bad outcomes?

Most of the time, the secret to making aligned ethical choices is adhering to dynamic choice theory. In this influencer context, one must always conduct due diligence before deciding and avoid stepping into the FOMO trap. Consider this perspective: If one does not have the right to make other people's choices, why would one allow others to influence one's decisions unduly? One cannot control attempts at influence, but everyone can choose to ignore external drivers.

Chapter Five

PONDEROUS ETHICAL SCENARIOS TO STIMULATE DEBATE

It is ostensibly fair to say the best way to understand the difficulty ethics adds to contemporary social contexts is to explore various ethical problems. However, since the author could produce an entire book with nothing but scenarios based on challenging ethical approaches, the five "ponderous ethical scenarios" included here are a minimal attempt to induce critical thinking about why ethics should be an essential topic for debate. Therefore, the author suggests that readers digest these five scenarios and discuss them with others to get a broad range of perspectives. Realistically, the scripts may also have a moral component for some readers, but readers should primarily focus on ethics.

FIRST RESPONDER'S NIGHTMARE"

*"We don't think about the first responders until we need them.
Like I don't unconsciously think every day about these people
and their lives, but that is what they are doing."*

Oliver Stark

*"When you first become an EMT, you are extremely gung-ho, with a sense
that you save lives; you are the antidote to all of life's miseries. You make
people rise from the dead. But when you are an EMT for a length of time,
you come to the grim reality that the number of lives that you save is small.
You stabilize people until they get to the hospital. You make sure they can
breathe and don't bleed to death and nothing more."*

Michael Stern

*"I've always seen first responders as unsung heroes and extraordinary people
because, when everyone else is running away from danger, they run into it."*

Dwayne "The Rock" Johnson

*"They know that tragedy is not glamorous. They know it doesn't play out
in life as it does on a stage or between the pages of a book. It is neither a
punishment meted out nor a lesson conferred. Its horrors are not attributable
to one single person. A tragedy is ugly and tangled, stupid and confusing."*

E. Lockhart

*F*irst responders are today's version of social heroes. Unfortunately, society tends to overlook police, fire, EMTs, and support personnel unless a) they find themselves in need of help or b) the first responders become "targets of derision" based on the actions of a few bad actors. It is challenging to embrace the police as helpful social actors; for example, if one assumes George Floyd's demise is a commonplace event. Statistically, bad outcomes are few when measured against a factual continuum of all possibilities. Fortunately, it is possible to fact-check the rarity of negative police interactions with the public. Still, one negative outcome becomes too many when victims emerge, leading to social outcry and protests.

One potential method for shifting the current social injustice narrative is to isolate the bad actors and effectively punish them for their actions. These evident social agents face challenges the rest of society would reasonably avoid at all costs; however, given the voluntary nature of pursuing law enforcement as a career, the presence of overwhelming stress should never be used as an excuse for making terrible choices or the discriminatory behavior often linked to overaggressive police misbehavior. Nevertheless, utilizing their high-stress environment was a natural choice for exploring the first of our ponderous ethical scenarios, which may serve to put a personal spin on being a first Responder.

Accidents are the most common scenarios where any number of first responders interact with the public they serve. Strangers are taking care of strangers. Well, what happens when the victims are family, not strangers? This familial context is the "first Responder's nightmare."

Two emergency crews get dispatched to an accident on a highway some distance away. The first report is five victims with various unknown levels of physical distress. While the crews speed on their way, a call reporting a second accident comes into dispatch. This newer accident has two victims, with one being critically injured. The dispatcher discerns from the transmitted narrative how the second accident involves the wife of one member of the two dispatched crews. Debating the actions occurring next is, by definition, an ethical problem. Two facts and one question must set the stage for keeping the debate "real."

One possible scenario, having one crew bypass the first accident, potentially reducing the number of available trained personnel "on the scene" where they might be essential to delivering proper care, could occur. Two, the response time for a critical victim is paramount for positive outcomes, meaning knowing the second accident has a severe injury adds a high-stress component to the scenario. The dispatcher does not know if the severe injury involves the wife or the other person, creating an "incomplete information dynamic." Three, how many ethical questions apply to the scenario? Be creative and explore where you may find conflicting decisions and potentially compelling answers based on your reality. Also, be aware of an essential fact; most jurisdictions and codes of ethics preclude first responders with familial ties from medically interacting with other family members except in rare, unavoidable contexts.

"FAMILY OR SOCIETY?"

*"Young man, should I press charges against your Mom?" These words
shocked the mom trying to get her son into his middle school one morning. As
she removed him from the car, a teacher approached and asked the question.
The assumption was that the parent was committing some form of abuse
by removing the child from the vehicle. Luckily, the son said, "No, that's my
mom. I am the one being a problem." Name withheld by request*

*"Have you ever noticed how parents can go from the most wonderful people
in the world to totally embarrassing in three seconds?"*

Rick Riordan

*"While we try to teach our children all about life, our children
teach us what life is all about."*

Angela Schwindt

*"There's nothing that makes you more insane than family. Or more happy.
Or more exasperated. Or more secure."*

Jim Butcher

*H*ow does one choose to traverse family issues having the potential
to spill over into society? The instinctual response would be to
isolate and protect the family or a family member while letting other
social players deal with the collateral effects. Unfortunately, with an

infinite level of possible scenarios to choose from, the selected story in this example is a version of the far-too-common situation involving bullying.

Bullying is present in all cultures globally. Some bullying, such as harassment, is overt and easily identified. Most bullying, however, is covert and hidden from prying eyes. This type of bullying is pervasive and involves the bully inducing constant fear within their victims. The bullying is especially devastating when the bully targets the family or comes from a family member.

Consider three versions of the dynamic:

A. One is when a family member is a perpetrator.

B. Two is when the family member is a victim.

C. Three is when both perpetrator and victim are members of the same family.

Joe is hard at work when he gets the dreaded call from the school. His son, Joe, Jr., has repeatedly been accused of picking on another student. Thus far, the administrators have handled the problem, but "junior" has reached a threshold where expulsion is required if parental notification and intervention do not work effectively. A second consideration creating a more profound problem is when "junior" claims he is merely copying what dad does at home. Junior's claim implies domestic abuse occurs within the home environment, which raises the situation to the level of mandatory reporting. The administrator has implemented the compulsory reporting protocols.

This exploration includes all three versions of the bullying dynamic. The twist shows how convoluted ethics can become when multiple factors include multiple players, primarily when a player (in this case, junior) might function as both perpetrator and victim. Does mandatory reporting create an opportunity for change or incite more problem behavior? Does the choice made by the administrator serve the parties, the general society, and at what level? Discuss this dynamic with peers and explore ways to change the dynamic for all involved and peripheral parties. Focus on how preventing future events serves the interests of society.

"CAMPUS HI-JINKS"

*"It doesn't matter, what you were wearing, what you look like,
nothing. Watch the nature channel. Predators go for the easy prey."*
Mindy McGinnis

"What you reckon to make him do a thing like that?"
"Beats me. Just nasty."
*"Well, they ought to take **her** out of school."*
*"Ought to. **She** carries some of the blame."*
Toni Morrison

*"Justifying a demonic act does not make the actor less demonic;
justifying makes the negator more complicit."*
Glenn Hefley

The most perceptibly challenging ethical discourse on campus is the contemporary approach to allegations of campus sexual assaults versus consensual sex. Repeatedly, reports of sexual assault evolve into a test of honesty, a "he said-she said" puzzle to navigate, and an assumption of unabated sexual promiscuity on campuses. The author shall not debate the issue of unconditional intimacy contexts in this forum. However, a deep dive into campus life is where ethics can be explored, especially in the context of socialization, dating, parties, and the word "no" versus a conceptual adoption of the importance of a "qualified yes."

Many students do not live on campus due to oppressive costs. The urban university and the online campus scenario have become the day's rule, where students commute to school or attend digitally. The dynamic may continue to evolve, but many students who seek to enjoy campus life outside the classroom still occupy dwellings on or near campus. Universally, the university world is suited to single life and co-ed interaction. The well-deserved image of "party central" is alive and well on most campuses. Students love to party!

Dating is a social reality when the environment includes many available people, which students commonly refer to as a "target-rich" environment. Unfortunately, "target" has become the operative word. Young men and women are prone to exploring boundaries and having an opportunity to "hook up," a contemporary reference for consensual sex. However, especially in party environments with flowing booze and the potential for available drugs, many students find themselves in the proverbial "yes-no" sexual scenario. Admittedly, many students seek ways to reduce inhibitions, but the choice to "open up" often leads to unintended consequences.

What happens when the participants are incapable of consent? The test for consensual sex has been defined as "no means no," with most of the conflict emerging from when "no" might be uttered. It is time to change the script, removing most, if not all, of the ambiguity from alleged campus sexual assaults.

Instead of a qualified "no," defined as an "opt-out" choice, both participants must "opt-in" with a suitable, unambiguous, unimpaired, and sustained "yes." Suppose either party is under the influence, up to or beyond the capacity to state a qualified yes based on levels of incoherence. In that case, the answer must be viewed legally and functionally as an automatic "no." The concept holds action potential if 100 percent of campus faculty and administrators transparently drive the initiative. Impairment removes consent as a possibility and creates an instantaneous barrier, adding to the time and distance element of "no." From an ethical perspective, sustaining the status quo is unacceptable when many courts are hesitant to apply justice within "he said-she said" scenarios.

Before moving to the following scenario, the "alone test," spend some time debating and exploring with peers how you see this high-charged ethical topic; the discussion should explore social norms, victimology, fairness, and be mindful of how justice has historically been unevenly applied based on how courts interpret distinct contexts under their jurisdictional microscope, often with confidentiality restrictions. Each case stands alone on its merits. Do not judge. Instead, explore the ethical perspectives.

"THE ALONE TEST"

*"Ultimately, the only power to which man should aspire
is that which he exercises over himself."*
Elie Wiesel

*"We achieve emotional equanimity and self-control by discovering how to
live in accord with our capabilities, character, and evolving ethical values."*
Kilroy J. Oldster

*"One's dignity may be assaulted, vandalized, and cruelly mocked,
but it can never be taken away unless it is surrendered."*
Michael J. Fox

*"The only real conflict you will ever have in your life won't
be with others but with yourself."*
Shannon L. Alder

*"Who you are in public is a test of your conviction;
who you are in private, integrity."*
Criss Jami

"No one should ever compromise the dignity of another human being."
Sarah Addison Allen

"Dignity is as essential to human life as water, food, and oxygen."

Laura Hillenbrand

Anyone who has ever played an individual sport has faced a version of the "alone test." The sports context is an extraordinary one because the only people confronting potential harm (to their honor or image, not any physical concept of damage due to injury) are involved in the sport or function as their immediate support group. Golf is a sport many people use as an example of the "alone test" since the rules require self-refereeing and self-imposed penalties. Other versions of the alone test may bridge morals and ethics; however, the lesson to be learned is specific to fundamental mental processes and how one projects self-imposed expectations. The "alone test" example shared here is one related to the author by a mentor long ago. The scenario exemplifies an "obligation" and consideration for "to whom it is required."

A senior-age husband visited his comatose wife in an assisted living home daily, often staying from early morning to well beyond the supper hour. The nursing staff could see the harmful effects of long hours on his health, and one suggested he take a day for himself. He politely declined. The caregiver questioned his logic by saying, "your wife will never know you were not here." His uniquely telling response, "I would know," indicates the ethical considerations involved were his and his alone.

The story comes across as a heart-wrenching display of noble character and a significant self-awareness about how one should perceive, then address self-expectations. The gentleman's resolve to project his love despite no possibility of recognition is well beyond anyone's expectations but his and is a quintessential exemplar of how dignity works in real-time.

Would any reasonable person question another person's need for respite? Probably not, but this gentleman ignored personal needs out of hand. The context shows virtue ethics in superb detail when doing the right thing at potentially high personal cost (in this case, his health and well-being) is often an individual choice applying to the one making a choice. A revealing but relevant question based on our exploration of ethics might be, "Would you have the fortitude to be this strong ethically?"

"EXPANDING BEYOND
THE TROLLEY DILEMMA"

*"When people consider the **trolley problem**, here's what brain imaging reveals: In the footbridge scenario, areas involved in motor planning and emotion become active. In contrast, in the track-switch scenario, only lateral areas involved in rational thinking become active. People register emotionally when pushing someone; when they only have to tip a lever, their brain behaves like Star Trek's Mr. Spock."*

David Eagleman

"If kids come to us from strong, healthy functioning families, it makes our job easier. If they do not come to us from strong, healthy, functioning families, it makes our job more important."

Barbara Coloroso

"Dharma or Ethics and Morals are the Fundamental Set of Rules created for those who want to Play the Game by those who are Inside the Game."

Vineet Raj Kapoor

"Although these days we commonly talk, hear, or read about 'ethical dilemmas,' those difficult situations in which we truly are perplexed as to the right course of action; it is crucial to recognize that these dilemmas, for most of us, represent the exception and not the rule in our lives. What typically is

*the rule in our daily lives is not a matter of knowing what is right and good
but having the character to do what is right and good."*

Russell W. Gough

*"For the vast majority of us who reside in the troubled middle,
there are no easy answers to the ethical dilemmas that biotechnology
can pose. As biotechnology moves forward, we'll have to carefully evaluate
each application on its own terms, trying to balance what's in the best
interests of an individual animal with what's good for its species
as a whole, for humanity, and for the world we all share."*

Emily Anthes

*"The philosopher Edmund Pincoffs has argued that consequentialists and
deontologists worked together to convince Westerners in the twentieth century
that morality is the study of moral quandaries and dilemmas. Where the
Greeks focused on the **character of a person and asked what
kind of person we should each aim to become**, modern
ethics focuses on actions, asking when a particular action is right or wrong.
This turn from character ethics to quandary ethics has turned moral
education away from virtues and toward moral reasoning. If morality is
about dilemmas, then moral education is training in problem-solving."*

Jonathan Haidt

Everyone who has reached any educational level involving philosophy or sociology has heard of and discussed the "trolley problem." Additionally, the consensus among students and faculty is that no viable solution exists. The term "dilemma" asserts a similar conclusion. A dilemma is defined as:

A situation in which a difficult choice has to be made between
two or more alternatives, especially equally undesirable ones;
a challenging situation or problem; an argument forcing an
opponent to choose between two unfavorable alternatives

Ancient Greek philosophers termed dilemmas a "double proposition." Modernity has expanded the Greek characterization to a broader domain where two or more solutions may exist with equally flawed or undesirable outcomes. Therefore, the sensible approach is to accept the one commonality, the universality of poor results, as the only option.

Since the trolley problem has been beaten to death, let's explore a few modern dilemmas. The three chosen are a political disclosure problem, conversations about challenging social issues with one's children, and factual versus bot reviews in digital marketing. These three are normalized dilemmas present in most people's lives.

Disclosing one's political leanings to business peers or clients can have devastating implications. So what are the potential paths one might take? Disclosing and risk altering relationships, avoiding disclosure and risk being badgered relentlessly, or refusing to disclose on personal principles are three common possibilities. So let's explore where each takes someone hypothetically.

Modernity politics has devolved into a contentious affair. Choosing a political party or cause to support has ramifications; many can or will impact one's social standing, sometimes for decades. Does one "fit in to get in" or take a more ethical position of full disclosure and risk a well-curated image? If taking a deeper look, would the potential impact on others, such as family and friends, shift the ethical perspective?

Integrity is essential; when considering one's position on this dilemma, no blaming, shaming, or judging can be included, so set aside one's preferences and explore this with a purely ethical discourse. If everyone is honest, no good solution presents itself. Regardless of choice, there are many negative artifacts and fewer positive ones. Let's consider the following dilemma, the second of three.

How would one approach a third-party bystander issue with one's children? Research shows that bullying is substantially reduced when a third party steps in to defend a victim, verbally or by getting assistance. However, taking action could expose one's child to future retaliation. Do you owe a duty of care to your child beyond teaching them what the appropriate action might be? There are many choices within this dilemma, one being role modeling actively intervening, another being an uninvolved witness taking future action, or avoiding the issue entirely, to name a few. Again, if honesty is essential, there are few good options because all may lead to future adverse consequences.

The third challenging scenario is broader in scope, so let's narrow it down. Should someone place disingenuous reviews online? Regardless of what form "disingenuous" takes, such as dishonest claims when never using the product or giving bad reviews because of a personal conflict that has nothing to do with the product itself, is it ethical to post or knowingly allow others to post without reporting the "in bad faith" act? The obvious answer is to inform someone about the improper review or not intentionally make a false representation.

Many other dilemmas exist across society. For example, should one download songs that require royalties without paying? Should one post a funny picture of a friend without considering the consequences, just for a few laughs? What about plagiarism in the modern information-dense digital space?

Contemporary humans often hinge their short-term ethical decisions on their risk exposure. Haidt's quote sums up modernity and why ethics are skewed. The ancient philosophers placed ethics squarely on character projection and asserted that humanity had zero wiggle room for error. No judging here; however, it seems the ancients, with their virtues, were at the upper end of the slippery slope of ethics, standing in relative safety compared to modern ethical perspectives. So, finding clarity through insight might come from the following two sections on interests.

"COMPETING INTERESTS-CONFLICTED MINDS"

*"Aristotle argued on the issue concerning the whole of ethics:
In many cases, a proper decision requires the application of a kind
of practical wisdom that cannot be reduced to a rote application
of precise rules. Context and choice remain critical factors."*

D Groll

*"What is life? Life is living in this moment, experiencing
and experimenting, but experience isn't life.
Life is reflecting and meditating, but reflection isn't life.
Life is helping and guiding, but philanthropy isn't life.
Life is eating and drinking, but food isn't life.
Life is reading and dancing, but art isn't life.
Life is kissing and pleasuring, but sex isn't life.
Life is winning and losing, but competition isn't life.
Life is loving and caring, but love isn't life.
Life is birthing and nurturing, but children aren't life.
Life is letting go and surrendering, but death isn't life.
Life is all these things, but all these things aren't life.
Life is always more."*

Kamand Kojouri

"You will prosper if you focus on competing with yourself and constantly challenging yourself to be a better person."

Happiness Shuma

"A whole mind cannot create chaos. A conflicted mind can create nothing else."

Hugh Prather

"We are all human, with evolving, never completely predictable thoughts and feelings. We are all complex, however much we do or don't acknowledge and express it. We are all human. We are all complex."

Shellen Lubin

People find themselves in "competing interests" scenarios often. A simple competing interest example aligns with being hungry versus needing to work out and avoid calories. Although this context has limited ethical markers beyond one's perception of an acceptable biological reality, it is a robust example. The example also corrals the secondary factor necessary for exploring competing interests: "How does one resolve the duality while experiencing a conflicted mind?" Enough of the shallow end. Let us dive into a deeper exemplar with action potential for conflict anchored in an ethical problem.

In a multigenerational family context, members of the younger generations face difficult decisions and the necessity of holding difficult conversations with and about elderly family members. One of the most engaging discussions is when to take away the car keys. One must consider the competing interests bidirectionally to enhance one's perspective.

"Grandpa" does not want to bother his children or become a burden; however, he presents as a risk to himself and others, having been involved in three fender-benders in the past six weeks. Our elderly gentleman also wants to keep his current evolving relationship with a "friend" hidden from prying eyes, specifically family eyes. Grandpa's competing interests are a) independence, b) privacy, and c) active aging versus his safety and the control of his descendants.

Grandpa's oldest son wants his father to be safe, so taking the keys becomes an awkward conversation with a potentially gut-wrenching decision on the horizon. Moreover, he suspects his father has a new love interest in his life, which throws a wrinkle into the looming conversation. The son's competing interests are the father's safety versus a) happiness of the father, b) preserving their mutual independence while avoiding interdependence, and c) the father's privacy while still socially involved.

Ethically, the son is primarily responsible for allowing his father to have a fulfilling lifestyle if functionally possible. The conflict arises from whether the father should still be driving. There are options, such as aging in place or entering a senior-focused accommodation to minimize driving intentionally. Unfortunately, these options often increase the conversation's difficulty instead of mitigating the problem because the elder participant perceives a loss of dignity and many personal freedoms. Other real-world considerations may or may not be present, such as asset management, whether the father has enough affluence to pursue any options or enough health to engage in active "anything." Ultimately, the loss of dignity, the most egregious psychological effect, implies social irrelevance and potentially causes irreparable harm.

The elder "inevitable slide into dementia and beyond" scenario is like a slithering snake. It can and does go through many convolutions and difficult conversations, serving as a crucible for the concept of competing interests for people at each end of the spectrum. Unfortunately, conflicted minds and sometimes actual conflict are the norm, not the exception.

Before heading into a younger generation example of an ethical problem, ponder how the scenario described might play out in your sphere of influence. As one who has experienced this scenario firsthand, the author can assure readers that this "bumpy ride" leaves scars on all participants and rarely leaves anyone fully satisfied. Take the position of the elder and the younger party in turn. Be imaginative but set a time limit for yourself. This type of exploration can become convoluted rather quickly and frustrating since each participant has unique play factors. It may be helpful to consider how many excellent outcomes are possible, but only when all parties exhibit universal positive regard.

"COMPELLING AND CONFLICTING INTERESTS"

"I think you have to do the stories that interest you and hope an audience likes them, rather than doing stories that you think the audience will like, whether you like them or not. I think there has to be something that you find compelling and interesting, and hopefully, an audience will agree with you."

David Shore

"It makes sense that whatever the topic is, it's more compelling if you can provide the audience with a range of perspectives, and you can cross disciplines. And you don't have to control what people take out of it."

Bernice Johnson Reagon

"Real motivation is that drive from within: You know where you are going because you have a compelling image inside, not a travel poster on the wall."

Denis Waitley

"In any moment of decision, the best thing you can do is the right thing. The next best thing is the wrong thing. The worst thing you can do is nothing."

Theodore Roosevelt

"The man on top of the mountain didn't fall there."

Vince Lombardi

"Never give up on something you can't go a day without thinking about."

Winston Churchill

"You will prosper if you focus on competing with yourself and constantly challenging yourself to be a better person."

Happiness Shuma

"I am competing with what I am capable of."

Michael Jordan

"Life is not a competition. Each one is on their journey. Live according to your choices, capacity, values, and principles."

Anonymous

The previous section explored competing interests and how they manifest through internal conflict. Here, a pivot will shift the exploration to a juxtaposed dyad of interests, compelling versus conflicting. So let's start with definitions.

> Compelling-evoking interest, attention, or admiration in a powerfully irresistible way; not able to be refuted; inspiring conviction; not able to be resisted; overwhelming

> Conflicting-incompatible or at variance; contradictory

Some illuminating ideas emerge from the definitions. At first blush, conflicting is a "bounded reality" concept, while compelling is comparatively infinite in scope. Although a conflict may arise within any environment and between any number of stakeholders, "conflicting" connotes a divisive context existentially. Finally, compelling can apply to a desire for or against some "thing." Therefore, "conflicting" and "compelling" form a harsh binary with compelling as the asymmetric power magnet.

However, when inserting ethics and interests considerations into the matrix, compelling and conflicting gain profoundly different meanings. A "compelling interest" overrides all other matters due to its insular focus. "Conflicting interests" have the unenviable trait of being equally compelling, confounding the drive normalized insular focal points create. For example, the interest matrix has entered the dilemma domain instead of offering an easy decision.

The optimal way to approach the juxtaposed contexts is through their extended ethical artifacts. In most scenarios, a compelling interest hinges on its "rightness." However, in outliers bound to one's compulsions, the negative traits may take someone down a dark path. Who hasn't faced temptations that anchor in some "thrill effect" due to risk factors? One must choose the ethical approach while overcoming temptation, especially when ignoring a fierce compulsion to act irrationally.

Let's utilize a different vector to compare interests. What happens when conflicting interests have equally negative risk factors? One should anchor the choice on an overarching compelling interest to reduce or avoid risk. Choosing to do nothing instead of increasing risk isn't always apparent, but it is the optimal choice.

A significant alternate interest matrix adds complexity to the picture. For example, how does one choose when a person has equally compelling passions to consider, and neither has risk in play? Given how humans universally regret the choices they "didn't make," any choice made under these circumstances will always create a conundrum leading to regret. Let's admit this is one of the "unresolvable" dilemmas; make a choice, and hope the intrinsic locus of control discussed earlier in the book manifests favorably.

Finally, all interests have a compulsion artifact. If the appeal within the interest triggers enough compulsion to make it transcendent, most people will choose to pursue the goal regardless of potential risk or tangible harm. Therefore, a hyperbolic, out-of-control compulsion creates significant risk irrespective of magnitude or directionality. Conversely, traversing life without experiencing compelling passions would be unthinkable for most people.

Does the irresistible draw of compelling interests add flavor to anyone's existence? Most behavioralists agree that the interests matrix aligns with one's risk tolerance versus risk aversion choices and may hinge entirely on how someone perceives risk within their worldview. Conceptually, the potential risk is the "spice of life;" some prefer less while others seek more and more. But, regardless of which end of the continuum someone occupies, should it matter as long as ethical behavior is included?

CONCLUDING THOUGHTS ABOUT ETHICS

"Any tool can be used for good or bad. It's really the ethics of the artist using it."

John Knoll

"The most important ingredient we put into any relationship is not what we say or what we do, but what we are. And if our words and our actions come from superficial human relations techniques (the Personality Ethic) rather than from our own inner core (the Character Ethic), others will sense that duplicity. We simply won't be able to create and sustain the foundation necessary for effective interdependence."

Stephen Covey

"In just about every area of society, there's nothing more important than ethics."

Henry Paulson

"Have the courage to say no. Have the courage to face the truth. Do the right thing because it is right. These are the magic keys to living your life with integrity."

W. Clement Stone

"So I think ethics is the broader thing that's less focused on prohibitions and is more perhaps looking at principles and questions and ideas about how to live your life."

Peter Singer

"Action indeed is the sole medium of expression for ethics."

Jane Addams

An infinite number of ethical contexts exist any interested party may consider, primarily embedded in philosophical works. The author has created Volume I, a "stand-alone" text, to be intentionally non-prescriptive and seeks to encourage debate. One of the favorite characterizations of the author is, "Life is messy. Deal with messy. While you are dealing with 'messy,' do not hurt others. Intentional harm would make life much messier."

However, several excellent quotes sum up ethics in the modern world. For example, Bill Moyers says, "Our very lives depend on the ethics of strangers, and most of us are always strangers to other people." His quote indicates that modern busy lives are anchored to the proper behavior of those normally invisible to others. Denying that reality becomes more challenging as people get more comfortable embedding ethics into their daily routines.

Ashley Montagu asserts, "It is the mark of the cultured man that he is aware of the fact that equality is an ethical and not a biological principle." Throughout the book, one theme consistently emerged; relationships and prosocial behavior anchor humanity, but proper behavior is an imperative eternally linked to one's ethical worldview.

Within the construct of ethical behavior, one context to consider is whether altruism is an act of beneficence or founded on being self-serving. Based on critical thinking, the answer becomes moot in the real world. Based on Maslow's hierarchy, every action should be a step toward transcendence; therefore, every purposeful act undertaken has considerable potential for enhancing one's self-image while being self-serving.

Ethics has many definable characteristics and possible forms, but, in context, all ethics stem from either deontological or teleological pursuits. Deontological (virtue) ethics require one to seek to do the right thing regardless of potential adverse outcomes. Teleological (ends justify the means) ethics obligate one to attempt to make a positively aligned choice based on creating optimal results for society over any consideration for the individual. Aristotle's eudaimonia resides in the balance between the two forms of basic ethics. Indeed, all types of contemporary ethics exist within a continuum somewhere between Deontological and teleological concepts.

Applied ethics is subjective and consists of choices aligned with interests and potential outcomes but attempts to prevent one from intentionally harming another. Socially aligned consequences depend on primes and triggers adopted through social discourse and are neither ethical nor unethical without context. Eudaimonia may be achieved through adherence to "unconditional equal consideration and intentional positive regard," which allows one to set aside the historical or learned behaviors attached to primes, biases, and triggers.

If no other lesson enters a reader's worldview, one should be memorialized. Whether or not someone can speak eloquently on ethics, one can live ethically. Actions are the only measure of "humanity" worth considering when contemplating prosocial engagement. Live based on the tenets of some version of the Golden Rule, even if those around you do not.

The concept of fairness should be absent from ethical consideration. Life can be fair, but "fair" does not ensure equality will follow; if equality is the prime consideration, any perception of "fairness" would always depend on perspective and context. In conclusion, no approach to ethics can guarantee the positive outcomes routinely associated with equality, equity, or the concept of fairness; nonetheless, everyone should acknowledge that the pursuit of all three should never cease.

Simply because something is unobtainable does not mean humanity should defer to less admirable goals. Thankfully, all paths to engaging in applied ethics have the potential for optimal conclusions if one pursues them to their natural end with an honorable intent. One should have an easy task completing any noble pursuit of an ethical existence if one's motivation focuses on achieving Maslow's version of transcendence or Aristotle's portrayal of eudaimonia.

EPILOGUE

Ethics seems to take a back seat to issues like a global pandemic. The global crisis sets the tone for subsequent renewal of the indomitable human spirit, making ethics an optimal consideration as humanity tries to get it right. Most people have shifted from wishing for the "old normal" to accepting change, allowing everyone to define their "new normal" uniquely. What could go wrong?

For starters, people tend to view new beginnings as a chance to change course without realizing the best approach would be to correct what went wrong with the past version first, basically cleaning out the refuse bin. That choice is like building a home on sand. Stability is lacking, and failure is guaranteed. The new normal will invariably take on the same flawed context as the old normal.

Besides, systemically endemic social problems require an ethical approach, first, during, and always. Using an ethical guideline as a foundation would shift humanity to a new place, unlike anything from prior societies. People would anchor on universal positive regard and abide by the tenets of altruistic reciprocity normatively. A community as described might take some getting used to for most people, but it would be a far superior place to occupy than most people face today. In the past, what has been tried to resolve endemic problems like social and racial injustice and discord has only marginally worked, with "marginally" falling far from the optimal target zone.

The book scratched the surface of what is a globally relevant topic. A third expanded edition is planned for circa 2030, hoping readers would contribute their thoughts to an appendix dedicated to their wisdom. The author holds no illusion about the completeness of this work and expects and invites dissenting comments. Unfortunately, the topic is too vast, with too many opposing viewpoints to include more than a minute portion.

Given how the book's purpose was to encourage meaningful dialogue between any imaginable group of participants, the author must take a measure of joy from the effort and wait to see how ethical consideration manifests itself. In the author's biography page, potential contributors, or those wishing to debate the finer points contained within, may find several points of contact to consider. Until the next book or conversation, blessings.

GROUP DYNAMICS AND ETHICS

Group dynamics is a broad topic too large to tackle here. However, since this book is on contemporary applied ethics, the focus will be on three areas aligning with ethical considerations. First, behavior in a dyad or triad versus behavior exhibited when someone is in a larger group, particularly a defined "in-group, should be anchored in prosocial approaches. Second, the interaction between self-interest and acting for another should be balanced. Finally, how the crowd's wisdom and herd mentality diverge should be based on critical thinking focused on context.

Relationships drive social interaction. The simplest form of a relationship is a dyad, a pairing of individuals. Triads emerge when a third party joins the pair. In relationship coaching, dyads are the preferred dynamic due to the inherent power balancing present. Working with triads introduces group dynamics where manipulation occurs based on asymmetric power imbalance, often encouraging conflict scenarios to develop. No one can choose sides when a side is defined as "one." Dyads produce solid and durable relationships, while triads more often result in discord comparatively. The illustration shows how complex dyadic entanglement can become, yet dyads remain the most potent social influencing context.

Moving to a group larger than three usually influences an in-group/out-group effect. Smaller in-groups suggest music groups, close neighbors, individual participant sports teams, a group of cheerleaders, a drama cast, or numerous other groups. The group has common goals and interests. Conflict is possible but rarely occurs, mainly because being the agent of disagreement usually gets one removed from the group. An excellent term for what drives in-group dynamics is "cohesion."

The out-group effect is a "barrier to inclusion" effect. In social interaction, someone usually must earn an invitation to join an in-group. Everyone without an invitation is "out." Being in or out influences self-esteem, self-image, a sense of belonging, or feeling like an outcast for whatever reason.

The ethics involved in the first area emerge from how falling on either side of a social line in the sand impacts one's perception of social relevance. Plus, competing interests enter the equation as someone moves from a dyad/triad scenario to a larger in-group/out-group context. For example, two opposites may interact well as a dyad regardless of differentiation artifacts like gender, race, heritage, or religion; however, behavior shifts to preserving one's place within an in-group at any cost, including damaging a dyadic relationship. Why? Fear of exclusion is the primary reason for otherwise damaging behavior, which prompts the second area under consideration.

Intuitively, one should act to preserve meaningful relationships regardless of all outside factors. Observed normative social behavior aligning with abandoning a friend to protect group identity is counterintuitive for humans. Unfortunately, the abandonment scenario plays out repeatedly across America. Ethically, the optimal choice would revolve around building relationships across barriers to mitigate the abandonment effect, which is usually soul-crushing to both dyad members. Historical adherence to a socio-cultural silo effect is front and center in this conflicting interests conundrum. Undoing the damage created by segregation requires acting altruistically for the "other."

Arguably, acting for the other seems counterproductive, but research shows this as a social fallacy. The connection between acting in self-interest and concurrently for others is reciprocity, which aligns with any version of the "Golden Rule" in existence. Working for others' benefit is easily more demanding, especially if one cannot guarantee that others will return the social gift of consideration. A measure of faith is required, perhaps some patience, as others may need time to recognize the need to reciprocate.

Consider a robust worldview one should adopt: being a better person through effective role-modeling, forgiving occasional missteps as others learn the ropes of prosocial engagement, and a willingness to mentor others into becoming role models. Finally, one must explore the social cousins, the wisdom of the crowd, and the herd mentality. The "wisdom of the crowd" aligns with optimal paths to social harmony.

People mimic what works well for others and ignore seemingly successful outliers. The best restaurant to choose is bustling because it must have some attractive attributes drawing people through the doors. A contemporary twist on the wisdom effect is "FOMO," the fear of missing out, a social context oldsters like me would characterize as keeping up with the neighbors.

Herd mentality is a weak version of the "wisdom of the crowd" context. People follow people because it appears to be the right thing to do, but without much aforethought. One example is a few drinks with the group from work to keep up appearances. Wisdom rarely enters the picture.

The divergence of the wisdom of crowds from herd mentality is linked to ethical choice. Herd mentality behavior leans toward an absence of ethical thinking, while the wisdom of crowds dynamic leans a bit toward "wanting" to make an ethically aligned choice. Some people would suggest the divergence is splitting hairs, and they may be right, depending on the context. The best advice is to do what "feels" right.

CHOICE DYNAMICS AND ETHICAL BEHAVIOR

The Flow of Behavior with a Focus on Choice Dynamics

Behavior, or misbehavior in some cases, defines human interaction and evolution. Each person has a mental process for understanding acceptable or unacceptable behavior. The process is inherent to the child-rearing process globally. What doesn't happen is any recognizable consistency in how humans across cultures apply their ethical ideology to the behavioral continuum. Instead, there is a flow to behavior that manifests, although inconsistently. The broad range of how humans perceive what activities are "acceptable" creates division and creates action potential for conflict. One may mitigate the negativity and increase understanding by exploring the Action Cycle and the Choice Dynamics Process.

Based on how any action occurs, there are four domains to understand. These four domains are cyclical, hence the name action cycle, and may take place out of sequence at times, but all are necessary for optimal performance. One area may hold predominance; however, this is subjective and aligned with one's base competencies. Let's begin with the details of the Action Cycle.

The action cycle process begins with acquiring or holding knowledge. The label for the first step or phenomenon is cognition (C), the seeking of knowledge through learning. How one determines the required information depends on the goals and accumulated knowledge one has before beginning the exploration. Once knowledge is acquired, a plan can evolve to utilize the knowledge effectively. Most people call this "strategy," while knowledge professionals call this metacognition (MC), the structuring of functional utility based on the acquired knowledge. These two domains evolve based on the contextual needs of how one chooses to pursue a goal, and one may define the pair as the cognitive base, which creates a human action potential.

Where the action takes place is defined as the behavioral track. One may find the two domains of motivation and actual behavior here. Motivation (M), primarily intrinsic, self-driven motivation, has infinite vectors for utilizing the action potential to drive behavior (B) toward optimal outcomes. Exploring motivation and the resulting actions would illuminate the subjectivity of choice and the subsequent vectors' infinite nature. One could choose to complete a goal with optimization depending on how the cycle progresses.

The Action Cycle is straightforward to conceptualize. For instance, the Action Cycle is omnidirectional, and one should treat the cycle as a living and evolving instrument (The Action Cycle has a separate in-depth article in Appendix C). Based on the Choice Dynamics Process, there are five phases for every action cycle. Competency in teaching others the "how-to" requires a solid understanding of the five components of choice dynamics. Failure to acquire the knowledge and implement the action cycle process creates gaps that manifest as delays or bad choices. Let's explore each step in the Choice Dynamics Process:

Phase one is the foundational period when all options align with one's growth environment, culture, primary sphere of influence, and significant caregivers. Each of these is a primary factor within most known and defined human developmental schemas; therefore, the domain is Primes (derived from "primal"). A prime is any knowledge that creates an action potential in each person to respond to any given stimuli. Primes, a universal construct, function within the neural environment and lead to many implicit biases. One may view primes as an instrumental part of one's worldview and the "why" of exploring others' actions. In bygone eras, one would "prime" a pump to get water to flow, an excellent example of how a prime creates an action potential leading to a result.

Phase two is the critical moment where any event, intrinsic or extrinsic, may function as a Trigger. A trigger stimulates an urge or compulsion to act or react to others. Triggers are objectively benign, existing as artifacts of primes. A prime may trigger a desire to hug a friend after a long absence; an alternate trigger may cause one to strike out viciously to counter a threat. Triggers exist because primes always create an action potential, meaning triggers are a universal given with a twist. Triggers are controllable. Every trigger has an on-off switch, unlike a prime, which one embeds from birth. The on-off switch aligns with personal choice.

Phase three is the DCP of the choice dynamics process, an instantaneous point in time. Up to this point, no action has occurred. The DCP, or decision choice point, is the first opportunity to define how an action potential may manifest. One version of the DCP is how the amygdala controls fight, flight, or freeze. Some DCP responses link to the human genome, such as many fears based on evolutionary predation or phobias. However, humans have relatively little control over these responses.

Higher-level responses are controllable and should have a more in-depth exploration. Neurologically, humans choose engaging, avoiding, or ignoring. Another recognized choice is liking or disliking.

The precepts to these options align with one's implicit biases; however, every human can set aside the implicit biases and make socially relevant choices, hopefully with an open mind. Note: All versions of the DCP are binary choices that fit nicely into a decision tree. No matter what happens in phases one or two, this third phase defines "who" one is.

Phase four is the manifested action domain (MAD). Hopefully, everyone who has access to the internet understands the permanency of anything posted. The choices resulting in actions are here today, everywhere tomorrow, and forever. The MAD defines the "who" one is through perspective-making. By projecting the DCP context into the minds of anyone who brushes up against either the actions themselves or the consequences of one's choices, one creates a permanent, challenging to enhance "image" of oneself and one's worldview or character.

Phases three and four often become cyclical and self-perpetuating when one MAD stimulates the creation of another DCP. Sometimes, this is within one person trying to undo the consequences of their actions. At other times, this influences another person to get triggered, which jump-starts their DCP. Everyone should be familiar with this binary domain. It is where conflict lives, constructed along a continuum of extreme responses on one end, and collaborative solution creation on the other end. So, what about Phase five?

Phase five is reflective and potentially evolving, also seen as enhancing self-awareness. Choices may influence a circling back process to phase three, then phase four, especially in highly divisive, polarized environments. Ideally, phase five would allow one to explore and comprehend the complexities of one's worldview embedded in phase one, creating a new action potential merging phases two and three into a "slower to trigger" DCP. Slower triggers would lead to the emergence of a potentially optimal choice paradigm and create a self-manifestation everyone should embrace.

Here is the Choice Dynamics Process envisioned as stairs. Note that the process has a life of its own, and any step may jump to the forefront, particularly reflection and evolution, which serves as a buffer zone limiting choices and protecting one's interests or existence:

5. SELF-AWARENESS (Experiential)

4. MAD (Manifested Action Domain)

3. DCP (Decision Choice Point)

2. TRIGGERS (Stressors)

1. PRIMES (Pre-conditions)

When considering the interaction between the Action Cycle and the Choice Dynamics Process, one must merge the two into an environment where all nine contexts can create momentum within a person. Again, each perspective is benign, absent of ethical or moral consideration, and may manifest anywhere within the behavior continuum. The subjective nature of any contemplation of "acceptable" creates the ethical or unethical, moral, amoral, or immoral projection humanity chooses to adopt based on context. The benign nature of primes assumes all worldviews are valid without attaching any preference to any worldview.

One prominent factor stands out among the nine contexts included in the Action Cycle and Choice Dynamics Process. Without exception, motivation links to the other eight, creating a fascinating matrix with evolving "compelling interests rationales" that can instantly force a pivot or course change. Moreover, outcomes of actions often dictate how one perceives goal achievement's viability or may even obfuscate a goal to the point where it becomes irrelevant.

Suppose an outcome creates an emerging, more vibrant, enticing goal. Would one be motivated to stay the course, pursue the old objectives, or be driven to change the target? Depending on the disparity between the two goals, the new duality may create another DCP to explore or navigate for optimization. Yes, the entire matrix is dynamic and continuously challenging. One should envision a format where nine factors can align with any other element within the template, which projects the possibility of infinite feedback loops and a new DCP.

Keep in mind the work of Dr. Glasser on the Choice Theory itself. Dr. Glasser, Choice Theory's founder, asserts that one may only control oneself in thoughts, words, and deeds. Therefore, the evolved projection of Choice Dynamics, an outgrowth of his theory, is a validated human process where society should progress positively, one person at a time.

BONUS ARTICLES ONE THROUGH TEN (EARLIER PUBLISHED WORKS OF THE AUTHOR UPDATED FOR THE BOOK)

CHANGING ONE'S WORLDVIEW-ONE CONCEPT AT A TIME
TODAY: "ACTION CYCLES-DESIGN AND UTILITY"

Actions Do Speak Louder Than Words and Have Consequences

The action cycle synthesizes the four-factor model, the multiple points of intelligence framework created by Sternberg and Detterman (1986), and how one's locus of control functions in dynamic contexts. The cycle works across all types of intelligence and supports growth universally.

The four-factor model intertwines mental and physical constructs into a cohesive framework. Cognition, basic knowledge, and meta-cognition, combining knowledge and application through strategy, are mental constructs. The material components are motivation, the why behind all choices, and behavior, the subsequent action following the other three factors complete the model.

Locus of control applies to the motivation portion of the action cycle. Motivation is generally split into intrinsic and extrinsic forms based on two concepts: locus of control within one's worldview and attribution. If someone believes they can dictate how the future should play out, they exhibit an internalized locus of control. When blaming, shaming, or victimology is present, people generally believe circumstance drives outcomes and harmful external locus of control has been activated.

Attribution follows a similar path. Humans are prone to a fundamental attribution error bias when they explore locus of control concepts. The error emerges in scenarios in perspective-making and perspective-taking models. For example, someone wishes to project victimization, blaming adverse outcomes on many external factors, but only when speaking of themselves. A familiar favorite is "the sun was in my eyes" to explain a failed attempt to do something done effortlessly otherwise. On the opposite side of attribution, the "why" of another person's similar outcome, the person's qualities come into play, an internal fault context.

Developing a positive action cycle requires one to set aside attribution outside of introspection. How does this work? The following questions point the way: Do I know everything necessary to move to the next step? Have I determined a strategy to accomplish my goal? Do I exhibit persistence, determination, and resolve to achieve my goal? Has the opportunity to act on my plan presented itself, and why haven't I taken the first step?

"Do I have the necessary knowledge" further explains how competency functions. Beginners approach a new activity with minimal or no ability through a lack of awareness labeled unconscious incompetence. As they gain knowledge, they are more aware of the activity's context but lack experience. Conscious incompetence is the best label for how people perceive this acquisition stage. Conscious competence, the subsequent step of knowledge gathering, combined with minimal but increasing utility, is where effective practice and focus gets the work done. Finally, unconscious competence is when expertise "happens" because the task or knowledge is fully embedded in the participant.

Determining a strategy is usually where action cycles are optimized. Failing to plan means planning to fail. A typical checklist should look like this:

Is knowledge acquired? Check.

Is the competency cycle complete? Check.

Has the outcome goal been determined? Check.

Does the subject demonstrate a willingness to follow through to completion? Check.

A strategy is the only variable missing. But how does one optimize a system to acquire a goal? First, ensure the relevant knowledge is sufficient for the task at hand. Are there any gaps in either expertise or competency? Part of any effective strategy is filling any gaps creating barriers to success. Doubts impact the next step deeply. Motivation, "why" someone actively engages the cycle, wavers if one doesn't believe the foundation is as perfect as humanly possible. Stay with strategy until the gaps disappear, mentally or figuratively.

A favorite statement one of my doctoral professors used when confronting a doctoral learner who was projecting doubts is, "Persistence and determination are far more important than intelligence." Actualized motivation hinges on that statement. When resolve is lacking, follow-through will also be absent, and action shall be impaired in academics and everything in one's quality world.

Consequences are the result of any process. Consequences imply a gentler approach to outcomes, preferable to projecting rewards or punishments. The goal is to influence an outcome favorably and reset the clock with another goal and action cycle. Life is dynamic, fundamentally a series of action cycles, like opening a door, crossing a room, and opening another door while rinsing and repeating.

The utility of action cycles should be apparent. Action cycles are coping mechanisms for mitigating procrastination while driving success. The adage, "A journey starts with a single step," applies here. Optimizing action cycles has qualifiers. Goals should be perceived as stretch goals to force intentionality while avoiding entropy or stagnation. Sharing the process with peers and interested stakeholders adds a layer of resolve. Anyone can endure failure, but facing the prospect of failing in someone else's eyes is unbearable, at least to most. Blessings.

CHANGING ONE'S WORLDVIEW-ONE CONCEPT AT A TIME TODAY: "TREATISE ON INTELLIGENCE MODELS" (FROM PAGE 33)

Three Models from Gardner, Spearman, and Sternberg

*I*n expanding Maslow's hierarchy and synthesizing how motivation and intelligence coexist, it was suggested that any intelligence theory functions as a practical canvas for exploring the four-factor model as it relates to humans and motivation. Many intelligence schemas exist. For simplicity, three were chosen to juxtapose similarities and differences between the models. Most notably, Intelligence Quotient (IQ), Emotional Intelligence (EQ), Social Intelligence (SQ), and Cultural Intelligence (CQ) do not appear in any model despite their ubiquitous presence in contemporary literature.

The Gardner Model exists as nine interconnected but distinct types of intelligence. The supposition within the framework asserts how all nine types exist in every human, however, at varying levels of magnitude. The resulting infinite combinations of intelligence create an exponentially higher number of manifested competency ranges leading to unique prodigies in every conceivable field. Gardner's theory has been refuted somewhat over time, but one aspect stands out. Intelligence magnifies through interconnectivity.

The Spearman Model separates intelligence into two categories, general and specific. Instead of labeling for types, Spearman focused on intertwining general intelligence (GI) with cerebral processes. The supposition is a primacy effect within GI and varying attribute expression levels for the five specific outlier processes. Again, all humans share the attributes but in unique patterns. Spearman's simplified model avoids the ultra-specificity found in Gardner's treatment, preferring to increase utility across all potential types of intelligence.

Sternberg created a model that reduces the intelligence debate to three interconnected, non-specific types through its innate simplicity. Sternberg covers every base included in the previously discussed models but avoids controversy by ignoring all attributions. Analytical, creative, and practical intelligence co-exist and co-create what defines human intelligence.

One must offer a position on the exclusion of IQ, EQ, SQ, and CQ by most intelligence theorists. For one, IQ is a measure of acquired intelligence with measurable biases due to levels of access to knowledge. Those with access will consistently score higher as a collective. The other three are context-specific and tend to increase exponentially through exposure to environments where they apply. One can learn EQ through interactions requiring emotional competency. Similarly, SQ and CQ are experientially enhanced; however, SQ and CQ carry historical baggage and need a tremendous introspection level to evolve. People with high self-esteem and positive self-images appear to acquire EQ, SQ, and CQ with relative ease compared to their image-challenged counterparts.

CHANGING ONE'S WORLDVIEW-ONE CONCEPT AT A TIME TODAY: "EMBEDDED SOCIALLY RELEVANT INTELLIGENCE"

The Role of CQ, EQ, and SQ

Cultural Intelligence (CQ), Emotional Intelligence (EQ), and Social Intelligence (SQ) have high standing when exploring human intelligence. Although Daniel Goleman has written multiple books on EQ and SQ, many experts do not elevate either concept to the longstanding prominence level of Intelligence Quotient (IQ), a long-established measure of relevant human intelligence. Combined with CQ, a newer addition to the field, one should perceive each as a treatment of application or utility, given how these three describe how humans navigate environments relevant to each theory.

For example, Goleman recently authored an article lamenting how consumers of his EQ context often misapply the theory with this quote: "Emotional intelligence is not about being nice to people; it is about optimizing behavior while understanding the emotions present in the moment." In short, it is appropriate social interaction between people.

Taking into consideration the environmental context, SQ and CQ should be perceived in the same manner. People capable of optimal behavior in cross-cultural or intra-cultural contexts demonstrate high CQ. Cultural intelligence is the field; the skill is cultural competency. All three forms of quasi-intelligence are composites of different mixtures of the types of intelligence described in Article II.

Enhancing socially relevant types requires focus and access to experiential knowledge, primarily through environmental immersion like optimal linguistics acquisition. Humans need interaction to establish a baseline of proper behavioral norms, especially when facing novel situations and contexts. Social and cultural gaffes are an ever-present reality early in an expatriates' career because they have not been immersed in the new schema long enough to acquire and adopt norms.

The barrier to competency in SQ and CQ is the same. Rigid social and cultural isolation prevents people from learning about dissimilar others. In America, historical distrust leading to silo-mentality is rampant. Overcoming the barrier means choosing to allow curiosity about others to manifest.

In today's intertwined global culture, all three socially relevant forms of intelligence must become focal points for any human wishing to optimize relationships critical to long-term success. One misstep, one perceived insult to someone's culture or social group, can spell disaster for one's future interests. The key to avoiding the life-altering affront is investing in EQ, SQ, and CQ before one faces challenging contexts. Embed the competency, and one can count on it when challenges surface.

CHANGING ONE'S WORLDVIEW-ONE CONCEPT AT A TIME TODAY: "ROLE OF BIAS IN OUR LIVES" (FROM PAGE 59)

Biases are Neither Positive nor Negative Without Context

What do humans need to know about biases in their world? First, bias indeed exists. According to several readily available sources accessible in two minutes or less online, there are well over 220 recognized biases; however, most have close cousins or duplicate minor differences. Assuming humans bias everything in their sphere of influence is a fantastic starting point for how uncontrolled bias can fracture human social reality. Second, recognizing bias is essential because biases impact relationships and create or influence conflict or harmony. Third, the potential impact of bias means one must develop coping mechanisms to mitigate the effects of biased preconceptions. Finally, coping processes are critical to sustainable human discourse. Let's examine the role of biases and coping mechanisms in the context of ethical discourse. The examination needs social context and must isolate particular tendencies relevant to choice dynamics.

Experts categorize bias by application, such as the four noted within the chart: Those leading to problematic thinking, such as too much information or not enough meaning, and those attached to the "choosing" domain, such as a need to act fast while still optimizing, or what one should remember. The chart breaks down each application but lacks essential details about the origin of distinct biases and their social relevancy.

Sociologists commonly speak about two types of relevant bias, implicit and explicit. Implicit may be differentiated further when considering origin points, subconscious, and developmentally implicit. Subconscious biases emerge from human prehistory and innateness, customarily based on in-group/out-group recognition patterns. Developmentally implicit biases align with conception, infancy, and artifacts linked to attachment styles and early learning environments. Finally, explicit biases come into play through early multigenerational family dynamics, social interactions, silo effects due to isolation from diversity, and many choice-laden contexts.

Many assume bias is a negative attribute; however, context is instrumental in any positive-negative bias perspective. For example, threat agency bias, a context where someone applies a past negative interaction to a future possibility, creates a fear response and can be life-saving whether the threat is real or imaginary. Therefore, the context must be the first consideration when examining bias.

One could spend considerable time exploring each bias but learning to recognize any bias's presence and effects is far more critical to positive social engagement. Coping mechanisms are not likely to develop in persons unaware of their predispositions, in persons who misunderstand how their biases influence behavior, or be adopted by anyone in denial of their known biases. Generally, uncontrolled biases lead to confrontation with people outside one's quality world, to good or ill effect. Luckily, bias mitigation is available to those motivated to change and avoid conflict.

The racial and social injustice protests of 2020 are an excellent (sadly) example of how bias impacts society. Applicable explicit cognitive biases are herd behavior, commitment effect, the availability heuristic, fundamental attribution errors, an overjustification effect, a self-serving bias, and projection. Of course, the list of potential biases in evidence during this contentious period could be expanded much further; however, these few are sufficient to demonstrate how biases of every conceivable type can impact society, no matter which side of an issue you support.

Bias challenges everyone. No one gets a free pass. However, society should focus on explicit bias over subconscious or implicit bias. Yes, all three forms are potentially damaging. But, unlike the other two, explicit bias comes with external baggage, making it a formidable challenge.

The external baggage is the requirement of an active "choice" to either sustain explicit bias or to actively mitigate the negativity inherent to most choices aligned with bias. One example of mitigation, a potentially optimal coping strategy, should be a catalyst influencing one's motivation to overcome our bias-laden tendency as a species.

Consider the dyads in your sphere of influence. When you focus on interacting with only one "other," regardless of who that other is, civility becomes paramount. The opposite effect may be equally valid. When you interact as a group, impressions and herd identity come into play, forcing most people to choose between competing interests: the dyadic relationship or the value inherent to group identity.

Depending on your resolve to act ethically, you must make a tough choice, or maybe not. But, regardless of how you choose, consequences shall follow. If you look closely enough, you will observe numerous scenarios where this coping strategy emerges. Choice dynamics suggests that only you may decide what path to take, what choices to make, and which potential consequences are acceptable.

One should take comfort in knowing that all humans must traverse this domain. Nevertheless, a society endures because enough people choose to act in one significant way: through altruistic reciprocity. The hope inherent to altruism is always how a good deed should continuously be repaid in kind, resulting in a beneficence feedback cycle.

Altruistic acts endure a level of risk. What if the other party acts selfishly? Ignoring the occasional negative outcome is where positive social change agents thrive. One must persist in choosing the civil act, prefer to support the relationships over all else, and resolve to turn the other cheek.

Modeling becomes a compelling example of an ethical choice for others to mimic. Over time, persistence shall win over the crowd. Turn negative biases on their proverbial heads. Blessings.

CHANGING ONE'S WORLDVIEW-ONE CONCEPT AT A TIME TODAY: "ROLE OF RELATIONSHIPS IN OUR LIVES" (FOLLOW-UP TO ARTICLE IV)

Dyadic Relationships are the Foundation to Peace and Harmony

Contemporary American culture is mired in two simultaneous, highly polarized, traumatizing conflict paradigms: global and domestic. It is crucial to consider the compounding effect of trauma and what it does to humans. First, I shall address the worldwide conflict and put it into an American perspective. Then, I shall touch on the social and racial injustice present in America from the historical context of slavery and the contemporary philosophy of 'self-segregation versus diversity in the community.' After each, I shall connect the two seemingly disparate conflicts by addressing the social role inherent to dyadic relationships and their importance to healing.

The International part of this discussion emerges from events unfolding over the last quarter-century, focusing solely on the Western versus Muslim context where most of the conflict lies. The initial attacks on the World Trade Center (1993), Mogadishu (1993), the attack on the USS Cole (2000), the collapse of the World Trade Center from terrorist attacks (2001), and numerous similar events have infuriated hard-core conservative Americans, leading to a belief system that embraces isolationism and hatred of all things and people not within their self-defined in-group. If the events are perceived as an ongoing collective, it becomes difficult to separate feelings from the group who initiated the attacks. Avoidance and hardline isolationism are egocentric reactions linked to the perception that Americans should pursue increased safety and security, the most basic human needs. The visceral responses have led to divisiveness, silos of self-segregation, and group-think reinforcement of differences, breaking down any semblance of conservative-thinking citizens embracing the social idea of community.

Agree or not, like it or not, this is the reality of the hard-core conservative stance. It is hyper-focused on the Muslim community but has ramifications beyond Christian-Muslim interaction. The discord creates perceptual disruptions in how most Americans see any other distinct group. Again, this is not an endorsement of any position, only clarifying and reframing facts with context. If taken from the opposing viewpoint, which becomes a justification for extremist groups like the Proud Boys, hard-core conservative Muslims seek to subvert all other people and religions globally to their belief system. The dynamic is not necessarily an American-centric problem, but hard-core conservatives in America see only the points that affect them and define their position, ignoring the broader context.

As for the racial conflict in America, it is necessary to set a foundation for the discussion. Most black citizens in America are descendants of a population forced into slavery. In American culture, it should be a well-established fact that slavery was abhorrent. Although it has been over 150 years since the end of the American Civil War, the truthfulness of the despicable treatment linked to slavery is permanently etched into the fabric of black culture, influencing the minority perspective, and rightfully so. Slavery in the New World, beginning in 1619, supposedly set aside in 1863 by President Lincoln, followed by a century of being treated 'less than' is impossible to ignore. Whites who hold contempt for blacks for any reason should contemplate this reality. How would you react to this historical yoke?

First, be honest. Slavery happened. If it didn't, the discussion would be about heritage and social injustice, not racial injustice. Throughout history, the conflict has been about land, resources, and a contemptuous form of colonial advantage over indigenous groups in multi-cultural contexts. Heritage was an underlying context, an artifact stirring emotions and getting people to engage in those conflicts; however, the most notable manifestation of all indigenous groups was skin color, making being "non-white" the dominant focal attribute.

However, it was not always a factor. Globally, more powerful groups enslaved weaker ones historically; this practice was experienced for multiple millennia and still exists in various contexts. In America, slavery ended "officially," but the effects linger. The current social and racial discord aspects stem from the empowerment of minorities to overcome 'less-than.'

How do these two conflicts inter-relate? Contempt. Hard-core conservatives, regardless of origin or group, American or fundamentalist, radicalized Muslim, hold others as 'less-than.' Wow. Straight out of humanity's handbook on slavery and cultural hatred. No one has the right to impose their will on another human, but that can be a conversation for another day. Let's examine a different path, shifting from conflict to peace and harmony, by delving into relationships, specifically dyads.

Dyadic relationships are the foundation of the social world. Regardless of the participant's background, race, heritage, socio-economic status, career choice, or age, dyadic relationships are where humans live and prosper. Two people establish some level of rapport to accomplish something (that something is immaterial, undefined, and infinite) together. In business. In one's personal life. Whenever, wherever. What is the key to how dyads become the pinnacle of human interaction?

Conflict exists in the area where interests collide, not rights. In America, rights are universal; however, exercising those rights is most assuredly not treated equitably for all groups. How does this affect dyads? Each party brings different baggage to the relationship. While pursuing interests, the baggage gets ignored for the most part, with peace and harmony intact. Conflict arises when a party looks to bring discord to the table. There are several relationships' truisms' to consider. "Those looking for a fight can always find one or start one." "You get what you seek." "Peace or discord, both are a choice. They are not inevitable based on any human standard."

In a different article, I detailed how I overcame historical hatred in a dyadic context between an Indian native and a Pakistani native working together at an organization. I convinced both to leave their baggage behind. They had to ignore the historical perspective of the conflict between their people. Instead, focus on their innate "sameness," focus on aligning interests, and enhance their mutual humanity. The actual dispute between the parties hinged on how unhealthy historical perspectives dehumanized people from the opposing reality. Dyadic relationship-building hyper-humanizes the interaction and secures an environment focused on peace and harmony, not conflict. Comparably, each time dyads achieve this type of collaboration in the Arab-Israeli world, peace becomes possible, even inevitable.

When hard-core conservatives on both sides start to pursue opposing interests, conflict increases between the parties. One may choose any of several regional disputes best suited to one's focal point or sphere of influence, regardless of global locale. Increased conflict due to competing interests remains a universal constant in every context. Dehumanization allows people to commit atrocities against others, humans, or the lower species they hold contempt for, which circles back to the "less-than" paradigm.

Do you want to move to a better, more peaceful place in your life? Engage in meaningful dyadic relationships while discarding the baggage (biases, preconceptions, labels, stereotypes). In examining every instance of discord stemming throughout my lifetime, each instance started with a collision between competing interests and an inescapable belief in an anchored position by one party or both. Solutions arose from allowing curiosity to emerge, which empowered both parties to drop any anchored certitude and embrace a level of uncertainty that could be overcome by taking a solution-seeking journey together. Together. What a concept.

Follow the five "Bs." Be brave. Be vulnerable at the same time. Be open to others. Be curious. Be flexible. Think about this. Buildings that are built to sway with tremors survive earthquakes. Buildings made as immovable objects are torn apart under the same stress levels. There might be a lesson there.

CHANGING ONE'S WORLDVIEW-ONE CONCEPT AT A TIME TODAY: "PERSPECTIVE AND SCHEMAS"

What, Please Tell Us, is a Dog?

*H*ow is it that dogs are such a varied species, and yet, without a doubt, humans and dogs can both perceive if a "dog" is a "dog?" Big ones, tall ones, short ones, small ones, but all defined as "dog." If you've seen one dog, you can identify them all.

That would be perspective-taking in a nutshell. Try other examples. One may see a window, a door, a roof, and perhaps a porch or garage, but I know this is a description of a house every time. One sees tires, wheels, side panels, headlights, doors, a steering wheel, and perhaps a roof. I recognize an automobile. My hat is off to Anthony McGowan, who wrote *How to Teach Philosophy to Your Dog*, for my outlook on man's best friend. Mr. McGowan projected perspective-making imaginatively, enhancing my point of view.

How does this work exactly? Humans love to categorize everything, putting labels on people, places, and things, a trait recognizable as specifically human throughout recorded history. One could easily say most humans are naturally-endowed experts at perspective-taking. Well, maybe so, but not as well as one might guess.

Humans do exceedingly well in the visual/spatial context but not so well in abstract thinking areas. Is a person a "good" person? One would think "good" depends on far more than appearances. Is the painting a "good" piece of art? Now we are getting to the deep end of the perspective pool. Judging art is subjective at best for most humans. Plus, there are nuances to the context. One might think some piece of artwork is technically perfect and not "like" the work.

Understanding perspective-taking needs to be juxtaposed with perspective-making, a process authors like Anthony McGowan utilize to significant effect, especially in abstract areas. Seeing a picture simplifies the process, but remove visualizations and describe your closest friend to someone else. Experts agree with the supposition that perspective-making is more complicated by several degrees than perspective-taking. For example, showing someone how to use a snowblower can be done post haste while describing the action takes many sentences, especially in scenarios where the receiver has never seen snow. Luckily, humans have shortcuts that make perspective easy.

Life is traversed through a series of "schemas." In social contexts, schemas are normative behavior aligned with one's physical location or circumstance. One example would be the difference between eating at the kitchen table versus the formal dining room, the school cafeteria, or a formal or casual dining establishment. Another well-known schema is how one dresses differently for work or play contexts.

Earlier in the book, the author created a schema to help define the reader's perspective-taking on location dynamics. By intentionally labeling the "me-to-us-to-others" continuum with relatable terminology, with me being "local," us being "quasi-local," and others being "global," the author utilized perspective-making to enhance a mental construct instead of a temporal context. Schemas can be functional when designed for a purpose.

Learning life's schemas is a balancing act between perspective-making by teachers, parents, and caregivers (familial or not) and perspective-taking by untried charges. Anyone who has taken a toddler to a restaurant for the first time can relate to this fact. Optimizing one's ability to navigate vastly different schemas can take a lifetime and tons of effort, and one needs the tools aligning with perspective to become a master during the process.

CHANGING ONE'S WORLDVIEW-ONE CONCEPT AT A TIME TODAY: "ASSIMILATION"

Assimilation is a Majority-Guided Myth

*I*n diversity training courses, facilitators tout assimilation as the optimal path to the panacea of belonging, but embracing assimilation is a load of excrement in the contemporary world. Why? Based on the definition of assimilation as applied to culture, assimilating is becoming like or "similar to" a majority member. The expectation is broader, with assimilation meaning to be indistinguishable from the majority. In other words, "invisible" is the expectation from the majority.

So, let's unpack this expectation through a critical thinking process. Fundamentally, the American administration of 2020 sees the world as "not white, not middle-class or upper-class, not Christian, God-fearing people," leading to "must not be American enough." It isn't enough to be born in America since many pundits ask others, "Where were you born?" This example of microaggression projects a misaligned version of entitled white superiority. The question insinuates how not being assimilated along a projected path of invisibility gives a majority group member the right to question their right to belong. Black, brown, Asian, and Latino (the use of the Latino descriptive as a catch-all bucket is too expansive to function as a viable paradigm for my taste) all get the same question. I know Mexican-American descendants whose families have been in this country for more than five generations.

Even funnier (sorry, not funny; quite pathetic, in fact) is when members of the white majority ask native American Indians to justify their existence somehow. It isn't despicable enough to consider that indigenous people have endured two-plus centuries of deplorably savage treatment; people still think of them as "inferior" because they can't assimilate along expected invisibility lines. The majority anchors on assimilation as an unreachable "holy grail" and utilizes the resulting differentiation to label those they deem "unworthy."

Now, a concise picture should be emerging. Assimilation is not an offer of equality, acting more as a stumbling block, an inescapable barrier to inclusion. Because the perception of a social barricade exists, many minority groups feel betrayed by those in their group who try to assimilate. Assimilation has become antithetical, a betrayal of hope, an illusion of openness tainted with the reality that those individuals from any minority group can never "assimilate." Assimilation is a myth and drives divisive conflict.

Does a better path to inclusion, social equality, and building optimal social equity methods exist? Yes, thankfully, one does exist. Next week, the series will move to a slightly better concept (still not optimal), the contemporary worldview on acculturation.

CHANGING ONE'S WORLDVIEW-
ONE CONCEPT AT A TIME TODAY:
"ACCULTURATION"

Acculturation is a Misguided Concept

Acculturation climbs above the quagmire beyond the concept of assimilation, opening society up to significant possibilities, yet, acculturation falls woefully short of acceptable. Where assimilation seeks invisible autonomy, acculturation steps out of the shadows, but how far? Acculturation takes a tolerance path instead of an expectation path, nudges the majority to allow cultural identity to exist, but falls short of embracing the power of vastly differentiated cultural norms. When any defined minority group interacts with the majority, expectation aligns with a minimalist cultural relevance approach. In simple terms, acculturation is socially defined as maintaining an appearance of assimilation while allowing the minorities to cling to their cultural heritage, hidden away under a self-selection, self-segregation fog.

Again, tolerance is a weak, unacceptance social projection of a majority power extended toward those they perceive as "lesser" within the crowd. The bridging effect forces interacting people to embrace PC, a meaningless gesture lacking a positivist environmental tone, existing as a deceptive projection of "kumbaya" on a massive scale. Kumbaya is a beautiful African song word suffering from a derisive connotation in contemporary usage. What started as "come by here" (translated) has evolved into "naïve trusting" without understanding social exploitation or blatant disregard since, "of course, we are completely tolerant of your cultural choices, as long as you keep them segregated and hidden from our expected norms."

Without a doubt, acculturation is socially preferential to assimilation. For instance, assimilation doesn't hide the contempt attached to the expectation of social integration through invisibility. Acculturation mitigates the condescension in many contexts, mainly where majority stakeholders utilize PC's precepts as realistic projections of voluntary inclusion. But, again, there are contexts where this falls short. Let's examine two:

One visible artifact of acculturation is the emergence of cultural appropriation. Cultural appropriation has a dark history based on how the colonial period led to forced annexation. Indigenous populations were incapable of blocking the removal of historical artifacts by colonialists, suffered from the loss of their cultural uniqueness, and were forced to participate in allowing their colonial overlord's attempts to adopt intriguing aspects of their daily lives. No debate is necessary about the negative approach to native populations during the colonial period of human history. For example, the colonialists perceived the appropriation as acceptable; the native population viewed the practice as a "misappropriation" of their world. And yet, there are bright spots if one can navigate claims of cultural misappropriation.

Cultural misappropriation hinges on an intentional act, taking, holding, copying, or using another culture's identity in any form. How does one determine "deliberate" or "intentional?" Contemporary examples of social indignation over claimed cultural misappropriation are rampant. Hairstyles, clothing worn to proms, and the naming of sandwiches in restaurants have been scrutinized by the cultural misappropriation police (social media). When thoroughly examined, the claims almost always lack substantive existence of deliberate misdoing by the person who supposedly overstepped.

Our contemporary society willingly embraces and exists in a constant state of cultural appropriation. I knowingly consumed Chinese, Mexican, Italian, South American, and Southeast Asian cuisines within the last month and devoured these items in establishments licensed to offer these delectable items locally. I select and wear clothing representing many global contexts through personal choice, and those choices are typically deemed appropriate regardless of my location. I own many clothing items I have acquired in my travels to foreign locations. Unless I am missing something, none of this has a negative slant, and I see the appropriation of all listed contexts as honoring and plausible based on my choices.

The second visible artifact of acculturation is our language. The English language is a mashup of global imports. Every interaction with another cultural group, especially those hidden from modern norms, gives our globally preferred communication mode a conduit to expand and become more concise. Linguists honor diversity and uniqueness by seamlessly adopting creative additions to the vocabulary and including them in the global linguistic catalog. During more than five decades of research, I have yet to observe any group becoming enraged about their inclusion into the global collective based on culturally appropriated language. As globalization continues along its inevitable journey, humans across the globe will invariably cease to see "English" as much as they will consider English as the overall "human" language, especially as the primary language of business and legal pursuits (Chinese is the native language with the most users but lacks global utility due to its lack of diffusion across populations).

I know this article only touches on the broad topic of acculturation. From a social perspective, acculturation still falls short of ideal but opens doors to a better concept. That higher order concept is "social amalgamation." The following article explores and amplifies the "amalgamation of cultures," the optimal social step for inclusion that can drive archaic views of assimilation and acculturation into virtual obsolescence.

Blessings.

CHANGING ONE'S WORLDVIEW-ONE CONCEPT AT A TIME TODAY: "SOCIAL AMALGAMATION"

Social Amalgamation-An Evolution of the Melting Pot Theory

*I*n contemporary social discourse, social amalgamation exists as the catalyst for blending many people and cultures into one group instead of allowing the masses to remain divided through disparate social-silo mentality choices. As noted in a previous article, assimilation ignores the potentially positive attributes of all people and cultures not identified as the majority, places an expectation of fitting in through invisibility, and creates barriers to minority inclusion at a visceral level. Acculturation, given birth as an artifact of colonial conquest, where the victors presumed much, such as they could take without giving compensation or consideration, has evolved as a bridge allowing for a measure of inclusion while maintaining the asymmetric power position of the majority. Social amalgamation stands as a path for society to upend the archaic, dysfunctional choices for decades voluntarily.

Historically, America has been called a melting pot. Wave after wave of immigrants reached her shores. Some people came here involuntarily, namely the ancestors of African Americans, as enslaved people forced from their homes and families to serve members of the old aristocratic colonialist regimes. Others came seeking freedom from oppression; others sought a better life. The ones who mirrored the physical appearance and acted like the majority fit within the era's norms and expectations (mostly, ask any Italian or Irish descendant for a rock-hard rebuttal).

In every other case, all others were and are still treated with disdain, although "disdain" is a mild word for most of what occurred and is ongoing during this sustained clash of cultures. As a result of antisocial treatment, contemporary America, even after two-plus centuries, is still mired in a context of a conflict between ideological forces within every segment of society, including indigenous people who are often absent from the equation. The sustained conflict collapses the melting pot ideology.

American exists as a contentious patchwork quilt. Silos of self-segregation are more the norm than the exception. The current Administration counts on this portrayal and attempts to drive larger wedges between the white majority and all other groups. The divisive discourse doesn't stop with race or culture. The efforts to create division seek to accentuate differentiation by attacking all groups equally. Members of the LGBT community, legal or illegal immigrants, and anyone not aligned with a misguided mantra of "Make America Great Again" are targets of the Administration.

Note: "MAGA" is a euphemism for "let's all go back to pre-1960 America," where blacks and all other minority groups knew and complied with their expected status within the broader concept of society. Should reasonably intelligent people view a "proven as dysfunctional" period in history as acceptable on any level? Certainly not "great" by any reasonable person's social outlook, which is debatable and depends on one's worldview and overall social perspective. MAGA portends an Administration wanting to control the patchwork quilt by dictating how many squares are in the quilt, who occupies the spaces, who their neighbors are, and whether some members of society belong in the context. The MAGA quilt represents a compromise between assimilation and acculturation, with no room for social amalgamation.

Amalgamation, defined as blending unique but separate parts into an alloy, thereby increasing utility, has measurable value when used in any social context. Beyond the base definition, especially during this divisive period in our country's history, socially-focused amalgamation becomes an optimal approach for every stakeholder to potentially embrace. Everyone can adopt or adapt to any cultural choice because everyone belongs equally regardless of demographic attributes.

Religion, specifically separated from the State by our Constitution, can become the ideal the Founding Fathers intended, a choice everyone may make without fear of reprisal. Every culture's best attributes should be allowed to emerge, coexist, or synthesize into new social realities through organic processes and personal preference for their natural place within society. If something doesn't fit, it will wither and die through natural selection, not by being forced out by violent clashes between misguided misanthropes.

Many readers may cling to the melting pot imagery, but this would be wrong. The melting pot projects and supports the ideas aligned with assimilation and acculturation, with all people's individuality dissolving into the soup. How do we replace the melting pot portrayal with a new perspective, as we must if we are to evolve into a superior version of our past selves?

Break the pot and constructively encourage the recreation of the quilt. Changing the narrative to align with and address existing dysfunctional microaggressions would be a fantastic starting point. Learn from the past, but keep it in the past, where it belongs. Penetrate the barriers to inclusion and collaboration, beginning with the silos of self-segregation. Breach the virtual walls separating groups where possible and create enough resolve through dialogue to soften the edges when knocking down the walls is problematic. Create a beautiful tapestry out of our society.

The pieces to this puzzle are all on the table; they need guiding hands to place each piece into a relevant, carefully collaborative projection of social beauty. Social amalgamation only happens by choice, not chance. Burn the quilt. Stop looking upon one another with fear, distrust, or hatred based on old, tired biases. We are all human; we should respect basic biological facts as the decisive reason to evolve beyond our shameful past of disenfranchisement and exclusion. Research shows dyadic interaction leads to familiarity and friendship if people come to the emerging relationships with open minds and hearts regardless of differentiation.

Yes, there will be temporary upheaval and adjustment. Historically, we know conflict will continue to emerge. Still, we have better choices than those occurring now, such as developing alternatives capable of mitigating hatred, replacing it with a curiosity about which options might optimize peace and commonality. Enlarging social inquisitiveness alone should be a bridging event, a path leading to robust relationships crossing, bridging, or crushing all prior social boundaries. The expansion of prosocial processes depends on extending one's hand at the right moment to the right person, who may not be like you in appearance or worldview but wants peace as much as you do. All it takes is curious dialogue, a willingness to learn about others, and an inclination to set aside any belief that "my way is the only way."

According to demographic projections linked to global migration patterns, birth rates, the impending disappearance of the "boomer" generation, and a natural pattern seen over centuries, not decades, America shall become a minority-majority nation before the year 2050. Minorities will, if they set aside their natural inclinations to self-segregate, become the biggest voting bloc in the new America. The white majority shall no longer exist, and no force known to man can alter this natural process from occurring. Members of the white majority may treat this as a call to arms, a bellwether projection of disastrous social upheaval, and take short-term actions to offset reality, to no avail. Nature marches on.

The rest of us, the global people willing to embrace a form of equality never realized on our planet, will extend a curious mind toward others, and we shall forge a fantastic future. The new reality will be "habituated normalization" based on a socially amalgamated outlook where we willingly choose our unique peace path. For centuries, humans have focused on differences instead of commonalities, and where has this taken humanity? A broken planet, many armed conflicts across the globe, numerically the largest and most significant number of displaced refugees in recorded history, and culture wars in virtually every country. Can there be any more compelling argument against an emphasis on differentiation?

America can be a great nation, be perceived as a great nation with admirable leadership, and have enormous potential for projecting a historical level of greatness globally, but not by embracing the obsolete past or seeking old ideologies like assimilation or acculturation. We only have one planet. Peace and inclusion on a global scale would allow the resources wasted on the military-industrial complex to hold optimal utility for more socially relevant needs.

History illustrates the difficulty of collaboration amongst our current global neighbor nations; however, common sense shows us that change must start domestically. America needs to build a boundless "virtual table," where stakeholders may exchange cultural ideas and enhance inclusion. A virtual table where everyone is welcomed to earn a seat via socially relevant processes, not held through legacy ownership or taken by force. "Out with the old" (unless it demonstrates a willingness to adapt) and in with the best chance for a better tomorrow. A social amalgamation of cultures where acceptance and inclusion replace the obsolescent projection of minimized tolerance and social disenfranchisement.

ANONYMOUS QUESTION FROM QUORA (SUMMER-2020):

"I'm conducting a study. Were you raised with any prejudices or biases towards any group of people? If so, how? What were you told? How do you feel now?"

Answer from Buddy Thornton-Author

MA-Human Services Counseling and Executive Leadership (Liberty University-2014); Doctoral Learner at Grand Canyon University

"Well, a thoughtful question, but not a well-informed one."

Every human ever born has subconscious biases. Genetic biases exist from early humankind's need to identify in-group safety from out-group threats. They have evolved over a half-million years and will never disappear. Experts identify these as subconscious biases because of their innateness and permanency. The boundary between a human's subconscious and innate genetic biases and implicit bias is blurry and delves into the nature-nurture debate.

Implicit biases emerge shortly after birth and are inherent in human development. For example, humans are most comfortable when they see themselves in the mirror of another. This type of bias connects to subconscious bias at many levels while concurrently acting as primes for one's action potential. These predispositions are also permanent, although they may be offset by consciously utilizing coping mechanisms. Unlike the blurred boundary between implicit and subconscious bias, a definable bridge connects internal forms of subconscious and implicit biases to one's explicit bias, the primary influencer for socially aligned behavior.

The most recognizable and damaging type is explicit bias, a learned behavior. Whether racial, gender, heritage, or choice-based during periods of early development, every in-group adheres to and learns explicit bias. People learn to differentiate themselves from others through organic exposure or multigenerational teaching. Sometimes, this leads to positive outcomes, but the efficacy of positive differentiation depends solely on safety and security contexts, absent any discernible evil purpose.

Consider this critical point: Humans from every identifiable group (but not all; there are outliers) pervert differentiation into a form of hatred for anyone outside their in-group. What is crucial about explicit bias? It is a choice and a trigger leading to action. Anyone anchored to any form of explicit biased thinking is making a choice. Once someone is aware of embedded explicit bias within themselves, acting on any of the three bias types becomes a choice regardless of context. All three of these biases have been professionally researched and are identifiable within a person through an "Implicit Attitude Test (AIT)."

Bias leading to hatred is where prejudice and bigotry live. Contexts supporting concepts of "better than" ideology is where social and racial injustice gains a voice. Bias leading to projected entitlement is where white privilege exists.

I am an older white man who grew up in a time when a horrific social value system based on differentiation was the norm, but I have chosen to be vulnerable and learn what makes a "right a right" and a "wrong a wrong" on many levels since my youth. My education has specifically targeted cross-cultural competency and social conflict management. As a result, my peers (and mentors in many cases) socially project as a diverse group, people of character I consider my equals or betters.

I choose to live and act based on a belief in social equity and equality. When I find injustice, I name it. I believe my stance is quite clear. I like diversity. Prejudice, bigotry, and racially motivated social injustice are the enemies of all humankind, and I hire diversely to mitigate their presence. I choose to respect all I encounter regardless of any potential differentiation, including race or origin, ostensibly choosing to stand against oppression and inequality. More importantly, "who is with me?"

EXPLORATIONS IN RELATED TOPICS

Engaging Meaningfully with Our Youth About Ethics

Engaging meaningfully with the youth in one's sphere of influence is contentious enough without adding the ethics topic to the discussion. Ethics is a vague, abstract concept for the youthful, inexperienced mind, suggesting that a parent or involved stakeholder should utilize a measured approach. A contextual framework for approaching the matter should emerge before adolescents begin independently creating their version of ethical behavior, preferably after they mature enough to join the conversation willingly. Plus, the framework needs some boundaries and context aligned with the young adult's typical growth environment.

As a parent coach, I build ethics into every session regardless of who is participating. Participants may include parents, teachers, familial caregivers, external agents, mentors, and community leaders involved with youth. All forms of training must be consistent when considering ethics.

One strong word of caution, however. Do not confuse ethics with morals. The two are intertwined and cross many commonalities, but ethics are more rigidly codified and embedded into the concept of

Law. Morals are individualized and subjective, with a broad continuum of acceptable behavior. Compelling moral examples are opposing contexts of hedonism and deep evangelical religious conviction. Both are considered permissible choices by contemporary moral standards but are rarely practiced by the same individual. A lack of ethical context defines the argument for or against either option.

From this point forward, parents will be a catch-all for any caregiver in a child's environment. Taking this tack, one acknowledges that all caregivers function as surrogate parents with limited roles to play, with parents maintaining primacy in decision-making contexts.

Parents have distinct roles in their children's lives, but only one over-arching responsibility. Every part a parent assumes stems from the requirement to provide a positive growth environment, allowing children to become functional prosocial adults. Prosocial behavior requires the inclusion of ethical constructs during early childhood and adolescent developmental periods, implying that ethical approaches must be integral to any parental role modeling process. Children observe and mimic everything around them, cementing how crucial parental role-modeling is in their quality world.

The essential nature of role-modeling means parents must optimize the choices they adopt when engaging in parenting. There is no value in the archaic "Do as I say and not as I do" schema. Pre-teens, tweens, and adolescent teens will reject that statement. Consider the "why" of this rejection: The mere suggestion that children must behave more ethically than their caregivers projects disrespect for the child's existence. How would children learn the value of self-image if parents project that adults do not value the "self?" From an ethical standpoint, role-modeling a positive "self" enhances understanding of dignity and respect and sends a clear message of "I am willing to be what I ask you to be" to children.

The framework for providing a positive growth environment is simplified by eliminating poor role-modeling. A layer of deception or dishonesty melts away, leaving a transparent, open projection of proper behavior for children to mimic and adopt for themselves. Earlier in the text, intrinsic motivation was shown as the preferred influencer leading to self-enhancement. The modeling of willful engagement in beneficial activities influences children to engage. Intentionality leads to optimal family dynamics and opens up a pathway to a broader concept, choice dynamics.

Ethics emerges and intertwines every aspect of choice dynamics. Parents should embrace the necessity of allowing children to make unique choices. Even in small children, controlling behavioral decisions can create a hostile growth environment where children seeking to please their caregivers learn compliance overshadows self-interest.

Later in life, decision-making is diminished in over-controlled children who lack choice-making skills, forcing them to seek affirmation from others before making decisions. Yet, even after receiving assurance, doubt and hesitation are usually present.

Parents have options surrounding choice dynamics. Control may form a limited slate of choices in some contexts in younger children. Parents should consider expanding the menu as children demonstrate the competency to make more informed and acceptable, optimal selections. Flexible boundaries are valuable tools for teaching and rewarding behavior for tweens and teens. As maturity and sensibility emerge, parents should undertake the next, possibly the most rewarding step in the choice dynamics arena, allowing co-creation to commence.

Many parents hesitate to consider letting children co-create aspects of the family dynamic. Allowing co-creation exploits the aforementioned intrinsic motivation effect. Research demonstrates that humans who engage in any decision-making process are more likely to comply with self-driven choices than any choice forced upon them. Co-creation fills the bill if a parent seeks any "golden ticket" to effective family dynamics.

Yes, parents still need to "parent" their charges, starting with effective role-modeling, setting negotiable dynamic boundaries, and consistently engaging in meaningful conversations centered on co-creation, all bound to a primary focus on ethical prosocial behavior. Essentially, ethics requires universal positive regard, something all parents should model. With practice and commitment, every parent can achieve the objective of developing socially adept children into adulthood.

SCHISMOGENESIS CONCEPTS INFLUENCING CONFLICT

What a strange word! The origins of schismogenesis break down into "schism," which means division, and "genesis," which means creation. The working definition is "creation of division." Schismogenesis, or the formation of division, is a critical aspect of how relationships function in many contexts. Let's break the concept apart and study the way it affects society.

Anthropologist George Bateson established the various aspects of schismogenesis in the 1930s to account for several social behavior types between and within groups. He suggested a balanced style of symmetric interaction between equals, often rivals of some kind, and an unbalanced style of complementary interactions between categorical opposites. It makes sense that the two forms would be labeled "symmetrical schismogenesis" and "complementary schismogenesis."

A third and fourth type aligns with the breakdown of cooperation due to communication failures. In sociolinguistics, usually characterized as communication within a dyad, complementary schismogenesis creates divergence due to different conversational styles. For example, one party may be outgoing and loud while the other prefers a quiet approach. As a result, the interaction elevates to discomfort, then aggravation.

In group interaction contexts, schismogenesis shows up as mutual levels of holding back collaboration and contribution. For example, one member wishes to take sole credit for an idea and chooses to withhold information. Others in the room follow suit, leading to the evolution or likelihood of a system of "holding back."

So, how does this journey into an oddly-named concept apply to an ethics treatment? Once one understands the impact schismogenesis imparts on participants and bystanders alike, knowing the concept's mere existence implies the need to adopt coping mechanisms mitigating the potential damage. For parents, recognizing early signs of conflict takes on more depth, and coping mechanisms are readily based on ethical approaches. An excellent way to describe the creation of division between siblings is "tit-for-tat on steroids."

How is this for a scenario? One child spills a drink on her sister's homework in this example. In response, the "victim" dumps the perpetrator's book into the garbage, resulting in a full-blown conflict disrupting the entire household. This all-too-common scenario is an excellent portrayal of damaging symmetrical interaction. Parents should be able to identify many instances where this context would apply.

Sociologists suggest all four types are harmful, but the holding back scenarios are egregiously damaging. In what amounts to reductions in collaboration and perceptible support, holding back leads to contempt between equals and disrupts an otherwise peaceful coexistence. How much energy is wasted pursuing what amounts to divisive processes instead of focusing on progress, innovation, and meaningful relationships?

REFERENCES

Adler, M.J. (1980). Aristotle for Everybody: Difficult Thought Made Easy. Bantam Doubleday Dell

Ambrose, D. (2017). Interdisciplinary Exploration Supports Sternberg's Expansion of Giftedness. Roeper Review, 39(3), 178–182.

Arauz, E. C. (2020). Cultural heritage, ethics and contemporary migrations. *INTERNATIONAL JOURNAL OF HERITAGE STUDIES*.

Aristotle. (1941). The Basic Works of Aristotle. Random House Publishing Group

Bolongaro, E. (2019). Between Plenitude and Responsibility: Notes on Ethics and Contemporary Literature. Philosophia, 47(1), 21.

Bouchard, T. J. (2009). Genetic influence on human intelligence (Spearman's g): How much? Annals of Human Biology, 36(5), 527–544.

de Vries, J. R. (2003). Why History? Ethics and Postmodernity & What Happens to History: The Renewal of Ethics in Contemporary Thought. CLIO, 32(2), 209.

Epicurus. (1993). The Essential Epicurus: Letters, Principal Doctrines, Vatican Sayings, and Fragments (E. O'Connor, Trans.) Prometheus Books (Original Works published ca. 280 B.C.E.)

Fairbairn, D. (2002). Eastern Orthodoxy Through Western Eyes. Baker & Taylor

Fernando, J., Sya, M., & Marta, R.F. (2019). Amalgamation as a Strengthening Ethic. Mimbar: Jurnal Sosial Dan Pembangunan, 35(2), 334–341.

Gabriel, I. (2013). Where difference matters: social ethics in the contemporary world. Journal of Ecumenical Studies, 48(1), 97–106.

Glasser, W. (1999). Choice Theory: A New Psychology of Personal Freedom. Harper Collins Publishers

Glasser, W. (1998). Choice Theory in the Classroom. Harper Collins Publishers

Johnson, P. E. (1998). Social Choice: Theory and Research. SAGE Publications, Inc.

Joneja, R. (2016). Study of Multiple Intelligences Model of Howard Gardner in Higher Education. Aweshkar Research Journal, 21(2), 13–18.

Leaf, M.J. (2014). The Anthropology of Eastern Religions: Ideas, Organizations, and Constituencies. Lexington Books

MacIntyre, A. (1966). A Short Story of Ethics. Simon & Schuster

MacIntyre, A. (2007). After Virtue: A Study in Moral Theory (3rd ed.). University of Notre Dame Press

Maslow, A. H. (2013). A Theory of Human Motivation. (Reprint of 1943 ed.). Martino Fine Books

Maslow, A.H. (1970). Motivation and Personality. Addison-Wesley Educational Publishers, Incorporated

Maslow, A. H. (1968). Toward a Psychology of Being. Wiley & Sons, Inc.

McGowan, A. (2020). How to Teach Philosophy to Your Dog. First Pegasus Books

Ng, T. W. H., Hsu, D. Y., & Parker, S. K. (2021). Received Respect and Constructive Voice: The Roles of Proactive Motivation and Perspective Taking. Journal of Management, 47(2), 399–429.

Olupona, J.K. & Gemignani, R. (Eds.). (2007). African Immigrant Religions in America. New York University Press

Plato. (2004). Republic. (C. D. C. Reeve, Trans.). Hackett Publishing Company. (Original work published ca. 380 B.C.E.)

Ristovski, L. (2020). Morality and Ethics in Politics in the Contemporary Societies. Journal of Liberty and International Affairs, 2(3).

Rossignac-Milon, M., Bolger, N., Zee, K. S., Boothby, E. J., & Higgins, E. T. (2021). Merged minds: Generalized shared reality in dyadic relationships. Journal of Personality and Social Psychology, 120(4), 882–911.

Takesue, H., Miyauchi, C. M., Sakaiya, S., Fan, H., Matsuda, T., & Kato, J. (2017). Human pursuance of equality hinges on mental processes of projecting oneself into the perspectives of others and into future situations. SCIENTIFIC REPORTS, 7.

Van Dyne, L., Ang, S., Ng, K. Y., Rockstuhl, T., Tan, M. L., & Koh, C. (2012). Sub-dimensions of the four-factor model of cultural intelligence: Expanding the conceptualization and measurement of cultural intelligence. Social and Personality Psychology Compass, 6(4), 295–313.

Warburton, N. (2013). Philosophy: The Basics (5th ed.). Routledge

Zhou, F., Yang, Y., Chen, X., & Stirk, N. (2004). Is positive self-regard a universal human need? Definitely, yes. INTERNATIONAL JOURNAL OF PSYCHOLOGY, 39(5–6), 435.

BUDDY'S BIO:

Buddy has been married 48+ years to his spouse, Sharon, who assists Buddy in most venue events. They have four children, seven grandchildren, and eight great-grandchildren. Buddy is a Vietnam-era veteran who served as a Hospital Corpsman in the US Navy (1972-1976). He earned his BS in Allied Health Sciences from UW-Milwaukee (1984), certifications in Mediation and Paralegal Studies from Lakewood College (2012), a certificate in Life Coaching from UDEMY (2014-recertification-2019), and his MA in Human Services Counseling and Executive Leadership from Liberty University (2014). Buddy is currently a DBA Doctoral Candidate at Grand Canyon University (2015 to present-all coursework completed, currently ABD). Buddy added a certified trainer competency for the Center for Teaching Effectiveness in November 2018. He is a member of the Maricopa County Association of Family Mediators (2012-present) (mcafm.org), a past Ethics Co-chair for MCAFM (2013-2014), and a past President of the Doctoral Learners Cohort at GCU (2017-2018). Buddy is also COO of the Brokenness to Healing Foundation, a non-profit working with disadvantaged youth through after-school mentoring programs, and serves as an advisory board member for multiple domestic companies.

Buddy is the creative mind behind the Slippery Slope series and the author of Book I, *Contemporary Society Through the Lens of Applied Ethics*.

He brands as "The Positive Social Change Agent Pro" and has been invited to be a Keynote Speaker and Program Presenter (Conflict Management, Parenting Dynamics, Cross-Cultural Topics), with one notable global invitation to Da Nang Vietnam in November 2017 and invited to speak on cultural topics at the IIRP World Conference in Bethlehem, PA-October 2019. Buddy routinely appears on the *Impact of Educational Leadership* podcast hosted by Isaiah Drone III. Buddy was awarded the *2022 Take Center Stage Writer's Journey Educational Award* for his work on the Slippery Slope series and his impact through mentoring other authors and aspiring authors during their non-fiction authorship journey.

CURRENT PROGRAMS OFFERED
BCT MEDIATIONS PLUS 2022-2024
COURSE OFFERINGS WITH DESCRIPTIONS

"My Life-My Voice-My Passion-My Choice" ©

This course paves a path to building a focused, noteworthy future for you! Starting with fundamental basics designed to help each person find themselves through a unique inward-looking journey of self-appraisal, followed by building a powerful voice in multiple dimensions, the four "My's" is an empowerment framework with utility geared to enhance one's lifetime. The first two modules open a doorway to one's infinite possibilities, and the final two optimize a "rinse and repeat" mindset that supercharges motivation and personal focus. Target: All age groups. Available in half-day or full-day intensive format for groups from eight to twenty-four participants or as a four-week, iterative course for individuals online.

"Choice Dynamics-A Rapidly Evolving Personal Success Platform" ©

This course is an emerging personal choice empowerment vehicle for all domains, focusing on the developmental years of teens and young adults. The curriculum also serves as a course-correction framework for those needing some guidance or a refresher course in overcoming self-doubt or recurring barriers. Target: Mature pre-teens into adulthood. Available in half-day or full-day intensive format for groups of twenty-four to one hundred participants in a school or corporate setting or as a three-day mastermind super-intensive for four to eight highly focused clients in an exclusive venue.

"TC-Squared" (was Tough Conversations-Tough Choices) ©

This course emphasizes Choice Dynamics concepts and utility in stressful interactions. Are you faced with difficult conversations and challenging negotiations that leave you exhausted? Nothing will prepare you for these contentious scenarios better than learning and optimizing your unique Choice Dynamics perspective, complete with a framework for navigating the process, from setting the tone to achieving co-creation of solutions to compliance and follow-through. Target: Those facing impending tough conversations or ongoing unresolved conflict. Available as a two-hour or half-day intensive. Please note how this class is taught to groups of four to twenty-four for general educational purposes; however, the preferred forum to gain optimal utility for a unique challenge is during a one-on-one with a BCT Mediations PLUS mediation professional highly skilled in these types of conversations. Special pricing is available for class participants.

"Why Our Choices Fail" ©

This course focuses on the seven deadly sins of failing to understand Choice Dynamics. BCT Mediations PLUS designed this course for the naysayers who need a compelling reason to learn and adopt Choice Dynamics. Since this offering targets skeptics, it has a uniquely low pricing structure and a follow-up discount feature for those participants choosing to take other courses. This proof framework is a challenge we are willing to offer. Is it one you are inclined to accept for those on the fence? Contact BCT Mediations PLUS for details on this "walk on the wild side" special peek at our world.

"It is Never about Intelligence" ©

This course focuses on the optimization of group dynamics and team performance. Although this course focuses on small to medium enterprise environments and embedded cultures, the concepts and coping strategies work equally well in school and home environments. In addition to identifying the flexible nature of the course material, participants explore multiple artifacts which appear throughout life that research shows impact success far more than intelligence. Would you like to know more? Target: Mentors, teachers, parents, administrators, HR professionals, counselors, and caregivers in every walk of life tasked with identifying or developing success markers. Available as half-day or full-day seminars, two-day blast conferences, or three-day mastermind intensives focused on optimizing organizational culture through human capital utilization. Freshest look at overcoming the "unicorn effect" and creating a sustainable world-class entity. Note: This topic is our most popular lunch-n-learn teaser offering that converts to training and more!

"The Immutable Laws of Choice" ©

This course explores and delineates eight interlinked laws that explore human choice. This course will change your perspective on making choices in every aspect of your life. The target consumer is everyone seeking a better choice framework. Private coaching is available.

"Bridging the "Culture" Gap: Beyond Assimilation and Acculturation to Social Amalgamation" ©

This timely offering explores concepts aligned with mitigating the devastation of social and racial injustice by eliminating isolation silos and misaligned in-group/out-group thinking. Indeed, Americans of every possible mindset must admit that what has been tried before has not achieved the results anyone can be proud of yet. Answers must come from multiple vectors and include those most aggrieved. The course material explores the failures of social projections and looks at innovative and fully inclusive cultural frameworks offering dignity and equity to all groups. Target: Keynote address for diversity conferences and shorter breakout sessions or panel discussions on social and racial discourse. BCT Mediations PLUS collaborates with the Brokenness to Healing Foundation, a 501-c3 non-profit, and all profits earned through this offering go to the Foundation.

"Contemporary Parenting Dynamics Project" Series ©

(Five Age-Specific Seminars and Workshops) Individual Modules:

> CPDP #1-Conception to Toddler Twos-The 1010 Effect ©
>
> CPDP #2-Toddler Twos to Wide-Eyed Sixes ©
>
> CPDP #3-Wide-Eyed Sixes to Pre-Teen Twelves ©
>
> CPDP #4-Those Crazy Early-Mid-Teen Years-Thirteen to Sixteen ©
>
> CPDP #5-Mid-Teens Through Early Adulthood (and Beyond) ©

This series of multivector offerings gives parents and caregivers a transparent look at parenting aligned with modern challenges and empowerment concepts for children within any age group, including the often-ignored period from conception to age two. The series' primary focus is how one builds an iterative framework for optimal choice dynamics within the core family based on developmental milestones and modern contexts. Available as individual modules in-person as seminar/workshops or online as webinars, or as a series of modules over a five-week course.

"The Power of Forgiveness and Universal Positive Regard" ©

This course teaches relationships, social realism and relativism, and mindfulness as they align with conflict and innovative coping competencies in a refreshing new light. One serious failing in modernity is a lack of meaningful forgiveness. Social policing leads to immediate and disruptive conflict, people feeling repressed, suppressed, or disrespected out of hand by people who may not even know them personally, and an increase in overwhelming social inequity. Normative civility comes from choosing a prosocial path, and this course explores how forgiveness and UPR create social change. Target: Conflicted stakeholders and aspiring social change agents. Available as a motivational, inspirational keynote and a four to eight-person three-day mastermind for passionate social leaders who need a recharge or a life-changing pivot.

"The Bias Trap and Optimal Coping Through Mindfulness" ©

This course exposes bias at its roots and explores contemporary coping strategies. Most theories of "bias" recognize over two hundred twenty human bias types, which stem from three primary origin points in human development. Avoiding or coping with the "bias trap" requires a specific skill set and a mindset pivot. So take the plunge and mitigate the bias-laden negativity in your sphere of influence. Target:

Conflicted stakeholders and those wishing to gain competency and optimal coping methodology for offsetting harmful biases. Available as a breakout session for conferences, a mini-keynote, a lunch-n-learn session, or a corporate seminar/workshop.

"The Ebb and Flow of Casual Social and Professional Environments" ©

Ever wonder why work-related and other non-intimate relationships tend to "timeout" over inane or innocuous, seemingly petty details? This detailed exploration of the "waxing and waning effect" of human interactions provides a culture-enhancing projection of how one creates and sustains a semblance of order within the chaos. Instead of dwelling on the stress from "losses," one gains competency and coping skills for re-inventing or re-energizing through an adapted mini-grief cycle.

Target: Corporate and school environments struggling with low-intensity cultures and people anchored to victimology. You shouldn't guess whether you fit here; dive in and learn to supercharge your relationship journey. Available as a four to sixteen-person lunch-n-learn, half-day seminar/workshop, or corporate in-person training module. Digital modules are coming soon. In addition, one-on-one training is available for select clients.

"Dyadics Empowerment: Leveraging Bronfenbrenner and Maslow (Soul-Searcher-Part One)" ©

This course explores two dynamic models of social realism for optimal utility. Primarily, relationships are the heart of human interaction, and intertwining the self-centered ecological model of Bronfenbrenner with the motivation model of Maslow allows participants to design a unique framework for stable relationships. Ever feel as if your grip on life was slipping away? This course strengthens your ability to not only hang on but to enhance and optimize relationships in every aspect of your life journey. Please note that this course, combined with its follow-up companion course, "You bring the conflict with you," is not for the faint of heart. Vulnerability and introspection are the pillars leading to conquering one's dyadic empowerment perspective. Target and availability are listed after the companion course.

You Bring the Conflict with You: The Barriers in Your Mind, Heart, and Soul (Soul-Searcher-Part-Two)" ©

This course explores self-inflicted pain and the destructive artifacts of victimology. Soul-searcher-part two releases many self-limiting barriers accumulated over time and helps participants develop coping methods and feedback cycles to limit the emergence of suboptimal habituations. Building off the structure provided in part one, participants often discover hidden passions and stretch goals to pursue. Target: Motivated, high-energy people who want to pivot or refocus their careers or private lives. Available in tandem with part one, "Dyadics empowerment," for a three-day super intensive limited to four to eight pre-qualified participants. In the two-course intensive, confidentiality is essential because sharing personal details and exhibiting vulnerability play a role in reframing each participant's life after the exclusive location event.

Corporate Culture and B2B Specific Courses "Process of Optimized Organizational Evolution Through the ACSRA Method" ©

This course explores adaptive HR from an empowered culture perspective. HR is constantly evolving, but it must address every aspect of human capital, from attraction to attrition and everything in between. Diversity and inclusion are essential to organizations tasked to build sustainable throughput in a divisive social climate. The ACSRA method opens windows of opportunity and answers many unresolved questions, answers capable of creating an optimal human capital environment. Target: C-suite executives, HR managers, and recruiters tasked with being innovative while seeking to outshine competitors in this challenging hiring environment. Available as a lunch-n-learn teaser, half-day or full-day training, and a three-day mastermind for C-suite executives seeking a path to a blue ocean paradigm. Individual coaching options are included.

Beyond the Legal Aspects-How to Create: Partnerships, Alliances, Innovation, and Culture" ©

This course explores various pathways to optimal business through leveraged relationships. Targeted to C-suite, Board members, and owners who want to "up their game," the curriculum explores what Google identifies as the soft skills of success. From a ten-year study, Google determined that seven were explicitly soft skills out of eight possible essential skills, with the eighth, technology proficiency, sitting dead last on the list. Although the study is well-known, many analysts have failed to leverage the utility or the potential embedded within the soft skills. COVID-19 has created a "reset the clock" environment that begs for disruptive innovation and provides a ripe opportunity for top-level individuals to change what they see in the mirror. Are you ready for a change, or do you have people in your organization who fit that profile? Target: Leaders looking to redesign the ladder. Available as a mastermind by negotiation only. The calendar is open, at least, so far. Schedule your career booster today!

Shortened versions for one-off lunch-n-learns are also available for any of these trendy topics and more, such as "Mitigating Sabotage," Developing an Ethical Framework or Culture," and "Walking the Talk." In addition, inspirational keynotes, workshops, and seminars for half-day or full-day are popular client choices. Contact Buddy at bct@bctmediationsplus.com or 480-861-1371 for more information today.

Five Inspirational Keynotes with Available Seminars and Workshops

My Choice Series-Foundational Presentation "Choice Dynamics" © Keynote

My Choice Series-Middle School "Self-Awareness" © Keynote

My Choice Series-Secondary School, "My Life-My Voice-Yes-Mine!" © Keynote

My Choice Series-Teen to Emerging Adult "It Has to Be Me!" © Keynote

My Choice Series-Teens and Parents "The Cyclical Nature of Choice" © Keynote

"Lunch-N-Learn and Half-day/Full-day Seminar" Series ©

"Choice Dynamics-Seven Deadly Sins of Not Honoring the Self" © Power Keynote

"It Was Never About Intelligence" © Inspirational Parenting Choice Dynamics Keynote

"Assimilation-Acculturation-Amalgamation" © Cross-Cultural Inclusion Intensive

"You Bring the Conflict with You" © Conflict and Bullying Reduction Intensive

"Tough Conversations-Tough Topics" © Keynote and Discussion Panel

"Why Competition Matters (or Doesn't)." © Optimal Focus on the Sports Domain

"The Barrier in Your Mind" © Inspirational Student Choice Dynamics Intensive

"Partnerships and Alliances Have a Time Stamp" © Business Development Intensive

"Accommodation-Service Industry Differentiator" © Business Development Intensive

Also, Buddy can customize any topic related to parenting, life choice, cultural awareness, or business development by agreement. Buddy does breakout sessions at conferences on a variety of hot topics. Pricing is by mutual understanding. Factors are the time required for the presentation, travel, accommodations, audience size, materials requested, and non-profit or academic settings. Buddy does an intake to explore needs and options to enhance open access to all participants. Buddy welcomes any special requests. Contact Buddy at (480) 861-1371 (Call or Text)

Website: www.bctmediationsplus.com

Email: buddypscapro@gmail.com

Alternate Emails: bct@bctmediationsplus.com or bthornton2@ my.gcu.edu.

Buddy's LinkedIn URL: www.linkedin.com/in/gcudoc1955

Buddy's Twitter: @buddypscapro